The Consumer Society

Theory, Culture & Society

Theory, Culture & Society caters for the resurgence of interest in culture within contemporary social science and the humanities. Building on the heritage of classical social theory, the book series examines ways in which this tradition has been reshaped by a new generation of theorists. It will also publish theoretically informed analyses of everyday life, popular culture, and new intellectual movements.

EDITOR: Mike Featherstone, *Nottingham Trent University*

THE TCS CENTRE
The Theory, Culture & Society book series, the journals *Theory, Culture & Society* and *Body & Society*, and related conference, seminar and postgraduate programmes operate from the TCS Centre at Nottingham Trent University. For further details of the TCS Centre's activities please contact:

Centre Administrator
The TCS Centre, Room 175
Faculty of Humanities
Nottingham Trent University
Clifton Lane, Nottingham, NG11 8NS, UK e-mail: tcs@ntu.ac.uk

The Consumer Society

Myths and Structures

Jean Baudrillard

SAGE Publications

London • Thousand Oaks • New Delhi

Originally published as *La société de consommation* © Editions
Denoël 1970
This edition 1998, Reprinted 1999

This translation is published with financial support from the
French Ministry of Culture

Published in association with *Theory, Culture & Society*,
Nottingham Trent University

SAGE Publications Ltd
6 Bonhill Street
London EC2A 4PU

SAGE Publications Inc.
2455 Teller Road
Thousand Oaks, California 91320

SAGE Publications India Pvt Ltd
32, M-Block Market
Greater Kailash - I
New Delhi 110 048

British Library Cataloguing in Publication data

A catalogue record for this book is available from
the British Library

ISBN 0 7619 5691 3
ISBN 0 7619 5692 1 (pbk)

Library of Congress catalog card number 97–061881

Typeset by Photoprint, Torquay, Devon
Printed in Great Britain by Redwood Books, Trowbridge, Wiltshire

Shower him with all earthly blessings, plunge him so deep into happiness that nothing is visible but the bubbles rising to the surface of his happiness, as if it were water; give him such economic prosperity that he will have nothing left to do but sleep, eat gingerbread, and worry about the continuance of world history.

Fyodor Dostoyevsky, *Notes from Underground*

Contents

Foreword

Jean Baudrillard's book *The Consumer Society* is a masterful contribution to contemporary sociology. It certainly has its place in the tradition which includes Durkheim's *The Division of Labour in Society*, Veblen's *Theory of the Leisure Class* and David Riesman's *The Lonely Crowd*.

Baudrillard analyses our contemporary Western societies, including that of the United States. This analysis focuses on the phenomenon of the consumption of objects which he has already tackled in *The System of Objects* (Gallimard, 1968; translation, Verso, 1996). In his conclusion to that volume, he formulates the plan of the present work: 'It has to be made clear from the outset that consumption is an active form of relationship (not only to objects, but also to society and to the world), a mode of systematic activity and global response which founds our entire cultural system.'

He shows with great perspicacity how the giant technocratic corporations foster irrepressible desires, creating new social hierarchies which have replaced the old class differences.

A new mythology has arisen in this way. As Baudrillard writes,

> The washing machine *serves* as an appliance and *acts* as an element of prestige, comfort, etc. It is strictly this latter field which is the field of consumption. All kinds of other objects may be substituted here for the washing machine as signifying element. In the logic of signs, as in that of symbols, objects are no longer linked in any sense to a *definite* function or need. Precisely because they are responding here to something quite different, which is either the social logic or the logic of desire, for which they function as a shifting and unconscious field of signification.

Consumption, as a new tribal myth, has become the morality of our present world. It is currently destroying the foundations of the human being, that is to say, the balance which European thought has maintained since the Greeks between our mythological roots and the world of the logos. Baudrillard is aware of the risk we are running. Let us quote him once again:

> Just as medieval society was balanced on God **and** the Devil, so ours is balanced on consumption **and** its denunciation. Though at least around the Devil heresies and black magic sects could organize. Our magic is white. No heresy is possible any longer in a state of affluence. It is the prophylactic whiteness of a saturated society, a society with no history and no dizzying heights, a society with no myth other than itself.

The Consumer Society, written in a concise style, should be carefully studied by the younger generation. Perhaps they will take up the mission of breaking up this monstrous, if not indeed obscene, world of the abundance of objects so formidably sustained by the mass media and particularly by television, this world which threatens us all.

J.P. Mayer
University of Reading

Translator's Acknowledgements

I would like to thank Marie-Dominique Maison, Leslie Hill, Mike Gane and Glynis Powell for various forms of linguistic assistance with this translation. Thanks are also due to Richard G. Smith for providing some invaluable background information.

For reasons of style, the author has made some very minor changes to the original text. I have personally taken the liberty of numbering the chapters.

C.T.

Introduction

George Ritzer

This English translation of *The Consumer Society: Myths and Structures* (originally published in 1970) will be both a treat and a revelation to admirers of the work of Jean Baudrillard not fluent in French. Here is an early work by a scholar who has come to be thought of by many as *the* leading postmodern social theorist.[1] Postmodernists will be gratified to find, at least in their rudimentary form, many of the ideas associated with Baudrillard's later, more postmodern theorizing. Modernists will find a Baudrillard who is a much more modern social thinker than he is usually thought to be; one who is apt to be far more to their liking than the Baudrillard of the last decade or so. Metatheorists[2] will find many rewards in this work including a greater sense of Baudrillard's theoretical roots and the challenge of understanding a work of a thinker who was clearly in the throes of a profound intellectual transformation. Most importantly, theorists and other students of consumer society will discover a treasure trove of insights and perspectives into the world of consumption. Thus, this is a rewarding book at many levels, although it has, as we will see, its flaws.

This is no dusty and outdated theoretical work that is of little more than historical interest. In fact, it is a highly contemporary work that reads very well over a quarter of a century after its initial publication.[3] There is, for example, Baudrillard's discussion of such timely issues as sexually ambiguous, hermaphroditic models not unlike those who adorn the controversial Calvin Klein advertisements these days; the booming interest in fitness; the desire for slimness and the resulting dieting mania; obesity and the obsession with low-calorie, low-fat foods; and the burgeoning use of sexuality for commercial purposes. More generally, and importantly, this is a book about consumption and it is clear that Baudrillard was far ahead of his time in focusing on this issue. While most of his contemporaries in France (and elsewhere) were mired in stale old debates about production, Baudrillard recognized that consumption was where the important new issues and problems were to be found. Time has clearly borne Baudrillard out. There has been an outpouring of work, especially in Great Britain (for an overview, see Gabriel and Lang, 1995), on consumption and postmodern society is now seen as being more or less synonymous with consumer society (Featherstone, 1991; Bauman, 1992).

Baudrillard's foresight as far as consumption is concerned is exemplified by the fact, among others, that he dealt with the issue of credit at this early stage in the development of the modern credit, especially credit card, system.[4] To this day, this issue has received virtually no attention from social theorists.[5] This is in spite of the fact that it is an absolutely central aspect of the booming consumer society. Yet, when Baudrillard was writing in the late 1960s the credit card industry was in its infancy and it was not to begin to profoundly transform society until long after *The Consumer Society* was published. Thus, Baudrillard was ahead of his time in recognizing the importance of this issue, and many other issues, associated with the consumer society.

A Modern Work

There are many ways in which *The Consumer Society* can be seen as a piece of modern social theory. The book offers a generally sustained and coherent argument. While this was also true of the previously published *The System of Objects* (1968/1996), and remained the case for a number of Baudrillard's works that followed in the 1970s and into the early 1980s, it is certainly not true of the more recent works which often read like pastiches of aphorisms with little or nothing to connect them. The modern reader who is put off by Baudrillard's more recent postmodern style will be more comfortable with the structure and development of *The Consumer Society*.

The scholarly format of the book will be familiar to most modern readers. Intellectual predecessors and antagonists are clear (something not always the case in postmodern works) and, as a result, so are the roots of many of Baudrillard's ideas. A powerful intellectual presence is John Kenneth Galbraith, especially his book *The Affluent Society* (1958/1964). Baudrillard uses many of Galbraith's ideas, and his critical analysis of them, to develop his own perspective on the affluent, that is consumer, society. For example, Baudrillard argues that there is no such thing as an affluent society; all societies combine 'structural excess' and 'structural penury'. Rather than an affluent society, Baudrillard argues that we live in a 'growth society'. However, this growth brings us no closer to being an affluent society. Growth produces *both* wealth and poverty. In fact, growth is a function of poverty; growth is needed to contain the poor and maintain the system. While he is not always consistent on this, Baudrillard argues that the growth society is, in fact, the opposite of the affluent society. Its inherent tensions lead to psychological pauperization as well as systematic penury (see later) since 'needs' will always outstrip the production of goods. Since both wealth and shortage are inherent in the system, efforts like those proposed by Galbraith to solve the problem of poverty are doomed to failure. Thus, in various ways, Baudrillard not only critiques, but also builds in very modern ways upon, Galbraith's work.

Baudrillard makes similar, albeit far less elaborate, use of the ideas of other important thinkers of the day such as Marshall McLuhan, Daniel Bell, David Riesman, Daniel Boorstin, and even the popular writer Vance Packard. In other words, the intellectual landscape explored by Baudrillard was one that would have been much the same had a thinker less associated with the move to postmodern theory approached the topic of the consumer society in the late 1960s. And he explores that landscape in ways that are very familiar to the modernist.

More importantly, the set of classic social theorists informing Baudrillard's work was much the same as affected the theorizing of more conventional thinkers of the day. The most powerful presence, at least overtly,[6] is Marx, but Durkheim, Veblen, and Lévi-Strauss also play central roles in this analysis (Tocqueville is there, as well). Furthermore, there is an effort to synthesize ideas from these theorists with a number of other theoretical inputs. A modern, mainstream social theorist would be quite comfortable with both the theoretical heritage and the synthetic efforts involved in this work.

The important role accorded to Marx and his ideas, especially commodities and their use-value and exchange-value, is interesting in light of the fact that Baudrillard was soon to break with Marx in *The Mirror of Production* (1973/1975) and move progressively away from a Marxian perspective. Marxian theory is only one of several inputs shaping this work and in at least one crucial way (to be discussed later) this book deviates dramatically from a Marxian orientation.

Part of the reason for his influence is the fact that Marx, the master theorist of production, also has much to offer to anyone concerned with consumption. There are many parallels drawn by Baudrillard between production and consumption (for example, just as wage labour extorted labour power and increases in productivity, credit extorts savings; the consumer is often seen as a worker, a productive force; there is a 'reserve army' of needs analogous to the industrial reserve army); the ideas that apply to production are often extended to consumption. One of the most interesting of these extensions is Baudrillard's use of the concept of surplus value in reference to the distribution of welfare to the larger community. His contention is that society is expending part of its surplus in order to keep the public in line. Public munificence is seen as both a kind of ideological constraint (engendering a myth of service rather than a view of the world where everything is bought and sold) and a kind of social control.

More importantly, for Marx, and interestingly still for Baudrillard in this work, production is accorded priority over consumption. There is still the sense in this work, both explicitly and implicitly, that production is the base and all else, including consumption and the culture of which it is such an integral part, is superstructure. This is clearly a limiting, if not a self-defeating, perspective in light of developments in both the social world and social theory. In terms of the latter, there is now a clear recognition of the independent importance, if not ascendancy, of culture and commodities. And few, even among diehard Marxian theorists, would subscribe to a limited base–superstructure argument.[7]

Beyond use-value, exchange-value, commodities, and base–super-structure, Baudrillard employs a rather lengthy litany of Marxian ideas in *The Consumer Society*. The concepts of ideology, commodity fetishism and reification clearly fit quite well into a Marxian approach to consumption. More generally, there is a great deal of dialectical thinking about, among other things, the contradictions that afflict consumer society (especially the inability of production to keep pace with the explosive growth of 'needs'; and the ideology of equality versus the increasing differentiation of consumer society). There is a sense that the tendency toward monopolization occurs not only in the world of production but also in the world of consumption. Even that old warhorse, alienation, is trotted out on occasion and, startlingly, is central to the title of the book's concluding chapter. There is talk of revolution, even a hope that con-sumption offers the possibility of 'deep crises', 'new contradictions', and even revolutionary change. However, in the end, Baudrillard's structur-alism, especially his interest in the immutability of the 'code', leads him to the view that no true revolution is possible. This is one of the many places in which Baudrillard's theoretical resources are at odds with one another and lead to a contradictory perspective on the consumer society. And this is one of the reasons why Baudrillard was soon to break with the Marxian tradition. Its optimistic view of the future was at logger-heads with his essentially pessimistic view of the world.

Émile Durkheim is a second classical theorist whose ideas had a profound influence on this work. As we will see below, Baudrillard had at this point not yet abandoned sociology so it is not surprising that he should be drawn to Durkheim, the premier French classical sociological theorist. One important effect of this is that Baudrillard focuses his attention on collective phenomena, on Durkheimian social facts. Indeed, he describes consumption in very Durkheimian terms as 'collective behaviour', 'something enforced, a morality, an institution', and 'a whole system of values'. He fully recognized that lots of intellectual baggage went with such a perspective including a sense of the importance of group integration and social control.[8] Similarly, consumption from this Durkheimian perspective is seen not as enjoyment or pleasure, but rather as something which is institutionalized, forced upon us, a duty. While not inconsistent with Marx's thinking on reified social struc-tures, these ideas (collective, morality, values, duty, integration, institu-tions, social control) clearly have far more to do with Durkheim than with Marx. This is also true of the idea of socialization and the fact, underscored by Baudrillard, that we must be trained, we must learn, to consume.

However, in modern society, the managed possession of consumer goods is individualizing and atomizing. It leads to distinction and differentiation, not to social solidarity. Thus, modern consumption is at odds with the inherently collective nature of consumption. While even modern consumption is not totally individualistic, it is being pushed in that direction. Furthermore, production, like consumption, is viewed as a collective phenomenon. Thus, the pressure towards individualization in modern consumption is seen as being at odds with the nature of *both* production and consumption.

Beyond his macroscopic or collective focus, throughout *The Consumer Society* Baudrillard does an incredible amount of Durkheimian function-alism.[9] In fact, given its macroscopic orientation and the functional analysis, the book sometimes reads as if it were written by a structural functionalist, a reality that can be traced to Baudrillard's continuing ties, at least at this point, to sociology. This orientation is made clear when, for example, Baudrillard critiques the general idea that waste within consumer society is dysfunctional[10] and argues for the need for socio-logical study that would show its true functions. He goes on to argue that it is wasteful, superfluous consumption that allows people and society to feel that they exist, that they are truly alive. In this sense, wasteful consumption is functional, not dysfunctional, and is analysable from the perspective of functional analysis. Similarly, he discusses the functionality of the fact that the heroes of production have been replaced by idols of consumption ('great wastrels') such as movie stars and sports heroes. It is they who fulfil the function of useless and inordinate expenditure. *The Consumer Society* is liberally studded with such func-tional analyses. One sometimes feels as if one is reading a work by a disciple of Talcott Parsons and not a book authored by someone whose work has become the antithesis of such mainstream sociology. While the signs of Baudrillard's rejection of that sociology, indeed all sociology, are to be found in this book, it also offers a considerable amount of the kind of sociology Baudrillard was to come to reject.

Another central concept in Durkheimian theory – anomie – plays a central role in this work. Indeed, while the Conclusion deals with the Marxian concept of alienation, the immediately preceding chapter has 'anomie' in its title. It is in this chapter that Baudrillard deals with various 'pathologies'[11] associated with the consumer society such as the violence perpetrated in it, the non-violence of those like 'hippies', and the 'fatigue' (seen as a form of concealed protest) of many within consumer society. Durkheim, of course, deals with such pathologies within the context of a modern, reformist orientation in which he discusses a variety of ways (e.g. occupational associations) to cope with them. While Baudrillard is far more modern in this work than he was to come to be, he is still not nearly modern enough to offer reforms to deal with a system that he clearly regards as inherently and inevitably corrupt.

Another major modern theorist of influence in *The Consumer Society* is Thorstein Veblen. This is somewhat surprising since Veblen has tended to be ignored by mainstream, modern theorists, but Baudrillard is drawn to him because of Veblen's pioneering work on consumption. Indeed, Veblen's image, as well as that of his famous concept of conspicuous consumption, is evoked by the opening line of the book which deals with the 'fantastic conspicuousness' of the wide array of consumer goods and services. Baudrillard not only usefully employs the notion of conspicuous consumption, but also spins off some interesting ideas of his own from it. For example, while the middle classes continue to engage in conspicuous consumption, the elites may engage in new forms of *in*conspicuous consumption in order to create new and more subtle differences between themselves and the rest of society. Similarly, Veblen's arguments on conspicuous leisure are used to yield interesting insights into time and leisure. One of Baudrillard's conclusions is that it is impossible to waste time since in spending time in that way people are in fact *producing* something of value – prestige for themselves. Then, Baudrillard examines the 'benevolence' of things like advertisements where a 'free' television programme is offered in exchange for a few minutes of commercials. He sees this and things like it as conspicuous displays of disinterestedness.

Yet, while he builds upon some of Veblen's ideas, Baudrillard ultimately finds them wanting. For example, he clearly critiques Veblen's orientation from the point of view of the structuralist perspective (see later) that is the true heart of *The Consumer Society*. Baudrillard rejects Veblen's concern with imitation, the study of prestige at the 'phenomenal' level, and his concern with superficial conscious social dynamics. Instead, Baudrillard argues for the study of signs, structural relations, the code and, more generally, unconscious social logic.

While outside the sociological mainstream, structuralism is certainly a modern perspective (it was the modern source of poststructuralism and to a lesser extent postmodernism). Furthermore, it was the dominant intellectual perspective in the France of Baudrillard's early years as a scholar. While the imprint of Marx is strong, *The Consumer Society* is most powerfully influenced by a range of structuralist ideas. This is made clear by the book's subtitle, *Myths and Structures*, and by much of the substance of the book. The world of consumption is treated like a mode of discourse, a language (and even, following Lévi-Strauss, like a kinship system). As a language, consumption is a way in which we converse and communicate with one another. Once we think of consumption as a language, we are free to deploy the whole panoply of tools derived from structural linguistics including sign, signifier, signified and code. As a result, instead of Marxian use-values and exchange-values, consumables become sign-values. And it is this view of commodities that dominates this book, not the array of Marxian concepts which, while coexisting uncomfortably, are subordinated to them.

Baudrillard tries to relate the two theoretical perspectives that play the greatest role in undergirding his work by arguing that there are two entangled social orders – the *order of production* and the *order of consumption*. He still accords, at least overtly, the order of production priority, but recognizes that the logic of significations, and the order of production that goes with it, are of increasing importance. Whatever their relative significance, it is important that society be analysed from the perspective of both orders and their interrelationship.

Later, Baudrillard puts this another way, arguing that consumption is constrained at two levels. One is the level of structural analysis where consumption is constrained by the *constraint of signification*. The other is the level of 'socio-economico-political' analysis in which the *constraint of production* is operant. Baudrillard could hardly be clearer: he is seeking to use *both* structuralist and traditional Marxian approaches.[12] However, he appears not to be trying to integrate them, but rather to have them operate side-by-side. For example, he argues that a true analysis of the social logic of consumption would focus not on the individual appropriation of the *use-value* of goods and services, but rather on the production and manipulation of social signifiers. It is structural analysis that is deemed the appropriate approach to the latter issue.[13] Not only are the two theories not integrated, but Baudrillard already clearly privileges structuralism. Because structural analysis takes priority over Marxian theory, Baudrillard is ultimately unable to offer a theory of revolution. The code prevents real social revolution. That type that it does permit – fashion revolutions – not only are harmless but serve to prevent genuine social revolutions.

When looked at from a structural perspective, what we consume is signs (messages, images) rather than commodities. This means that consumers need to be able to 'read' the system of consumption in order to know what to consume. Furthermore, because we all know the 'code', we know the meaning of the consumption of one commodity rather than another. Commodities are no longer defined by their use, but rather by what they signify. And what they signify is defined not by what they do, but by their relationship to the entire system of commodities and signs. There is an infinite range of difference available in this system and people therefore are never able to satisfy their need for commodities, for difference. It is this that in Baudrillard's view helps account for the seeming insatiability and continual dissatisfaction of consumers. And this, in turn, is one of the reasons for Baudrillard's dissatisfaction with the use of the concept of 'needs' – needs can, by definition, be satisfied and therefore cannot account for the insatiability of consumers. What people seek in consumption is not so much a particular object as difference and the search for the latter is unending.

There is a sense that there is a series of structures that, in playing out their nature and relationship to one another, produce the consumer society. In contrast to a Marxian approach, there are no agents in such a structuralist orientation. For example, Baudrillard contends that the 'system' maintains itself by producing wealth *and* poverty, dissatisfactions and satisfactions, disturbances and progress. Furthermore, it is not deliberately bloodthirsty capitalists who are to blame for poverty, but rather the 'system' and its structures 'obeying its own laws'.

To take another example, there is the issue of individual differentiation or personalization. The usual sociological approach to this topic is to think of individuals as consciously seeking to distinguish themselves from others. However, in Baudrillard's view, it is the code, or the system of differences, that causes individuals to be similar to, as well as different from, one another. In the very act of particularizing themselves, people are reading and conforming to the code. Baudrillard concludes that the sociological study of consumption (and everything else) must shift from the superficial level of conscious social dynamics to the unconscious social logic of signs and the code. In other words, the key to understanding lies at the level of deep structures. It is those structures that constrain people who are only able to decode messages unconsciously.

Thus, structuralism represents the most powerful theoretical input into *The Consumer Society*. However, Baudrillard is already here a post-structuralist because he is supplementing structuralism with a series of other theoretical ideas derived from, among others, Marx, Durkheim, and Veblen. More generally, Baudrillard is still functioning as a sociologist and that further enriches (and complicates, even muddies) his analysis. In light of his later defection from, and acerbic remarks about, sociology, it is surprising to see Baudrillard employ sociology throughout this book. That involves not only utilization of a general sociological orientation, but more specific orientations such as the Durkheimian and functional analyses discussed earlier.

Although he utilizes an essentially structuralist approach to the issues, the impact of being a sociologist is most obvious in Baudrillard's concern with, and analysis of, inequality, social differentiation and social stratification.[14] (Of course, there is no necessary contradiction between structuralism and sociology, there is a 'structuralist sociology', although Baudrillard criticizes sociologists for seeing individuals as free and creative and for being 'wary of "deep motivation"'.) For example, because of their training, the upper classes are seen as having some degree of mastery over the code. It is the middle and lower classes who are the true consumers because they lack such mastery. As a result, they fetishize objects and seek to prove themselves and to find salvation in the consumption of objects.[15] Baudrillard urges the abandonment of the 'individual logic of satisfaction' (needs and so on) and a central focus on the 'social logic of differentiation'.[16] He argues that while 'primary penury' (a lack of goods) has largely been overcome in the modern world, 'structural penury' is built into the structure of modern growth society. That is, growth leads to privilege and that, in turn, leads to penury for many, at least in comparison to the state of those with privilege. He concludes that society's social logic is condemning people to a luxurious and spectacular penury. Since the cause lies in the social logic, it can only be solved by a revolution at that level, a revolution that, given his commitment to structuralism, Baudrillard believes unlikely, if not impossible.

There are times when Baudrillard adopts the perspective and mantle of sociologist (and structuralist) to critique the work of others. There is, for example, his critique of Galbraith for portraying individuals as passive victims and, in the process, ignoring sociological factors such as class, caste and social structure, as well as the more structural factor of the social logic of differentiation. In so doing, however, Baudrillard seems to be combining, perhaps more critically conflating, a structuralist approach ('the logic of differentiation') with a sociological orientation (to 'class', 'caste', and 'social structure'). In fact, this conflation is a confounding factor throughout the book.

In spite of his seeming commitment to a sociological approach, Baudrillard critiques traditional sociologists, as he does the economist Galbraith, for focusing on individual needs for differentiation. He seems to often equate sociologists with 'psycho-sociologists' who focus on such individual, phenomenological matters.[17] Instead, Baudrillard supports a sociology that focuses on structures, especially the unconscious structures of interest to structuralists. This can only be accomplished by abandoning the individual logic of satisfaction and according central importance to the social logic of differentiation. Thus, Baudrillard's support for sociology is, once again, support for a structural sociology. Indeed, he sometimes takes the position that sociology involves a focus on such structural issues as 'social logic'. While Baudrillard explicitly takes this position, we must not forget the many places in this work in which he does more conventional (i.e. Durkheimian, functional) analyses and focuses on such traditional sociological issues as social stratification.

Intimations of Postmodernism

While *The Consumer Society* has a number of modern characteristics, it also anticipates many of the ideas that one associates with Baudrillard's later work, ideas that have now become essential aspects of postmodern social theory. However, as we will see at the close of this Introduction, *The Consumer Society* is also assailable from a postmodern position because it is still embedded, at least in part, in a modern paradigm.

While Baudrillard is already, for the reasons discussed above, a poststructuralist in *The Consumer Society*, it is clear why even that designation will come to be an uncomfortable, even an inappropriate, label to describe his orientation. The fact is that there is an uncomfortable

and unstable mix of theoretical ideas in *The Consumer Society.* It seems
clear in retrospect that the only option open to Baudrillard was to leave
most of them behind and create a theoretical perspective unlike *any* that
had come before. Many of the elements of that theory, at least in a
rudimentary form, are to be found in *The Consumer Society,* but they do
not yet come together to form a distinctive theoretical orientation. That
had to await later theoretical work and intellectual development.

Let me begin with Baudrillard's privileging of primitive over modern
society, as well as the concept of symbolic exchange, ideas which were to
be more fully developed in later works, especially *Symbolic Exchange and
Death* (1976/1993). It is clear that Baudrillard is critical of modern
society[18] and that critique emanates from a sense of the importance of the
symbolic, especially symbolic exchange, as it exists, in part, in primitive
society and more generally in an abstract model of such an exchange
process. There are many places in which Baudrillard offers a critique of
modern practices in light of what they were like in more primitive
society. For example, communication, especially through the mass
media, has a 'technical, aseptic' form and '*is no longer achieved through a
symbolic medium*'; it lacks 'real symbolic or didactic processes'. In modern
society people display a kind of 'ludic curiosity' about things; they 'play
with combinations'. What is lost is 'passionate play', with passion
implying total involvement and intense symbolic value. Modern consumption involves the external manipulation of signs and it lacks,
among other things, the symbolic values involved in creation.

This aspect of Baudrillard's thinking is also well illustrated by what he
has to say about time. Our modern sense of time, especially as something
to be used, even wasted, in leisure is a product of our culture and
economic system. Thus, time becomes a commodity like any other, albeit
one that is rarer and more precious, in the consumer society. It can be
exchanged with any other commodity, especially money. Leisure time is
separated from work time and one is obligated, constrained to spend it.
This all stands in stark contrast to Baudrillard's view of primitive society
where there is no time; where it is meaningless to ask whether or not one
has time. Time in this context is nothing more than the rhythm of
collective activities, especially the rituals of eating and feasting. It is
impossible to dissociate time from such activities, or to plan or manip-
ulate time. Time in primitive societies is integral to symbolic exchange.

Waste is another area in which Baudrillard seeks to contrast modern
and primitive society and to privilege the primitive form of waste. In
the primitive world, waste is a festive ritual and a symbolic act of
expenditure. However, in the modern world it has become a bureaucratic
caricature in which wasteful consumption is obligatory. Baudrillard's
overall position on the transition from primitive to modern society is that
the fundamental characteristic of the latter is the loss of spontaneous,
reciprocal, and symbolic human relations.

In this light, Baudrillard's discussion of the work of the anthropologist

Marshall Sahlins on hunting-gathering societies is quite relevant and instructive. Baudrillard uses Sahlins's work not only to privilege primitive society, but also as one of many bases to critique Galbraith's ideas on the affluent society. Baudrillard argues, following Sahlins, that primitive societies can be seen as affluent while modern 'industrial and productivist' societies are 'dominated by scarcity'.

Hunter-gatherers like those of the Kalahari suffered from absolute poverty in the sense that they had few, if any, personal possessions. They did no 'work' in the contemporary sense of the term, made no economic calculations and did not amass a store of goods. They shared everything they did have with other members of the group and were confident (or foolish) enough to consume everything immediately. They managed to rest easy because they trusted in the abundance of natural resources. In contrast, modern society is characterized by anxiety and despair about a variety of insufficiencies. As a result, it was because they knew true affluence that the hunter-gatherers could afford to be what we would consider improvident.

To Baudrillard, following Sahlins, poverty involves not the quantity of goods a group possesses, but the nature of its human relationships. In the case of primitive hunter-gatherers there are transparent and reciprocal human relationships. There is no accumulation or monopolization of raw materials, technologies, or products that would serve to interfere with free exchange and lead to scarcity. What there is, and what is the source of their wealth, is symbolic exchange. Wealth is based not on goods but on human exchange; and, since the latter is endless, wealth is unlimited. The small number of goods that do exist create general wealth because they circulate continually among the members of the group.

While these primitive societies bask in the 'wealth' of the dialectic of human relationships, modern societies are characterized by the 'dialectic of penury'. In a society characterized by such a dialectic there is unlimited and insatiable need; a constant sense that one does not have enough. Rather than a reciprocal sharing of what people have, modern society is characterized by differentiation and competition which contributes to the reality and the sense that there is never enough. Since the problem lies in social relationships (or in the social logic), it will not be solved by increases in production, by innovations in productive forces, or by what we usually think of as even greater abundance. The only solution to the problem lies in a change in social relationships and in the social logic. We need a social logic that brings with it the affluence of symbolic exchange, rather than one that condemns us to 'luxurious and spectacular penury'. This is an attractive (structural) sociological argument, although one wonders how Baudrillard thinks such a revolution is to come about since he has given up hope in a Marxian-style revolution and in a revolutionary agent. Later we will see how he seeks to deal with this problem.

Another concept that is apparent throughout *The Consumer Society* is simulations. As was the case with the notion of symbolic exchange, it too was later to become a focal concern, as well as the title, of a book (Baudrillard, 1983/1990). The concept of a simulation makes sense when one looks at it in light of Baudrillard's thinking on symbolic exchange and the privileging of primitive society. For example, in primitive society nature is seen as an original and specific presence which stands in contrast to culture. However, in the modern world nature has tended to be reduced to something carefully groomed, managed, policed and tailored to the needs of humans. Nature in this form is a simulation of what it is in primitive society. It has become a sham; simulations can be defined as 'sham objects' and it is such objects that define our consumer society. They are objects that offer an abundance of signs that they are real, but in fact they are not.

Another major example of simulations is found in Baudrillard's discussion of *kitsch* – 'trashy objects', 'folksy knick-knacks', 'souvenirs'. These are defined by Baudrillard as pseudo-objects not to be confused with 'real' objects. Kitsch can also be defined as objects which, while they have a superabundance of signs, lack any real signification. The popularity of kitsch is closely tied to the development of a mass-production market and society. Rather than an aesthetics of 'beauty and originality', kitsch offers an aesthetics of simulation, of objects that reproduce, imitate, ape, and repeat. Yet another type of simulation is the *gadget*, a useless, impoverished object which simulates a function without having any real, practical referent. As such, the gadget is part of a broader process (growing numbers of useless, simulated objects) affecting society as a whole. As a result, all of society is suspected of uselessness, artificiality and fakery. More specifically, we act with gadgets in a ludic rather than a symbolic or utilitarian manner and this, too, is only part of a broader process since the curious play with combinations is coming to characterize more and more aspects of society. In other words, the world is coming to be increasingly dominated by simulations and we are reduced to playing with them rather than using them, or relating to them, symbolically.

Baudrillard argues that the mass media have greatly enhanced and generalized the simulation process. Instead of reality, people are treated to simulations involving the constant recombination of various signs, of elements of the code. Baudrillard has a problem here, and elsewhere, because lacking an Archimedean point, he cannot (or, at least, should not) label these simulations as false. Thus, he designates them 'neo-reality' because he recognizes that we need to find a way of avoiding using language which speaks of the 'false' and the 'artificial'. Yet, in other places that is just what Baudrillard does, as, for example, when he labels simulations 'sham objects'.[19]

Modern society is characterized not only by simulated objects, but also by simulated relationships. For example, advertisers are seen as imitating intimate, personal modes of communication in an effort to produce a sense of intimacy where, in fact, none exists. A simulated intimacy is created between people doing the advertising and potential customers, as well as between the latter and the products being advertised. This is but one part of what Baudrillard sees as a generalized game of human relations. Instead of the reciprocity characteristic of primitive societies and symbolic exchange, in modern society we have a gigantic simulation model of such reciprocal human relations.

More specifically, consumer society is one in which most of us are obliged to be solicitous of others. However, it is a simulated solicitousness which is forced, bureaucratized and counterfeit. As a result, we find ourselves surrounded by emotions and personal relations that are carefully orchestrated. Many of those we interact with are instructed to keep smiling and to be sure to tell us to 'Have a nice day.'

Symbolic exchange and simulations are two of a number of concepts that make their appearance, at least in rudimentary form, in *The Consumer Society*, concepts destined for further development in Baudrillard's later work. Other such ideas include the referendum, the examination, the ludic, cancerous and ecstatic growth, Americanism (Baudrillard, 1986/1989), fatality, and so on. The last concept which, like symbolic exchange and simulations, was fated to become part of the title of a later book by Baudrillard (1983/1990), makes one of its appearances at the close of *The Consumer Society*. It constitutes Baudrillard's way of dealing with the issue of how a revolution is to come about without a revolutionary subject rationally bringing it to fruition. In his view, the revolution will occur because it is fated to happen, just as the fabled and formative (for Baudrillard) student rebellion of 1968 was destined to come about in France.

It is not surprising that Baudrillard anticipated many of his own ideas in *The Consumer Society*. What is surprising is the degree to which it anticipated later postmodern concerns with such issues as time, space, sexuality and the body. The latter two ideas are more associated with the work of Michel Foucault, but Baudrillard was already dealing with them in his early work.[20] Naturally, he examines both through the lens of consumption.

The body emerges as something that can be used to sell commodities and services as well as being itself a consumed object. In order to be used as an object to sell things, the body must be 'rediscovered' by its 'owner' and viewed narcissistically rather than merely functionally. Once the body is seen in this way, people are free to adorn it with objects and to pamper and seek to improve it with a variety of services. In other words, people are free to consume goods and services on behalf of the body and capitalists are free to produce and market all manner of goods and services (suntan lotions and exercise regimens, for example) aimed at the body. However, Baudrillard contends that it is not bodily drives that are liberated in this way, but merely the drive to buy more goods and services. Thus, the body, like labour power in Marxian theory, must first be liberated (at least as a factor in consumption) so that it can then be exploited.[21]

Once 'liberated' as an object, the body takes its place in the system of objects. However, it is not merely one of the mass of objects to be manipulated and consumed, it is the 'finest' of those objects. People have come to make increasingly great psychological investments in their bodies; in Marxian terms they have come to *fetishize* their bodies. The body has become the object that people lavish more attention *and* money on than any other object. We have become consumers of our own bodies and as such we consume a wide variety of goods and services in order to enhance them. Baudrillard argues that a historical transformation has taken place and instead of seeking salvation through the soul we have come to seek salvation through the body. The latter is evident, among other places, in the therapies, treatments, regimes and sacrifices associated with the body.

Closely tied to the issue of the body, especially its beauty, is that of sexuality. Baudrillard addresses, as Foucault was to later, the explosion of interest in sexuality. What concerns Baudrillard, however, is the role played by sexuality in the consumer society. Not only does sexuality tinge everything that is offered for consumption, but sexuality is itself offered for consumption. There are at least two main reasons for the centrality of sexuality in consumer society. On the one hand, and most obviously, sex sells and it is used to sell myriad objects and services. On the other hand, and perhaps more profound, is the fact that sexuality is expressed in consumption so that it will not become a force to disrupt and perhaps overthrow the existing social order. Thus, Baudrillard differentiates between eroticism as a domain of signs and exchange and the more basic and 'genuine' human desire. In the consumer society eroticism in its more commercial form comes to predominate and it serves to control and subvert the explosive potential of desire.[22]

Consumption

While from both a prospective and a retrospective point of view *The Consumer Society* is fascinating theoretically and metatheoretically, it is clearly above all a work about consumption. While we have already touched on a number of issues relating to consumption, Baudrillard's thoughts on that process will concern us more directly in this section. Unfortunately, it is no easy matter to unravel what Baudrillard means by consumption. It is not that he does not try to define the concept, rather it is that he defines it in many different ways, perhaps because of the many different theoretical inputs into this work.

To Baudrillard, consumption is *not* merely a frenzy of buying a profusion of commodities, a function of enjoyment, an individual function, liberating of needs, fulfilling of the self, affluence, or the consumption of objects. Consumption *is* an order of significations in a 'panoply' of objects; a system, or code, of signs; 'an order of the manipulation of signs'; the manipulation of objects as signs; a communication system (like a language); a system of exchange (like primitive kinship); a morality, that is a system of ideological values; a social function; a structural organization; a collective phenomenon; the production of differences; 'a generalization of the combinatorial processes of fashion'; isolating and individualizing; an unconscious constraint on people, both from the sign system and from the socio-economico-political system; and a social logic.

If one tries to summarize all of the things that consumption is and is not, it seems clear that to Baudrillard consumption is *not*, contrary to conventional wisdom, something that individuals do and through which they find enjoyment, satisfaction and fulfilment. Rather, consumption *is* a structure (or Durkheimian social fact) that is external to and coercive over individuals. While it can and does take the forms of a structural organization, a collective phenomenon, a morality, it is above all else a coded system of signs. Individuals are coerced into using that system. The use of that system via consumption is an important way in which people communicate with one another. The ideology associated with the system leads people to believe, falsely in Baudrillard's view, that they are affluent, fulfilled, happy and liberated.

In the modern consumer society we consume not only goods, but also human services and therefore human relationships. People involved in those services are, as mentioned earlier, very solicitous of us. However, it is through such solicitousness that they serve to pacify us. Thus, pacification is added to the constraint and repression of the system and the code. Ultimately, what is being consumed in the consumer society is consumption itself. The last point is best exemplified by advertising. In watching or reading advertisements people are consuming them; they are consuming consumption.

Baudrillard seeks to extend consumption from goods not only to services, but to virtually everything else. In his view, 'anything can become a consumer object.' As a result, 'consumption is laying hold of the whole of life.' What this communicates is the idea that consumption has been extended to all of culture; we are witnessing the commodification of culture. This, in turn, leads to one of the basic premises of postmodernism – the erosion of the distinction between high and low culture. Art, for example, has increasingly become indistinguishable from any other commodity. A good example is the production and sale of a large number of numbered prints. These mass-produced works of art become commodities like all others and are therefore valued in the same way as other commodities. They are evaluated in a relative manner within the same system of objects as, for example, Levi's jeans or

McDonald's hamburgers. Art, jeans and burgers all acquire their meaning and their value relative to one another as well as to the entire system
of consumer objects. A work of art is now consumed in the same way as,
say, a washing machine. Indeed, they (or at least their signs) are
substitutable for one another. Ultimately, cultural objects are subjected to
the same demand for signs as all other commodities and they come to be
created in order to satisfy that demand. Art, and culture more generally,
come to be subject to the fashion cycle. Instead of being part of a process
of symbolic exchange, art (like much else in the modern world) becomes
just one more 'ludic and combinatorial practice'. Art is thus abolished by
consumer society, but Baudrillard holds to the dream of an art that,
instead of being in the thrall of consumer society, would be able to
decipher it.

Pop art comes under Baudrillard's special scrutiny. Pop is a type of art
that fits well within a society dominated by the logic of signs and
consumption. Pop art is a system which produces 'art' objects that
become just some of many 'sign objects' within the realm of consumption. It is virtually impossible to see pop art as high culture and to
distinguish it from low culture. Indeed, one of the major subjects of pop
artists is low culture as represented in Andy Warhol's work on Campbell
soup cans and Marilyn Monroe. Art, or at least pop art, has ceased to be
creative or subversive; it is merely one more set of objects to be included
in the system of objects. It no longer creates or contradicts the world of
consumer objects;[23] it is part of that world.

Within his body of thought on consumption, and often ignored
because it does not fit well with his primary focus on signs, sign systems
and the code, is Baudrillard's innovative ideas on the 'means of consumption'. Here is a term that is obviously derived from Marx's sense of
the means of production[24] and it has a similar material connotation. In
that sense, it runs counter to the main thrust of Baudrillard's work with
its focus on signs and sign systems. The concept's existence is reflective,
yet again, of the theoretical tension that exists within *The Consumer
Society*. While clearly most influenced by structuralism and moving in a
poststructuralist and ultimately postmodernist direction, Baudrillard is
still influenced by Marxian theory in general and, in this case, by
Marx's thinking on the material means of production such as tools, raw
materials, labour power, technologies and factories. The means of consumption discussed throughout *The Consumer Society* are similarly
material phenomena.[25]

Baudrillard's paradigm of the means of consumption was the French,
especially the Parisian, drugstore. This was different from its modern
American counterpart; it was more like a mini department store or
shopping centre (indeed, Baudrillard appears to equate the shopping
centre and the drugstore). As a paradigm, the drugstore can become a
whole community as it does in Parly 2 with its gigantic shopping centre,
swimming-pool, clubhouse and housing development. The shopping

centre, indeed the entire community, can be seen as the 'drugstore writ large'. In addition to drugstores, shopping centres, and planned communities, Baudrillard also mentions ski resorts, Club Med and airports under the broad heading of the new means of consumption. Also discussed in this context is the credit card.[26]

Baudrillard actually does relatively little with these new means of consumption given his primary interest in the non-material signs associated with consumer society. However, he was quite prescient in recognizing the importance of these phenomena at this early stage in their development. While from a contemporary American, and even global, point of view he may have picked the wrong paradigm (drugstores), since the time that Baudrillard wrote we have witnessed a massive expansion in the number and significance of the new means of consumption. The shopping centres, or malls, that he mentions have become a major presence. The credit card, as well as derivatives like the ATM and debit card, have undergone meteoric expansion. Ski resorts and Club Med have expanded, but to them should be added the far more important cruise ships, Las Vegas-like casino/hotels, and theme parks like Disney World or Euro Disney (in Baudrillard's France). Among the new means of consumption not mentioned by Baudrillard, but clearly part of the same domain, are fast-food restaurants (Ritzer, 1996), home shopping television networks, and cybermalls.

I have come to think of the new means of consumption as 'fantastic cages'. That is, they combine the material reality of Marx's means of consumption (or better Weber's iron cage) with a fantasy world of goods and services (Williams, 1982). While Baudrillard does not describe the means of consumption in these terms, there is support in his work for such a perspective. For example, he contends that affluence and consumption are both lived as myth and endured as objective processes. More generally, in addition to its constraining effect, consumption is described by Baudrillard as a magical, miraculous, fantastic world.[27] The new means of consumption offer the consumer fantastic, mythical images (signs) *and* they are objective structures that constrain the behaviour of consumers.

These new means of consumption are not only important as sites within which people consume signs, but also important in their own right as structures that lead people to consume more and different things. In that sense, they are consistent with Baudrillard's concern with constraint throughout *The Consumer Society*. Terms like 'totalitarian', 'omnipotent', 'tyrannical', 'repressive' and 'terroristic' are frequently applied to the system of signs, the code, the consumer society, the media, leisure, affluence and so on. Baudrillard's world is characterized by not only obligatory consumption, but also obligatory leisure. However, there is also a sense here that society, as successful as it has been in its effort to control people, is doomed to ultimate failure. It cannot forestall the violent and non-violent (e.g. of 'hippies') reactions against consumer society. These reactions are 'fated' to occur.

While there is much criticism here of consumer society, Baudrillard is at pains to differentiate his position from that of mainstream critics such as Galbraith. He sees mainstream criticisms as an 'anti-discourse' which, along with the discourse in praise of consumption, creates the great myth of consumption in modern society. That counter-discourse focuses on the problems associated with consumer society and the tragedy to which it dooms society. However, to Baudrillard, both the counter-discourse and the positive discourse are part of the code and as such they *both* serve to reinforce it. Baudrillard appears to believe[28] that he avoids this problem, perhaps because his main target is the code rather than consumption *per se*. It is the code and its constraints that are the problem. They cannot be attacked through efforts to mobilize people to revolt against them. We are back to Baudrillard's fatal world and the only hope there is: a reaction that cannot be rationally mobilized; a reaction that is unforeseen but nonetheless certain.

Conclusion

The Consumer Society is a significant piece of social theory. The English-speaking world will find an intellectual banquet in this translation. Let me iterate the reasons why I think this is a superior contribution to social theory.

First, it is relatively timeless. Yes, there are a few things that date the book, but in the main the book reads as well today as it must have in 1970. Furthermore, it is a book that will prove to be relevant, if not required, reading for decades to come, for as long as consumerism is a dominant aspect of the social world. Since consumerism is apt to accelerate in the coming years, decades, even centuries, this book will be of continuing relevance.

Second, it is of general, if not universal, significance. This is not a book about France; it reads at least as well from the context of American society. Indeed, it is relevant to any society in the thrall of consumerism, or which is moving inexorably in that direction.

Third, it made a radical break with the productivist orientation that predominated in the France of the day. This was a difficult break for any French social thinker interested in the economy and even more difficult for Baudrillard because he was operating, at least in part, from the overwhelmingly productivist Marxian perspective. Interestingly, today, almost three decades after the publication of *The Consumer Society*, much of the academic world, especially in the United States, has still not made the transition made almost three decades ago by Baudrillard. This is especially true of American sociology and social theory, both of which remain firmly embedded in a productivist paradigm. Thus, while there are well-established subfields like industrial sociology, the sociology of work, and the sociology of occupations, there is no subfield in the United States devoted to the sociology of consumption. It is stunning that such a contention can be made about a sociology at the centre of the world of consumption as it approaches the millennium, but that is the reality.

Fourth, the book shows a theorist (and a theory) in transition, one who is in the midst of struggling, sometimes unsatisfactorily, with a series of often incompatible theoretical perspectives. With the benefit of hindsight we can now see not only where Baudrillard was coming from, but where he was ultimately to go. Indeed, we can see where Baudrillard *had* to go given the tensions and predilections found in *The Consumer Society*.

Fifth, it shows a theorist at work who is sensitive *both* to the most important classical and contemporary theories and to the most important social issues of the day.

Sixth, this is a work that can be read profitably today for theoretical perspectives and ideas that can help us to think better about the consumer society. One example, of particular importance to me, is the idea of the (new) means of consumption. This, as we've seen, is almost a throwaway idea in *The Consumer Society*, one that is little developed by Baudrillard, but it is one that I think is worthy of much greater exploration. There are many such ideas in this book, and that says nothing of the central ideas (e.g. simulation) that have already proven of great utility to many observers of the social world.

This is important social theory, but it is also flawed, perhaps even deeply so. While from one angle there is theoretical richness to be found here, from another a range of theoretical perspectives can be seen as coexisting uncomfortably. As we have seen, this book draws upon Marx (and Marxian theory), Durkheim, Veblen, structuralism, and sociology in general. There is even some Freudian theory thrown into the mix, although Freudian ideas play far less of a role here than they did in *The System of Objects*. The coexistence of a number of theoretical perspectives, without any effort to integrate them, creates a number of problems, many of which have been pointed out previously. Thus, the materialism of a Marxian perspective and its concern for things like the means of production and consumption coexists uncomfortably with the (linguistic) structuralism that leads Baudrillard to accord much greater importance to such non-material phenomena as signs. In the end, of course, Baudrillard privileges the latter over the former, but the issue of the relationship between material and non-material phenomena is unexplored and unresolved.

There is considerable confusion about Baudrillard's views on the sociological perspective and how it relates to structuralism. On the one hand, Baudrillard is critical of sociology which he often associates with psycho-sociology. On the other hand, Baudrillard often explicitly does sociological analyses. At times they are quite straightforwardly sociological, such as when he analyses inequality and social stratification, or when he does one of his functional analyses. However, at other times he is, in fact, doing structural analysis when he says he is operating from a sociological perspective. For example, he often uses the term 'sociology' when he analyses, as he frequently does, the 'logic' of the social system. Yet, it most often seems that he is thinking of something like the structuralist's code when he is dealing with social logic. The fact is that much of this is quite muddy and he is clearly conflating a range of theoretical perspectives.

Relatedly, while Baudrillard has been able to move from production to consumption, a productivist bias continues to haunt this work. There is often a clear sense that production continues to retain its primacy over consumption. Furthermore, as pointed out previously, Baudrillard is often led to make some highly questionable analogies between production and consumption. Part of the reason for this is that Baudrillard had yet to part company with Marxian theory and its productivism. Another part, however, may have been that France of the late 1960s was a society still dominated by production; the shift in emphasis to consumption was in its earliest stages. As we approach the new millennium, the centrality of consumption over production is far clearer in France, the United States and other developed nations.

Furthermore, many of the ideas to be explored and fleshed out dramatically in later works – especially simulations and symbolic exchange – exist here in their rudimentary forms. This is clearly an early work in a career that was to lead to much more fully developed theorizing in the coming years. Thus, for example, one would probably miss the full implications of symbolic exchange were it not for knowledge of Baudrillard's later work. Indeed, it is clear that Baudrillard is only at the early stages of exploring these and other ideas and is himself only dimly aware of their full implications.

On the other hand, this early work bears none of the arrogant disregard for academic canons that characterizes his most recent work. In *The Consumer Society* Baudrillard is clearly working hard at the academic craft. He is reading the relevant literature, adopting its useful insights, critiquing its weaknesses and using all of it, as well as a sensitive eye towards the social world, to develop his theoretical ideas. While *The Consumer Society* is not nearly as important, at least theoretically, as say *Symbolic Exchange and Death*, it is far better and far more important than works like *Cool Memories* (1980–5/1990) or *America* (1986/1989).

Finally, it is worth critiquing this work from a postmodern perspective. From that point of view, itself heavily influenced by Baudrillard's later work, *The Consumer Society* is clearly still mired, at least to some degree, in a modern paradigm; it has all of the modernist characteristics discussed earlier. But rather than rehash all of those from a postmodern perspective, let me emphasize the point that this book is dominated by that *bête noire* of postmodernists, a grand narrative. Fundamentally, and in many different ways, Baudrillard paints a picture of a world that has fallen from the glories of primitive society and the symbolic exchange that characterizes it.[29] During the industrial era, symbolic exchange was replaced by exchange dominated by use-values and exchange-values. When Baudrillard was writing this book, he clearly felt that we had moved into an era dominated by the exchange of sign-values.[30] However he describes the period in which he was writing, it comes off badly in comparison with primitive society and its symbolic exchange. While the terms are different, this is precisely the kind of grand narrative that postmodernists such as Lyotard (1979/1984) have lambasted. In addition to all of the other examples discussed previously, the following are just a few of the other ways in which Baudrillard expressed this grand narrative: the loss of spontaneous, symbolic human relations; more and more of society falling under the logic of signs and the code; the substitution of ludic and combinatorial practices with cultural signs for culture as a symbolic system; the achievement of communion through technical rather than symbolic means; sexuality as a spectre rather than as symbolic rejoicing and exchange; and the loss of authentic relationships.

In the years that followed, Baudrillard actually clarified and extended this grand narrative. However, most recently, his work has become more obscure and elusive on this issue, and many other issues. Nonetheless, a good portion of it remains embedded in a grand narrative much like the one described above. Of course, a critique of Baudrillard from a post-modern perspective may be dismissed by him since he generally rejects the designation of a postmodernist and refuses to use the term.

Another criticism of *The Consumer Society* may be traced to the fact that Baudrillard was in the process of transforming himself into less of a modernist and more of a postmodernist. Baudrillard is clearly trying to distance himself from the modern tendency to develop an Archimedean point (such as Marx's species being) from which to criticize society. However, while he may be making such an effort at an overt level, he seems to implicitly employ such an Archimedean point, symbolic exchange, throughout this book and ensuing works. Thus, Baudrillard had not yet shaken off his modernist inclinations and they were to continue to influence his work for some years to come.

As a result of his Archimedean point, Baudrillard is led into a number of other problematic positions. For example, he is uniformly positive about primitive society. He fails to see anything wrong with it and, more generally, with symbolic exchange. For another, he fails to see anything positive about, or right with, modern (or postmodern) consumer society. He is unremittingly critical of that society. An even slightly more balanced portrait of *both* primitive and modern societies would have enhanced Baudrillard's analysis.

As we turn Baudrillard's work around in our minds, it is clear that it has many flaws from many different perspectives. Yet, what important work in social theory is flawless? In exploring the weaknesses we must not lose sight of the fact that *The Consumer Society* is a significant contribution to social theory, and Jean Baudrillard demonstrates here something that was to become even clearer as his work progressed in the ensuing decade or so – that he is a major social theorist.

Notes

1 The other major possibility would be Michel Foucault, but he is perhaps better thought of as a poststructuralist than as a postmodernist. Baudrillard eschews the post-structural label and Foucault abhorred all attempts to label him.

2 I am using this term to mean those who take sociological theory as a subject of study (Ritzer, 1991).

3 There are a few exceptions; a few things that do date the book. Examples include the discussion of a now-forgotten 1960s radio quiz show, Brigitte Bardot as a paradigm of female beauty, and the hippies and their rejection of modern consumer society.

4 He had dealt with it in greater detail in his previous book, *The System of Objects* (1968/1996). He also dealt with consumption, both directly and indirectly, in this earlier work, but in nothing like the detail in which it was to be analysed in *The Consumer Society*.

5 Two exceptions are *Expressing America: A Critique of the Global Credit Card Society* (Ritzer, 1995) and *Credit Card Nation: America's Dangerous Addiction to Consumer Debt* (Manning and Williams, 1996).

6 Although his name is rarely mentioned, I think *the* most powerful presence is Ferdinand de Saussure and the structuralism and structural linguistics he played such a central role in creating.

7 Fredric Jameson (1991) is one postmodernist who is often accused of this.

8 Consumption is also described as a system of communication, but while this idea too can be traced to Durkheim, it is better associated with other theoretical inputs into his work (see later).

9 Of course, there are those who see a great deal of functional thinking in Marx's work (e.g. Cohen, 1978/1986).

10 While he is doing functional analyses, there is no clear indication that Baudrillard had read Merton (1968) and his work on the functional paradigm.

11 Other pathologies dealt with by Baudrillard are a series of environmental 'nuisances' (air, water and noise pollution), cultural 'nuisances' (like grim housing developments, planned obsolescence, insecure employment), as well as poverty.

12 There is, of course, a Marxian strand of structuralism (Althusser, Poulantzas, etc.).

13 To this he adds a more sociological analysis of social differentiation and stratification. And this has both a lived and a structural aspect. As a result of the latter, people are permanently controlled by a code that they are, in the main, unable to fathom.

14 In Chapter 4, note 1, Baudrillard seems to acknowledge that there is a difference between a modern (presumably including modern sociology) and a structural approach to inequality.

15 Using a more sociological approach, Baudrillard also argues that the lower classes engage in consumption in an effort to compensate for their lack of upward mobility.

16 The key here is the notion of 'social logic' which Baudrillard clearly intends in a structural sense, but also associates with a sociological approach.

17 Baudrillard also critiques psycho-sociologists for being part of the service sector and for being interested in solving social problems by being therapists involved in dealing with communication problems.

18 At this stage in his work, Baudrillard *never* discusses postmodern society. While the term 'postmodern' had some early precursors, and C. Wright Mills had used it as early as 1959, it was not to begin to be used widely until the 1970s.

19 To take another example, he contends that desire is the truth of the body, implying that the body's modern sexuality or eroticism is false.

20 The body had come under Foucault's scrutiny in the *Birth of the Clinic* (1963/1975), but sexuality was not to become a focal concern until *The History of Sexuality* (1978/1980).

21 This is one of the many places in this work where Baudrillard remains locked in a Marxian perspective, causing him, among other things, to make a series of analogies between consumption and production. This is one of the key areas in which it is abundantly clear that Marxian theory is at least as much of a hindrance as it is a help to Baudrillard. It is this kind of tension that sets the stage for Baudrillard's later abandonment of a Marxian perspective.

22 Although Baudrillard does not explicitly make the point, desire would predominate in a society characterized by symbolic exchange.

23 The implication, once again, is that art in primitive society, in symbolic exchange, would play such a contradictory role.

24 In fact, Marx (1981: 471) used the term 'means of consumption' and distinguished it from 'means of production'. The former are commodities that enter individual consumption (as necessities or luxuries), while the latter enter productive consumption. However, Marx is not using 'means of consumption' as it is employed by Baudrillard and here to mean structures that serve to make consumption possible. They are to Marx consumer goods used by the proletariat (means of subsistence) and the capitalist (luxuries).

25 Although they can be seen as signs themselves (McDonald's, Burger King and Wendy's are part of the sign system that is the fast-food industry) as well as settings which permit people to consume signs.

26 Credit cards might better be seen as 'meta-means of consumption', facilitating the use of means of consumption such as shopping malls and ski resorts.

27 Although it is a simulated fantasy world since truly meaningful dreamwork is in Baudrillard's view no longer possible. Yet again, the presumption is that truly meaningful dreamwork is only possible in primitive societies and/or those characterized by symbolic exchange.

28 Obviously, this author is dubious about Baudrillard's belief that he avoided falling into the trap that ensnared Galbraith and others.

29 It is interesting to note that Baudrillard (1968/1996: 54) had earlier noted his resistance to the idea of romanticizing the past.

30 Baudrillard (1976/1993; 1983/1990; 1990/1993) is later more explicit about this historical model and takes it further.

References

Baudrillard, Jean (1968/1996) *The System of Objects*. London: Verso.

Baudrillard, Jean (1973/1975) *The Mirror of Production*. St Louis: Telos.

Baudrillard, Jean (1976/1993) *Symbolic Exchange and Death*. London: Sage.

Baudrillard, Jean (1983/1990) *Simulations*. New York: Semiotext(e).

Baudrillard, Jean (1980–5/1990) *Cool Memories*. London: Verso.

Baudrillard, Jean (1986/1989) *America*. London: Verso.

Baudrillard, Jean (1990/1993) *The Transparency of Evil: Essays on Extreme Phenomena*. London: Verso.

Bauman, Zygmunt (1992) *Intimations of Postmodernity*. London: Routledge.

Cohen, G.A. (1978/1986) *Karl Marx's Theory of History: A Defence*. Princeton, NJ: Princeton University Press.

Featherstone, Mike (1991) *Consumer Culture and Postmodernism*. London: Sage.

Foucault, Michel (1963/1975) *The Birth of the Clinic: An Archaeology of Medical Perception*. New York: Vintage.

Foucault, Michel (1978/1980) *The History of Sexuality. Vol. 1: An Introduction*. New York: Vintage.

Gabriel, Yiannis and Lang, Tim (1995) *The Unmanageable Consumer: Contemporary Consumption and its Fragmentation*. London: Sage.

Galbraith, John Kenneth (1958/1984) *The Affluent Society*, 4th edn. Boston: Houghton Mifflin.

Jameson, Fredric (1991) *Postmodernism, or the Cultural Logic of Late Capitalism*. Durham, NC: Duke University Press.

Lyotard, Jean-François (1979/1984) *The Postmodern Condition: A Report on Knowledge*. Minneapolis: University of Minnesota Press.

Manning, Robert and Williams, Brett (1996) *Credit Card Nation: America's Dangerous Addiction to Consumer Debt*. New York: Basic.

Marx, Karl (1981) *Capital*, Volume II. New York: Vintage.

Merton, Robert (1968) *Social Theory and Social Structure*. New York: Free Press.

Ritzer, George (1991) *Metatheorizing in Sociology*. New York: Lexington.

Ritzer, George (1995) *Expressing America: A Critique of the Global Credit Card Society*. Thousand Oaks, CA: Pine Forge.

Ritzer, George (1996) *The McDonaldization of Society*, rev. edn. Thousand Oaks, CA: Pine Forge.

Williams, Rosalind (1982) *Dream Worlds: Mass Comsumption in Late Nineteenth-Century France*. Berkeley, CA: University of California Press.

PART I
THE FORMAL LITURGY
OF THE OBJECT

1

Profusion

There is all around us today a kind of fantastic conspicuousness of consumption and abundance, constituted by the multiplication of objects, services and material goods, and this represents something of a fundamental mutation in the ecology of the human species. Strictly speaking, the humans of the age of affluence are surrounded not so much by other human beings, as they were in all previous ages, but by **objects**. Their daily dealings are now not so much with their fellow men, but rather – on a rising statistical curve – with the reception and manipulation of goods and messages. This runs from the very complex organization of the household, with its dozens of technical slaves, to street furniture and the whole material machinery of communication; from professional activities to the permanent spectacle of the celebration of the object in advertising and the hundreds of daily messages from the mass media; from the minor proliferation of vaguely obsessional gadgetry to the symbolic psychodramas fuelled by the nocturnal objects which come to haunt us even in our dreams. The two concepts 'environment' and 'ambience' have doubtless only enjoyed such a vogue since we have come to live not so much alongside other human beings – in their physical presence and the presence of their speech – as beneath the mute gaze of mesmerizing, obedient objects which endlessly repeat the same refrain: that of our dumbfounded power, our virtual affluence, our absence one from another. Just as the wolf-child became a wolf by living among wolves, so we too are slowly becoming functional. We live by object time: by this I mean that we live at the pace of objects, live to the rhythm of their ceaseless succession. Today, it is we who watch them as they are born, grow to maturity and die, whereas in all previous civilizations it was timeless objects, instruments or monuments which outlived the generations of human beings.

Objects are neither a flora nor a fauna. And yet they do indeed give the impression of a proliferating vegetation, a jungle in which the new wild man of modern times has difficulty recovering the reflexes of civilization.

We have to attempt rapidly to describe this fauna and flora, which man has produced and which comes back to encircle and invade him as it might in a bad science fiction novel. We have to describe these things as we see and experience them, never forgetting, in their splendour and profusion, that they are *the product of a human activity* and are dominated not by natural ecological laws, but by the law of exchange-value.

> The busiest streets of London are crowded with shops whose show cases display all the riches of the world, Indian shawls, American revolvers, Chinese porcelain, Parisian corsets, furs from Russia and spices from the tropics, but all of these worldly things bear odious, white paper labels with Arabic numerals and the laconic symbols £.s.d. This is how commodities are presented in circulation. (Marx)[1]

Profusion and the Package

Profusion, piling high are clearly the most striking descriptive features. The big department stores, with their abundance of canned foods and clothing, of foodstuffs and ready-made garments, are like the primal landscape, the geometrical locus of abundance. But every street, with its cluttered, glittering shop-windows (the least scarce commodity here being light, without which the merchandise would be merely what it is), their displays of cooked meats, and indeed the entire alimentary and vestimentary feast, all stimulate magical salivation. There is something more in this piling high than the quantity of products: the manifest presence of surplus, the magical, definitive negation of scarcity, the maternal, luxurious sense of being already in the Land of Cockaigne. Our markets, major shopping thoroughfares and superstores also mimic a new-found nature of prodigious fecundity. These are our Valleys of Canaan where, in place of milk and honey, streams of neon flow down over ketchup and plastic. But no matter! We find here the fervid hope that there should be not enough, but too much – and too much for everyone: by buying a piece of this land, you acquire the crumbling pyramid of oysters, meats, pears or tinned asparagus. You buy the part for the whole. And this metonymic, repetitive discourse of consumable matter, of the *commodity*, becomes once again, through a great collective metaphor – by virtue of its very excess – the image of the *gift*, and of that inexhaustible and spectacular prodigality which characterizes the *feast*.

Beyond stacking, which is the most rudimentary yet cogent form of abundance, objects are organized in *packages* or *collections*. Almost all the shops selling clothing or household appliances offer a *range* of differentiated objects, evoking, echoing and offsetting one another. The antique dealer's window provides the aristocratic, luxury version of these sets of objects, which evoke not so much a superabundance of substance as a *gamut* of select and complementary objects presented for the consumer to choose among, but presented also to create in him a psychological chain reaction, as he peruses them, inventories them and grasps them as a total category. Few objects today are offered *alone*, without a context of objects which 'speaks' them. And this changes the consumer's relation to the object: he no longer relates to a particular object in its specific utility, but to a set of objects in its total signification. Washing machine, refrigerator and dishwasher taken together have a different meaning from the one each has individually as an appliance. The shop-window, the advertisement, the manufacturer and the *brand name*, which here plays a crucial role, impose a coherent, collective vision, as though they were an almost indissociable totality, a series. This is, then, no longer a sequence of mere objects, but a chain of *signifiers*, in so far as all of these signify one another reciprocally as part of a more complex super-object, drawing the consumer into a series of more complex motivations. It is evident that objects are never offered for consumption in absolute disorder. They may, in certain cases, imitate disorder the better to seduce, but they are always arranged to mark out directive paths, to orientate the purchasing impulse towards *networks* of objects in order to captivate that impulse and bring it, in keeping with its own logic, to the highest degree of commitment, to the limits of its economic potential. Clothing, machines and toiletries thus constitute object *pathways*, which establish inertial constraints in the consumer: he will move *logically* from one object to another. He will be caught up in a *calculus* of objects, and this is something quite different from the frenzy of buying and acquisitiveness to which the simple profusion of commodities gives rise.

The Drugstore

The synthesis of profusion and calculation is the drugstore. The drugstore (or the new shopping centre) achieves a synthesis of consumer activities, not the least of which are shopping, flirting with objects, playful wandering and all the permutational possibilities of these. In this respect, the drugstore is more representative of modern consumption than the department stores. There, the quantitative centralization of the products leaves less margin for ludic exploration, the arrangement of departments and products imposing a more utilitarian path on the consumer. And, generally, the large stores retain something of the period in which they emerged, when broad classes of the population were first gaining access to *everyday* consumer goods. There is a quite different meaning to the drugstore: it does not juxtapose categories of merchandise, but *lumps signs together indiscriminately*, lumps together all categories of commodities, which are regarded as partial fields of a sign-consuming totality. In the drugstore, the cultural centre becomes part of the shopping centre. It would be simplistic to say that culture is 'prostituted' there. It is *culturalized*. Simultaneously, commodities (clothing, groceries, catering etc.) are also culturalized in their turn, since they are transformed into the substance of play and distinction, into luxury accessories, into one element among others in the general *package* of consumables.

> A new art of living, a new way of living, say the adverts – a 'switched-on' daily experience. You can shop pleasantly in a single air-conditioned location, buy your food there, purchase things for your flat or country cottage – clothing, flowers, the latest novel or the latest gadget. And you can do all this in a single trip, while husband and children watch a film, and then all dine together right there.

There's a café, a cinema, a bookshop, places to buy trinkets, clothing and lots more in the shopping centres: the drugstore takes in everything in kaleidoscopic mode. If the department store offers the fairground spectacle of commodities, the drugstore presents the subtle recital of consumption, the whole 'art' of which consists in playing on the ambiguity of the sign in objects, and sublimating their status as things of use and as commodities in a play upon 'ambience'. This is generalized neo-culture, where there is no longer any difference between a delicatessen and an art gallery, between *Playboy* and a treatise on palaeontology. And the drugstore is to modernize itself to the point of introducing 'grey matter':

> Just selling products doesn't interest us. We want to put a bit of grey matter in there too . . . Three levels. A bar, a dancefloor and sales outlets. Knick-knacks, records, paperback books, intellectual books, a bit of everything. But we aren't trying to flatter the clientele. We are really offering them 'something'. A language laboratory operates on the second level. Among the records and books, you can find the major movements which are stirring our society. Experimental music, tomes which explain our times. This is the 'grey matter' that goes with the products we sell. It's a drugstore, then, but a new-style drugstore with something extra – a little intelligence, perhaps, and a bit of human warmth.

The drugstore can become a whole town: this is the case with Parly 2 with its giant shopping centre in which 'art and leisure mingle with everyday life' and each group of residences radiates out from its swimming-pool, where the local clubhouse becomes its focus. A church built 'in the round', tennis courts ('the least we could do'), elegant boutiques and a library. The tiniest ski resort borrows this 'universalist' model of the drugstore: all activities there are encapsulated in, systematically combined around and centred on the basic concept of 'ambience'. Thus Flaine-la-Prodigue offers you a complete, all-purpose, combinatorial existence:

> Our Mont Blanc, our spruce forests; our Olympic runs, our children's 'plateau'; our architecture carved, chiselled and polished like a work of art; the purity of the air we breathe; the refined ambience of our Forum (modelled on the forums of Mediterranean towns. A lively time is to be had there after a day on the slopes. Cafés, restaurants, shops, skating-rinks, a night club, a cinema and a cultural and amusement centre are all located in the Forum to make the life you live off-piste particularly rich and varied); our internal TV system; our world-scale future (we shall soon be listed as a cultural monument by the Arts Ministry).[2]

We are at the point where consumption is laying hold of the whole of life, where all activities are sequenced in the same combinatorial mode, where the course of satisfaction is outlined in advance, hour by hour, where the 'environment' is total – fully air-conditioned, organized, culturalized. In the phenomenology of consumption, this general 'air-conditioning' of life, goods, objects, services, behaviour and social relations represents the perfected, 'consummated' [*consommé*] stage of an evolution which runs from affluence pure and simple, through inter-connected networks of objects, to the total conditioning of action and time, and finally to the systematic atmospherics built into those cities of the future that are our drugstores, Parly 2s and modern airports.

Parly 2
'The biggest shopping centre in Europe.'
'Printemps, BHV, Dior, Prisunic, Lanvin, Franck et Fils, Hédiard, two cinemas, a drugstore, a Suma supermarket, a hundred other shops – all in a single location!'
In the choice of shops, from grocery to high fashion, two imperatives: commercial dynamism and aesthetic sense. The famous slogan, 'Ugliness doesn't sell', is now *passé*. It might be replaced by: 'The beauty of the setting is the prime requirement for happy living.'
A two-storey structure organized around a central mall, which is the split-level main thoroughfare – the triumphal avenue. Small- and large-scale traders reconciled. The modern pace of life reconciled with age-old idle wandering.
The unprecedented comfort of strolling among shops whose tempting wares are openly displayed on the mall, without even a shop-window for a screen, the mall itself being a combination of the rue de la Paix and the Champs-Elysées. Adorned with fountains, artificial trees, pavilions and benches, it is wholly exempt from changes of season or bad weather: an exceptional system of climate control, requiring 13 kilometres of air-conditioning ducts, makes for perpetual springtime.
Not only can you buy anything here, from shoelaces to an airline ticket; not only can you find insurance companies and cinemas, banks or medical services, bridge clubs and art exhibitions, but you are not a slave to the clock. The mall, like any street, is accessible night and day, seven days a week.
Naturally, for those who want it, the centre has introduced the most modern style of payment: the 'credit card'. This frees shoppers from cheques or cash – and even from financial difficulties. To pay, you just show your card and sign the bill. There's nothing more to it. And every month you get a statement which you can pay off in full or in monthly instalments.
In this marriage of comfort, beauty and efficiency, the Parlysians are discovering the material conditions of happiness which our anarchic cities denied them.

We are here at the heart of consumption as total organization of everyday life, total homogenization, where everything is taken over and super-seded in the ease and translucidity of an abstract 'happiness', defined solely by the resolution of tensions. The drugstore writ large in the form of the shopping centre, the city of the future, is the *sublimate* of all real life, of all objective social life, in which not only work and money disappear, but also the seasons, those distant vestiges of a cycle which has at last also been homogenized! Work, leisure, nature and culture: all these things which were once dispersed, which once generated anxiety and complexity in real life, in our 'anarchic and archaic towns and cities', all these sundered activities, these activities which were more or less irreducible one to another, are now at last mixed and blended, climatized and homogenized in the same sweeping vista of perpetual shopping. All are now rendered sexless in the same hermaphroditic ambience of fashion! All at last *digested* and turned into the same homogeneous faecal matter (naturally enough, this occurs precisely under the sign of the disappearance of *liquid cash* – too visible a symbol still of the *real* faecality of real life, and of the economic and social contradictions which once inhabited it). That is all over now. *Controlled*, lubricated, *consumed* faecality has passed into things; it seeps everywhere into the indistinctness of things and social relations. Just as the gods of all countries coexisted syncretically in the Roman Pantheon in an immense 'digest', so all the gods – or demons – of consumption have come together in our Super Shopping Centre, which is our Pantheon – or Pandaemonium. In other words, all activities, labour, conflicts and seasons have been united and abolished in the same abstraction. The substance of life unified in this way, in this universal digest, can no longer have in it any *meaning*: what constituted the dreamwork, the labour of poetry and of meaning – in other words, the grand schemata of displacement and condensation, the great figures of metaphor and contradiction, which are based on the living interconnection of distinct elements – is no longer possible. The eternal substitution of homogeneous elements now reigns unchallenged. There is no longer any symbolic function, but merely an eternal combinatory of 'ambience' in a perpetual springtime.

2

The Miraculous Status
of Consumption

The Melanesian natives were thrilled by the planes which passed overhead. But those objects never came down from the skies to them, whereas they did descend for the whites, doing so because there were, in certain places, similar objects on the ground to attract the flying aircraft. So, the natives themselves set about building a simulacrum of an aeroplane from branches and creepers. They marked out a landing-ground, which they painstakingly illuminated by night, and patiently waited for the real aircraft to alight on it.

Without calling the anthropoid hunter-gatherers who today wander through our urban jungles primitives (though why not?), we might see this as a fable of the consumer society. The beneficiary of the consumer miracle also sets in place a whole array of sham objects, of characteristic signs of happiness, and then waits (waits desperately, a moralist would say) for happiness to alight.

I do not mean to present this as a principle of analysis. What we have here is simply the private and collective consumer *mentality*. But at this rather superficial level, we may venture this comparison: consumption is governed by a form of *magical thinking*; daily life is governed by a mentality based on miraculous thinking, a primitive mentality, in so far as that has been defined as being based on a belief in the omnipotence of thoughts (though what we have in this case is a belief in the omnipotence of signs). 'Affluence' is, in effect, merely the accumulation of the *signs* of happiness. The satisfactions which the objects themselves confer are the equivalent of the fake aircraft, the Melanesians' models, i.e. the anticipated reflection of the potential Great Satisfaction, of the Total Affluence, the last Jubilation of the definitive beneficiaries of the miracle, from whose insane hope daily banality draws its sustenance. These lesser satisfactions are as yet only exorcistic practices, means of calling down or summoning up total Well-being or Bliss.

In everyday practice, the blessings of consumption are not experienced as resulting from work or from a production process; they are experienced as a *miracle*. There is, admittedly, a difference between the Melanesian native and the viewer settling down in front of his TV set, turning the switch and waiting for images from the whole world to come down to him: the fact is that the images generally obey, whereas planes never condescend to land by magical command. But this technical success is not sufficient to show that our conduct is realistic and the natives' behaviour imaginary. For the same psychical economy ensures on the one hand that the natives' confidence in magic is never destroyed (if the process fails to work, it is because they have not performed the necessary acts) and on the other that the miracle of TV is perpetually brought off, *without ceasing to be a miracle* – this latter by the grace of technology, which wipes out, so far as the consumer's consciousness is concerned, the very principle of social reality, the long social process of production which leads to the consumption of images. And does this so well that the TV viewer, like the native, experiences the appropriation as a *capturing* in a mode of miraculous efficacy.

The Cargo Myth

Consumer goods thus present themselves as *a harnessing of power*, not as products embodying work. And, more generally, once severed from its objective determinations, the profusion of goods is felt as a *blessing of nature*, as a manna, a gift from heaven. On contact with the whites, the Melanesians (to turn again to them) developed a Messianic form of worship: the cargo cult. The whites, they reasoned, lived lives of plenty, whereas they had nothing. This was because the whites knew how to capture or divert the goods that were destined for them, the blacks, by their ancestors who had withdrawn to the ends of the earth. One day, when the white men's magic had been foiled, their ancestors would return with the miraculous cargo, and they would never again know want.

Thus 'underdeveloped' peoples experience Western 'aid' as something natural and expected, something long due to them. As a magical remedy – having no relation to history, technology, continued progress and the world market. But if we look at all closely at them, do not the Western beneficiaries of the economic miracle behave collectively in the same way? Does not the mass of consumers experience plenty as an *effect of nature*, surrounded as they are by the fantasies of the Land of Cockaigne and persuaded by the advertisers' litany that all will be given to them and that they have a legitimate, inalienable right to plenty? Faith in consumption is a new element; the rising generations are now inheritors: they no longer merely inherit goods, but *the natural right to abundance*. And so the cargo myth lives again in the West whereas it is declining in Melanesia. For even if abundance is becoming a banal, daily fact, it continues to be experienced as a daily miracle, in so far as it does not appear to be something produced and extracted, something won after a historical and social effort, but something *dispensed* by a beneficent mythological agency to which we are the legitimate heirs: Technology, Progress, Growth, etc.

This does not mean that our society is not firstly, objectively and decisively a society of production, *an order of production*, and therefore the site of an economic and political strategy. But it means that there is entangled with that order an *order of consumption*, which is an order of the manipulation of signs. To that extent, we may draw a (no doubt venturesome) parallel with magical thought, for both of these *live off signs and under the protection of signs*. More and more basic aspects of our contemporary societies fall under a logic of significations, an analysis of codes and symbolic systems – though this does not make these societies primitive ones, and the problem of the *historical production* of these significations and codes remains fully intact – that analysis having to articulate itself to the analysis of the process of material and technical production as its theoretical continuation.

The Consumed Vertigo of Catastrophe

The usage of signs is always ambivalent. Its function is always a conjuring – both a conjuring up and a conjuring away: causing something to emerge in order to capture it in signs (forces, reality, happiness, etc.) and evoking something in order to deny and repress it. We know that, in its myths, magical thought seeks to conjure away change and history. In a way, the generalized consumption of images, of facts, of information aims also *to conjure away the real with the signs of the real*, to conjure away history with the signs of change, etc.

Reality we consume in either anticipatory or retrospective mode. At any rate we do so at a distance, a distance which is that of the sign. For example, when *Paris-Match* showed us the secret forces assigned to protect the General [de Gaulle] training with machine-guns in the basement of the Prefecture, that image was not read as 'information', i.e. as referring to the political context and its elucidation. For every one of us, it bore within it the temptation of a superb assassination attempt, a prodigious violent event: the attempt will take place, it *is going to* take place; the image is the forerunner to it, and embodies the anticipated pleasure; all perversions have their acting-out. What we see here is the same inverse effect as in the expectation of miraculous abundance within the cargo cult. Cargo or catastrophe – in both cases, we have an effect of consumed vertigo.

We may, admittedly, say that it is, then, our fantasies which come to be signified in the image and consumed in it. But this psychological aspect interests us less than what comes into the image to be both consumed in it and repressed: the real world, the event, history.

What characterizes consumer society is the *universality of the news item* [*le fait divers*] in mass communication. All political, historical and cultural information is received in the same – at once anodyne and miraculous – form of the news item. It is entirely *actualized* – i.e. dramatized in the spectacular mode – and entirely *deactualized* – i.e. distanced by the communication medium and reduced to signs. The news item is thus not one category among others, but **the** cardinal category of our magical thinking, of our mythology.

That mythology is buttressed by the all the more voracious demand for reality, for 'truth', for 'objectivity'. Everywhere we find *'cinéma-vérité'*, live reporting, the newsflash, the high-impact photo, the eye-witness report, etc. Everywhere what is sought is the 'heart of the event', the 'heart of the battle', the 'live', the 'face to face' – the dizzy sense of a total presence at the event, the Great Thrill of Lived Reality – i.e. the **miracle** once again, since the truth of the media report, televised and taped, is precisely that *I was not there*. But it is the truer than true which counts or, in other words, the fact of being there without being there. Or, to put it yet another way, the *fantasy*.

What mass communications give us is not reality, but *the dizzying whirl of reality* [*le vertige de la réalité*]. Or again, without playing on words, a reality without the dizzying whirl, for the heart of Amazonia, the heart of reality, the heart of passion, the heart of war, this 'Heart' which is the locus of mass communications and which gives them their vertiginous sentimentality, is precisely *the place where nothing happens*. It is the allegorical sign of passion and of the event. And signs are sources of security.

So we live, sheltered by signs, in the denial of the real. A miraculous security: when we look at the images of the world, who can distinguish this brief irruption of reality from the profound pleasure of not being there? The image, the sign, the message – all these things we 'consume' – represent our tranquillity consecrated by distance from the world, a distance more comforted by the allusion to the real (even where the allusion is violent) than compromised by it.

The content of the messages, the signifieds of the signs are largely immaterial. We are not engaged in them, and the media do not involve us in the world, but offer for our consumption signs as signs, albeit signs accredited with the guarantee of the real. It is here that we can define *the praxis of consumption*. The consumer's relation to the real world, to politics, to history, to culture is not a relation of interest, investment or committed responsibility – nor is it one of total indifference: it is a relation of **curiosity**. On the same pattern, we can say that the dimension of consumption as we have defined it here is not one of knowledge of the world, nor is it one of total ignorance: it is the dimension of **misrecognition**.

Curiosity and misrecognition denote one and the same form of overall behaviour towards the real, a form of behaviour generalized and systematized by the practice of mass communications and characteristic, therefore, of our 'consumer society'. This is the denial of the real on the basis of an avid and repeated apprehending of its signs.

We can at the same time define *the locus of consumption*: daily life. This latter is not merely the sum of daily doings, the dimension of banality and repetition: it is a *system of interpretation*. Everydayness is the separation of a total praxis into a transcendent, autonomous and abstract sphere (of the political, the social, the cultural) and the immanent, closed, abstract sphere of the 'private'. Work, leisure, family, acquaintances: the individual reorganizes all these things in an involutive mode, this side of the world and of history, in a coherent system based on the closure of the private, the formal freedom of the individual, the securitizing appropriation of the environment, and misrecognition. Everydayness is, from the objective point of view of the totality, impoverished and residual, but it is, by contrast, triumphant and euphoric in its effort totally to autonomize and reinterpret the world 'for internal consumption'. It is here that there is profound, organic collusion between the sphere of private everydayness and mass communications.

Everydayness as closure, as *Verborgenheit*, would be unbearable without the simulacrum of the world, without the *alibi* of participation in the world. It has to be fuelled by the images, the repeated signs of that transcendence. As we have seen, its tranquillity needs the vertiginous spin of reality and history. Its tranquillity requires perpetual *consumed* violence for its own exaltation. That is its particular obscenity. It is partial to events and violence, provided the violence is served up at room temperature. The caricature image of this has the TV viewer lounging in front of images of the Vietnam War. The TV image, like a window turned outside-in, opens initially on to a room and, in that room, the cruel exteriority of the world becomes something intimate and warm – warm with a perverse warmth.

At this 'lived' level, consumption makes maximum exclusion from the (real, social, historical) world the maximum index of security. It seeks the resolution of tensions – that happiness by default. But it runs up against a contradiction: the contradiction between the passivity implied by this new value system and the norms of a social morality which, in essentials, remains one of voluntarism, action, efficacy and sacrifice. Hence, the intense sense of guilt which attaches to this new style of hedonistic behaviour and the urgent need, clearly outlined by the 'strategists of desire', to take the guilt out of passivity. For millions of people without histories, and happy to be so, passivity has to be rendered guiltless. And this is where spectacular dramatization by the mass media comes in (the accident/catastrophe report as a generalized category of all messages): in order for this contradiction between puritanical and hedonistic morality to be resolved, this tranquillity of the private sphere has to appear as a value *preserved only with great difficulty*, constantly under threat and beset by the dangers of a catastrophic destiny. The violence and inhumanity of the outside world are needed not just so that security may be experienced more deeply as security (in the economy of enjoyment [*jouissance*]), but also so that it should be felt *justifiable* at every moment as an option (in the economy of the morality of salvation). The signs of destiny, passion and fatality must flourish around the preserved zone in order that everydayness may seize back the grandeur and sublimity of which it is, precisely, the reverse side. Fatality is thus evoked and signified on all sides, so that banality may revel in it and find favour. The fact that road accidents play so extraordinarily well on radio and TV, in the press, in individual conversation and in the talk of the nation proves this: the crash is the finest exemplar of 'daily fatality'. If it is exploited with such passion, this is because it performs an essential collective function. The litany of road deaths is rivalled only by the litany of weather forecasts. In fact the two form a mythic couple – the obsession with the sun and the litany of death are inseparable.

Everydayness thus offers this curious mix of euphoric justification by 'social standing' and passivity, on the one hand, and the *delectatio morosa* of potential victims of destiny on the other. The whole forms a specific mentality or, rather, 'sentimentality'. The consumer society sees itself as an encircled Jerusalem, rich and threatened. That is its ideology.[1]

3

The Vicious Circle of Growth

Collective Expenditure and Redistribution

Consumer society is not characterized merely by the rapid growth of individual expenditure. It is also accompanied by the growth of expenditure met by third parties (by the government in particular) for the benefit of private individuals, the purpose of some of this being to reduce the inequality of the distribution of resources.

This proportion of collective expenditure meeting individual needs has risen from 13 per cent of total consumption in 1959 to 17 per cent in 1965. In 1965, the percentage of needs met by third parties was:

- 1 per cent for food and clothing ('subsistence');
- 13 per cent for housing expenses, transport and communication networks ('the environment');
- 67 per cent in the fields of education, culture, sport and health ('protection and development of the person').

Collective expenditure is clearly channelled more towards human beings, then, than into the goods and material equipment made available for their use. Similarly, public expenditure is at its highest under the budget heads which look set to grow fastest. But it is interesting to note, with E. Lisle, that it was precisely in this sector where the community assumes the greater part of expenditure, in the sector which it has developed most intensively, that the crisis of May 1968 broke out.

In France, the 'social budget of the nation' redistributes more than 20 per cent of gross internal production (the national education system alone absorbs the total of taxes on personal incomes). The heavy disparity between private consumption and collective expenditure which Galbraith attacks seems much more characteristic of the United States than of the European nations. But this is not the issue. The real problem is whether *this state expenditure makes for an objective equalization of social chances.* Now, it seems clear that this 'redistribution' has little effect on social discrimination at all levels. As for inequality of standards of living, comparison of the two studies on family budgets made in 1956 and 1965 shows no reduction in the discrepancies. We know the incurable, hereditary disparities which apply in the field of education: where other mechanisms more subtle than the economic are in play, the use of economic redistribution alone very largely amounts to reinforcing the mechanisms of cultural inertia. The proportion of 17-year-olds in full-time education is 52 per cent: 90 per cent for the children of senior managers, professionals and teachers, less than 40 per cent for farmers and workers. In higher education, the chances of access for boys in the former category are more than 33 per cent, but only 1 or 2 per cent for the latter.

In the health field, the redistributive effects are not clear: among the active population, there would seem to be an absence of redistribution, as though each social category were at least intent on getting back what it paid in contributions.

As regards taxation and social security, let us examine what E. Lisle has to say on the topic.

> Growing public consumption is financed by the development of taxes and other contributions: where social security alone is concerned, the ratio of contributions to total wage costs has risen from 23.9 per cent in 1959 to 25.9 per cent in 1967. Social security thus costs employed workers a quarter of their resources, it being fair to regard the so-called 'employers' contributions' as a deduction at source from workers' incomes, as is also the 5 per cent fixed-rate contribution. The total of these deductions is much higher than the sum deducted in income tax. Since the latter is progressive, but social security contributions and the fixed-rate contribution are regressive, the *net effect of tax and other deductions is regressive*. If we accept that indirect taxation, which mainly takes the form of VAT, is proportional to consumption, we may conclude that direct and indirect taxation and the social contributions paid by households and very largely earmarked for the financing of collective consumption *would not, overall, have any effect of reducing inequality or any redistributive impact*.
>
> So far as the effectiveness of public amenities is concerned, the available studies show frequent 'deflections' from the intentions of the authorities. When these amenities are designed for the most deprived, we gradually see their 'clientele' becoming more varied, with this diversification leading to an affective rejection, more for psychological than financial reasons, of the poor. When the amenities are intended to be open to all, the elimination of the weakest members of the community occurs from the outset. The effort to achieve open access usually ends in a segregation reflecting the social hierarchy. This would seem to indicate that in a highly inegalitarian society, political actions aimed at ensuring formal equality of access more often than not have increased the degree of inequality. (Commission du Plan, *Consommation et Mode de Vie*)

Inequality with regard to death rates remains very great.

Once again, then, the unadorned figures have no meaning and the increase in available resources – a green light to affluence – has to be interpreted in its real social logic. Social redistribution and, in particular, the effectiveness of public action has to be questioned. Should we regard this 'deviant' performance on the part of 'social' redistribution, this restoration of social inequalities by the very mechanisms which are supposed to eliminate them, as a temporary anomaly due to the inertia of the social structure? Or should we, rather, formulate the radical hypothesis that the mechanisms of redistribution, which are so successful in preserving privilege, are in fact an integral part, a tactical element, of the power system – and hand in glove in that regard with the educational and electoral systems? There would then be no point deploring the repeated failure of a social policy: we should, rather, have to conclude that it was performing its *real* function to perfection.[1]

In spite of certain findings, the evaluation of the effect of transfers, as regards both redistribution and the orientation of consumption, must be delicately handled. If the overall effect of transfers has, in the long run, made it possible to reduce the range of net incomes by half, the relative stability of this distribution of net incomes has only been achieved at the cost of a very great increase in the sums redistributed.

Environmental Nuisance

The advances of affluence – that is to say, of the possession of ever more goods and individual and collective amenities – have been accompanied by increasingly serious 'environmental nuisances' which are a consequence, on the one hand, of industrial development and technical progress, and, on the other, of the very structures of consumption.

First, we have seen the degradation of our shared living space by economic activities: noise, air and water pollution, environmental destruction, the disruption of residential zones by the development of new amenities (airports, motorways, etc.). Traffic congestion produces a colossal deficit in technical, psychological and human terms. Yet what does this matter, since the necessary excess of infrastructural building, the extra expenditure on petrol, the costs of treatment for accident victims, etc. will all be totted up as consumption, i.e. will become, under cover of the gross national product and statistics, an indication of growth and wealth! Does the flourishing mineral water industry permit us to speak of a real increase in 'affluence' since, to a large extent, it is merely a response to the deficient quality of urban water? And so on. We should never be done with listing all the productive and consumer activities which merely counteract internal nuisances generated by the system of growth. Once it has passed a certain threshold, extra productivity is almost entirely wiped out, swallowed up, by this *homoeopathic treatment of growth by growth*.

The 'cultural nuisance effects' caused by the technical and cultural effects of rationalization and mass production are, of course, strictly incalculable. Moreover, value judgements prevent us from defining common criteria. It would not be possible objectively to characterize the 'nuisance effect' of a grim housing estate or a 'Z feature' movie, as we might do with water pollution. Only a civil service inspector could propose, as happened at a recent congress, the creation, alongside a 'clean air ministry', of a 'crime of offending the intelligence' to protect the populace against the effects of the sensationalist press! But we may admit that nuisance effects of this kind are growing at the same pace as affluence.

The built-in obsolescence of products and machines, the destruction of old structures by which certain needs were met, and the increasing number of bogus innovations that are of no appreciable benefit to our lives may all be added to the balance sheet here.

Perhaps even more serious than the downgrading of products and machinery is the fact, pointed out by E. Lisle, that

the cost of rapid progress in the production of wealth is the mobility of labour, and therefore the instability of employment. A turnover and retraining of human beings which has very serious social costs and, most importantly, produces a general sense of *insecurity*. The psychological and social pressures of mobility, of status and competition at all levels (income, prestige, culture, etc.) are becoming more burdensome for everyone. It takes longer to recover, to get back to one's best, and offset the psychological and nervous wear-and-tear produced by the wide range of nuisances: the journey to work, overpopulation, continual stress and aggression . . . In short, the major cost of the consumer society is the sense of generalized insecurity it engenders.

Which leads to the system, as it were, devouring itself:

In this rapid growth . . . which inevitably engenders inflationist tensions . . . a non-negligible fraction of the population is not able to keep up with the pace. These people are 'left on the scrapheap'. And those who stay the course and achieve the mode of life which is proposed as the model do so only at the cost of an effort which leaves them diminished. With the result that society finds itself compelled to cushion the social costs of growth by redistributing a growing proportion of the gross internal product into social investments (education, research, health) which are designed, above all, to serve growth. (E. Lisle)

Now, these compensatory expenditures, whether private or collective, which are intended to cope with dysfunctions rather than increase positive satisfaction, are *added in*, in all the accounts, *as part of the rise in the standard of living*. Not to mention the consumption of drugs, alcohol and all the other conspicuous or compensatory expenditures, or the military budgets, etc. All of this is growth and, hence, affluence.

The growing number of categories of people 'dependent on society', though not actually a nuisance as such (the battle against illness and the decline in mortality being one of the aspects of 'affluence' – a consumer demand), nonetheless puts a heavy financial burden on the process itself. Ultimately, writes J. Bourgeois-Pichat, 'one might imagine the part of the population whose activity is devoted to maintaining the good health of the country's inhabitants growing larger than the part that is actually involved in production.'

In short, we are everywhere reaching a point where the dynamic of growth and affluence is becoming circular and generating only wheel-spin and where, increasingly, the system is exhausting itself in its own reproduction. A threshold where the wheels turn, but do not advance, where the entire increase in productivity goes into maintaining the system's conditions of survival. The only objective result, then, is the cancerous growth of figures and balance sheets. In all essentials, how-ever, we are returning, in strict terms, to the primitive state, which is that of absolute penury, the state of the animal or the native, all of whose energies are devoted to survival. Or the state of those who, as Daumal has it, 'plant potatoes so as to be able to eat potatoes, so as to be able to plant potatoes again, etc.' Now, a system is inefficient when its cost is equal to, or higher than, its output. We are not at that point. But, through nuisances and the social and technical correctives to those nuisances, we can see on the horizon a general tendency towards a *tentacular internal functioning of the system*. With 'dysfunctional' consumption, both individual and collective, rising more quickly than the 'functional', the system is basically becoming parasitic upon itself.

The Accounting of Growth or the Mystique of GNP

In this reference to mystique, we are speaking of the most extraordinary collective bluff on the part of modern societies – of an operation of 'white magic' on the figures which in reality conceals a black magic of collective bewitchment. We are speaking of the absurd gymnastics of *accounting illusions*, of national accounts. Nothing enters into these except factors which are visible and measurable by the criteria of economic rationality, and that indeed is the central principle of the magic. Research, culture and women's domestic labour are all excluded from these accounts on this basis, though certain things which have no business there do figure in them, *merely because they are measurable*. Moreover, like dreams, they have no conception of the negative and lump together everything – nuisances and positive elements – in the most total (though by no means innocent) illogicality.

Economists lump together the value of all products and services of all kinds, making no distinction between public and private services. Nuisances and palliatives to them figure in the accounts on the same basis as the production of objectively useful goods. 'Motion pictures, television, cars, and the vast opportunities which go with mobility, together with such less enchanting merchandise as narcotics, comic books, and pornographia, are all included in an advancing gross national product.'[2]

The deficit side – damage and obsolescence – does not figure in the accounts or, if it does, it figures *positively*! The costs of travel to work, for example, are accounted as consumer expenditure! This is the logical result, expressed in figures, of the magical goal of production for its own sake: *every article produced is sacralized by the very fact of its being produced*. Every article produced is *positive*, every measurable thing is positive. The 30 per cent reduction in the luminosity of air in Paris over the past 50 years is regarded as external and non-existent by the accountants. But if it results in a greater expenditure of electrical energy, of light bulbs and spectacles, etc., then it exists – and exists, moreover, as an increase in production and social wealth! Any restrictive or selective infringement of the sacred principle of production and growth is met with cries of sacrilege ('We shall not touch one screw of Concorde!'). As a collective obsession consigned to the accounting ledgers, productivity primarily has the social function of a *myth*. And anything can be used to fuel that myth – even the conversion of objective realities which refute it into figures which confirm it.

But there is perhaps in this mythic algebra of financial accounts a profound truth, **the** truth of the economico-political system of growth societies. It seems paradoxical to us that the positive and the negative should be added together indiscriminately. But it is perhaps quite simply *logical*. For the truth is perhaps that it is the 'negative' goods, the nuisances compensated, the internal operating costs, the social costs of 'dysfunctional' endoregulation, the subsidiary sectors of useless prodigality *which play the dynamic role of economic engine in that set-up.* This latent truth of the system is, of course, hidden by the figures, the magical addition of which conceals this admirable circularity of the positive and the negative (alcohol sales and hospital building, etc.). And this would explain the impossibility, despite all efforts and at all levels, of rooting out these negative aspects: the system lives by them and cannot rid itself of them. We shall meet this problem again in connection with poverty, that 'balancing counterforce' of poverty which growth societies 'drag along behind them' as a defect and which is in fact one of their most serious 'nuisances'. We have to accept the hypothesis that all these nuisances somewhere enter into the equation as positive factors, as continual factors of growth, as boosters of production and consumption. In the eighteenth century, in *The Fable of the Bees*, Mandeville proposed the theory (already regarded as sacrilegious and libertine in his day) that a society achieves equilibrium not through its virtues but through its vices, and that social peace, progress and human happiness are obtained by the instinctive immorality which leads them continually to break the rules. He was, of course, speaking of morality, but we may construe his words in a social and economic sense. It is, precisely, by its hidden defects, its balancing forces, its nuisances, and what seem like vices when compared with a rational system, that the real system prospers. Mandeville was accused of cynicism: it is the social order, the order of production, which is objectively cynical.[3]

Waste

We know how much the affluence of rich societies is linked to waste, given all the talk of a 'throwaway society' and the fact that some have even envisaged a 'garbage-can sociology': 'Tell me what you throw away and I'll tell you who you are!' But the statistics of waste and rubbish are not interesting in themselves: they are merely a redundant marker of the volume of goods on offer, and their profusion. We can understand neither waste nor its functions if we see in it only the residual scraps of what is made to be consumed but is not. Once again, we have here a simplistic definition of consumption – a moral definition based on the imperative utility of goods. So, all our moralists rail against the squandering of wealth – from the actions of the private individual who no longer respects that kind of *moral law internal to the object which its use-value is taken to be* and the object's time-span (the individual who throws his goods away or changes them to comply with the whims of prestige or fashion, etc.) to waste on the national and international scale – and even on a kind of global scale, where the human race is seen as squandering wealth in its general economy and its exploitation of natural resources. In short, waste is always considered a kind of madness, of insanity, of instinctual dysfunction, which causes man to burn his reserves and compromise his survival conditions by irrational practice.

This vision at least betrays the fact that we are not in an era of *real* affluence, that every present-day individual, group or society, and even the species as such, stands under the sign of scarcity. Now, it is generally the same people who maintain the myth of the inevitable coming of affluence who deplore waste, linked to the menacing spectre of scarcity. At any event, this whole *moral* vision of waste as dysfunction needs to be reviewed from the perspective of a *sociological* analysis which would bring out its true functions.

All societies have always wasted, squandered, expended and consumed beyond what is strictly necessary for the simple reason that it is in the consumption of a surplus, of a superfluity that the individual – and society – feel not merely that they exist, but that they are alive. That consumption may go so far as *consumation*, pure and simple destruction, which then takes on a specific social function. In potlatch, for example, it is the competitive destruction of precious goods which sets the seal on social organization. The Kwakiutl sacrifice blankets, canoes, etched 'coppers', which they burn or throw into the sea to 'maintain their rank,' to assert their value. And, again, it is by 'wasteful expenditure' that the aristocratic classes have asserted their pre-eminence down the ages. The notion of utility, which has rationalistic, economistic origins, thus needs to be revised in light of a much more general social logic in which waste, far from being an irrational residue, takes on a positive function, taking over where rational utility leaves off to play its part in a higher social functionality – a social logic in which waste even appears ultimately as the essential function, the extra degree of expenditure, superfluity, the ritual uselessness of 'expenditure for nothing' becoming the site of production of values, differences and meanings on both the individual and the social level. Within this perspective, a definition of consumption as consumation – i.e. as productive waste – begins to emerge, a perspective contrary to that of the 'economic' (based on necessity, accumulation and calculation) and one in which, by contrast, the superfluous precedes the necessary, and expenditure takes precedence in terms of value over accumulation and appropriation (even if it does not precede them in time).

'O reason not the need! Our basest beggars/ Are in the poorest thing superfluous./ Allow not nature more than nature needs,/ Man's life is cheap as beast's,' writes Shakespeare in *King Lear* [Act II, Scene iv]. In other words, one of the fundamental problems posed by consumption is the following: do human beings organize themselves for purposes of survival, or in terms of the individual or collective meaning they give to their lives? Now, this value of 'being', this structural value may involve the sacrifice of economic values. And this problem is not metaphysical. It is at the centre of consumption and may be expressed as follows: *does not affluence ultimately only have meaning in wastage?*

Should we define affluence in terms of foresight and the laying in of provisions, as Valéry does?

> When one contemplates piles of imperishable foodstuffs, is one not looking at time in hand and activity spared? A box of biscuits is a whole month of idleness and life. Pots of conserves and fibre baskets stuffed with seeds and nuts are a storehouse of quietude; a whole winter of tranquillity lies hoarded up in their aroma . . . Robinson Crusoe could smell the presence of the future in the coffers and chests in his store-room. His hoard radiated idleness. A sense of time emanated from it, in the way an absolute heat emanates from certain metals . . . Humanity only raised itself up slowly by finding a footing on that which endures. Foresight and the laying in of provisions gradually freed us from the rigours of our animal necessities and the 'word-for-word' character of our wants . . . Nature suggested this: it so arranged matters that we carried with us the means of resisting somewhat the inconstancy of events; the fat which is on our limbs, the memory which stands ready in the depth of our souls are models of stores laid up which our industry has imitated.

This is the *economic* principle to which Nietzsche's (and also Bataille's) vision of the living being, who wants above all to 'expend his strength', stands opposed:

> Physiologists should think again before positing the 'instinct of preservation' as the cardinal drive in an organic creature. A living thing wants above all to *discharge* its force: 'preservation' is only a consequence of this. Beware of *superfluous* teleological principles! The entire concept 'instinct of preservation' is one of them . . . The 'struggle for existence' – this formula refers to an exceptional situation; the rule is much rather the struggle for power, the ambition to have 'more' and 'better' and 'quicker' and 'more often'. (Nietzsche, *The Will to Power* [Fragment 650])

This 'something more' by which value asserts itself may become the 'something of one's own'. This law of symbolic value, which states that the essential element always lies beyond what is indispensable, is best illustrated in expenditure, in loss, but it may also be verified in appropriation, provided that the latter has the differential function of being extra, of being 'something more'. As witness the Soviet example: the worker, the cadre, the engineer and the party member have a flat which does not belong to them: whether rented or granted for life, it is accommodation which goes with the job, tied to the social status of worker and active citizen, not to the private person. This good is a social service, not a piece of property, nor even less a 'consumable'. On the other hand, the secondary residence, the dacha in the country with its garden, is something which belongs to them. Neither is this a lifetime possession, nor is it revocable, and it can survive them and become hereditary. Hence the 'individualistic' infatuation attaching to it: all efforts are directed towards the acquisition of that dacha (for want of automobiles, which to some extent play this same 'second home' role in the West). The dacha has a prestige value and a symbolic value: it is the 'something more'.

In a way, it is the same with affluence: for this to become a *value*, there has to be not simply enough, but *too much*. A significant difference has to be maintained and manifested between the necessary and the superfluous. This is the function of waste at all levels. By this, I mean that it is illusory to wish to reduce it, to aspire to eliminating it, for it is waste, in some way, which orientates the whole system. Indeed, just like the gadget (where does usefulness end, uselessness begin?), it can be neither defined nor delimited. All production and expenditure beyond the needs of strict survival can be termed waste (not just fashion in clothing and the food 'dustbin', but military super-gadgets, the 'Bomb', the superfluous agricultural equipment of certain American farmers, and the industrialists who renew their machinery every two years rather than getting the full value out of it: not only consumption, but production too – not to mention politics – largely obeys the laws of ostentatious processes). Profitable and sumptuary investments are everywhere inextricably interlinked. An industrialist who had invested 1,000 dollars in advertising declared: 'I know half of it is wasted, but I don't know which half.' This is always how it is in a complex economy: you cannot isolate what is useful or try to remove what is superfluous. Moreover, the (economically) 'wasted' half is not perhaps the half which takes on the least value, in the long term or, viewed more subtly, even in the very act of being 'lost'.

We have to interpret the immense wastage of our affluent societies this way. It is that wastage which defies scarcity and, contradictorily, signifies abundance. It is not utility, but that wastage which, in its essence, lays down the psychological, sociological and economic guidelines for affluence.

Is not the fact that the glass packaging can be thrown away the mark of **the golden age**?

One of the great themes of mass culture, as analysed by Riesman and Morin, illustrates this in an epic register: this is the theme of the *hero of consumption*. In the West, at least, the impassioned biographies of heroes of production are everywhere giving way today to biographies of heroes of consumption. The great exemplary lives of self-made men and founders, pioneers, explorers and colonizers, which succeeded those of saints and historical figures, have today given way to the lives of movie stars, sporting or gambling heroes, of a handful of gilded princes or globe-trotting barons – in a word, the lives of *great wastrels* (even if the imperative is often that they be shown, by contrast, in their daily 'simplicity', doing their shopping, etc.). With all these great dinosaurs who fill the magazines and TV programmes, it is always the excessiveness of their lives, the potential for outrageous expenditure that is exalted. Their superhuman quality is the whiff of potlatch that attaches to them. In this way, they fulfil a very precise social function: that of sumptuary, useless, inordinate expenditure. They fulfil this function by proxy for the whole social body, like the kings, heroes, priests or great parvenus of bygone ages. Like them, indeed, they are never so great as when, like James Dean, they pay for this elevated position with their lives.

The essential difference is that, in our current system, this spectacular squandering no longer has the crucial symbolic and collective signification it could assume in primitive feasting and potlatch. This prestigious consumption, too, has been 'personalized' and mass-mediafied. Its function is to provide the economic stimulus for mass consumption, which is defined in relation to it as a subculture of labour. The caricature of the magnificent dress which the star wears for just one evening are the 'disposable panties' which, 80 per cent viscose and 20 per cent non-woven acrylic, can be put on in the morning and thrown away at night, and need no washing. Above all, this sublime, de luxe wastage highlighted by the mass media merely replicates, on the cultural level, a much more fundamental and systematic wastage which, for its part, is integrated directly into economic processes, a *functional*, bureaucratic wastage produced by the production system as it produces material goods, a wastage built into them and, therefore, obligatorily *consumed* as one of the qualities and dimensions of objects of consumption: their fragility, their built-in obsolescence, their condemnation to transience. What is produced today is not produced for its use-value or its possible durability, but rather with an *eye to its death*, and the increase in the speed with which that death comes about is equalled only by the speed of price rises. This alone would be sufficient to throw into question the 'rationalistic' postulates of the whole of economic science on utility, needs, etc. Now, we know that the order of production only survives by paying the price of this extermination, this perpetual calculated 'suicide' of the mass of objects, and that this operation is based on technological 'sabotage' or organized obsolescence under cover of fashion. Advertising achieves the marvellous feat of consuming a substantial budget with the sole aim not of adding to the use-value of objects, but of *subtracting value from them*, of detracting from their time-value by subordinating them to their fashion-value and to ever earlier replacement. And we may leave aside here the colossal quantities of social wealth sacrificed on military budgets and other state and bureaucratic prestige expenditure: that kind of prodigality no longer has any symbolic odour of potlatch about it; it is a desperate, but vital solution for an economico-political system in distress. This 'consumption' at the highest level is part of the consumer society, of the same order as the convulsive craving for objects at the level of the private individual. The two conjointly ensure the reproduction of the order of production. And we have to distinguish individual or collective waste as a symbolic act of expenditure, as a festive ritual and an exalted form of socialization, from its gloomy, bureaucratic caricature in our societies, where wasteful consumption has become a daily obligation, a forced and often unconscious institution like indirect taxation, a cool participation in the constraints of the economic order.

'Smash up your car, the insurance will do the rest!' Indeed, the car is without doubt one of the main foci of daily and long-term waste, both private and collective. Not only is it so by its systematically reduced use-value, its systematically increased prestige and fashion coefficient, and the outrageous sums invested in it, but – without doubt much more deeply than this – by the spectacular collective sacrifice of sheet-metal, machinery and *human lives* in the Accident. The Accident: that gigantic 'happening', the finest offered by consumer society, through which society affords itself in the ritual destruction of materials and life the proof of its excessive affluence (a proof *a contrario*, but one that is much more effective in the depths of the imagination than the direct proof by accumulation).

The consumer society needs its objects in order to be. More precisely, it needs to *destroy* them. The use of objects leads only to their *dwindling disappearance*. The value created is much more intense in *violent loss*. This is why destruction remains the fundamental alternative to production: consumption is merely an intermediate term between the two. There is a profound tendency within consumption for it to surpass itself, to transfigure itself in destruction. It is in destruction that it acquires its meaning. Most of the time in daily life today, it remains subordinate – as a managed consumptivity – to the order of productivity. This is why, most of the time, objects are present *by their absence*, and why their very abundance paradoxically signifies penury. Stock is the excessive expression of lack and a mark of anxiety. Only in destruction are objects there *in excess* and only then, in their disappearance, do they attest to wealth. At any rate, it is clear that destruction, either in its violent and symbolic form (the happening, potlatch, destructive acting-out, both individual and collective) or in its form of systematic and institutional destructiveness, is fated to become one of the preponderant functions of post-industrial society.

PART II
THE THEORY OF CONSUMPTION

4
The Social Logic of Consumption

The Egalitarian Ideology of Well-Being

The whole of the discourse on needs is based on a naïve anthropology: that of the natural propensity to happiness. Happiness, written in letters of fire behind the least little advert for bathsalts or the Canary Islands, is the absolute reference of the consumer society: it is the strict equivalent of *salvation*. But what is this happiness which haunts modern civilization with such ideological force?

Here again one has to revise all spontaneous conceptions. The ideological force of the notion of happiness does not originate in a natural propensity on the part of each individual to realize that happiness for himself. It derives, socio-historically, from the fact that the myth of happiness is the one which, in modern societies, takes up and comes to embody *the myth of Equality*. All the political and sociological virulence with which that myth has been charged since the industrial revolution and the revolutions of the nineteenth century has been transferred to Happiness. The fact that Happiness initially has that signification and that ideological function has important consequences for its content: to be the vehicle of the *egalitarian* myth, Happiness has to be *measurable*. It has to be a *well-being* measurable in terms of objects and signs; it has to be 'comfort', as Tocqueville put it, already noting this trend of democratic societies towards ever more well-being as a reduction of the impact of social misfortune and an equalization of all destinies. Happiness as total or inner enjoyment – that happiness independent of the signs which could manifest it to others and to those around us, the happiness which has no need of *evidence* – is therefore excluded from the outset from the consumer ideal in which happiness is, first and foremost, the demand for equality (or distinction, of course) and must, accordingly, always signify with 'regard' to *visible* criteria. In this sense, Happiness is even further removed from any collective 'feast' or exaltation since, fuelled by an egalitarian exigency, it is based on *individualistic* principles, fortified by the Declaration of the Rights of Man and the Citizen which explicitly recognize the right to Happiness of everyone (of each individual).

The 'Revolution of Well-Being' is heir to, or executor of, the Bourgeois Revolution, or simply of any revolution which proclaims human equality as its principle without being able (or without wishing) *fundamentally* to bring it about. The democratic principle is then transferred from a real equality of capacities, of responsibilities, of social chances and of happiness (in the full sense of the term) to an equality before the Object and other *manifest* signs of social success and happiness. This is the *democracy of social standing*, the democracy of the TV, the car and the stereo, an apparently concrete but, in fact, equally formal democracy which, beyond contradictions and social inequalities, corresponds to the formal democracy enshrined in the Constitution. Both of these, the one serving as an alibi for the other, combine in a general democratic ideology which conceals the *absence* of democracy and the non-existence of equality.

In the mystique of equality, the notion of 'needs' is indissociable from that of well-being. Needs point to a reassuring universe of ends, and this naturalistic anthropology lays the ground for the promise of a universal equality. The implicit argument is as follows: all men are equal before need and before the principle of satisfaction, since all men are equal before the *use-value* of objects and goods (whereas they are unequal and divided before *exchange-value*). Need being indexed to use-value, we have here a relationship of *objective* utility or natural finality, in the face of which there is no longer any social or historical inequality. At the meat-and-drink level (use-value), there are no proletarians, no privileged individuals.

Thus the complementary myths of well-being and needs have a powerful ideological function of reducing, of eliminating the objective, social and historical, determinations of inequality. The whole political game of the welfare state and consumer society consists in surmounting their contradictions by increasing the volume of goods, with the prospect of an automatic equalization by quantity and a level of final *equilibrium*, which would be that of total well-being for all. Communist societies themselves speak in terms of equilibrium, of 'natural' individual or social needs, needs 'harmonized' and free of all social differentiation or class connotation. In this, they too drift from a *political* solution to a definitive solution by abundance, substituting the formal equality of goods for the social transparency of exchanges. Thus we also see the 'Revolution of Well-Being' taking over from the social and political revolution in the socialist countries.

If this perspective on the ideology of well-being is correct (namely, that that ideology is a vehicle for the myth of formal equality 'secularized' in goods and signs), then it is clear that the eternal problem of whether consumer society promotes or hinders equality, whether it is a fully achieved democracy (or on the way to being so) or the opposite – merely restoring earlier inequalities and social structures – is a *false problem*. Whether or not one is able to prove that consumption possibilities are being equalized (income differentials being flattened out, social redistribution, the same fashion for everyone, along with the same TV programmes and holiday destinations), this means nothing, since posing the problem in terms of the equalization of consumption is already to substitute the pursuit of objects and signs (level of substitution) for the real problems and their *logical* and sociological analysis. All in all, analysing Affluence does not mean seeking its verification in the statistics, which can only be as mythic as the myth, but radically changing focus and approaching the myth of Affluence with a logic other than its own.

Analysis does, of course, require that we assess affluence in terms of figures, that we draw up the balance sheet of well-being. But the figures do not speak for themselves, and they never provide any counter-argument. Only interpretations speak, sometimes to one side of, sometimes against, the figures. Let us listen to what they have to say.

The most stubborn and unyielding of these is the idealist version:

- growth means affluence;
- affluence means democracy.

It being impossible to conclude that this state of total felicity is imminent (even at the statistical level), the myth becomes more 'realistic' and we have the ideal-reformist variant: the large-scale inequalities of the first phase of growth are diminishing, there is no 'iron law' any longer, incomes are becoming harmonized. The hypothesis of a smooth, continuous progress towards ever more equality is, of course, refuted by certain facts (the 'Other America': 20 per cent living in poverty, etc.). But these point to a temporary dysfunction, to teething troubles. Growth, while producing certain inegalitarian effects, implies an overall, long-term democratization. Thus, in Galbraith's view, the problem of equality/inequality is no longer relevant. It was linked to the problem of wealth and poverty and the structures of the 'affluent' society have resolved the problem, despite an unequal redistribution. The 'poor' (the 20 per cent) are those who remain, for one reason or another, outside the industrial system, outside growth. The principle of growth itself remains inviolate; it is homogeneous and is tending to homogenize the entire social body.

The basic question which arises at this level is the question of this 'poverty'. For the idealists of affluence, it is 'residual'; it will be cleared up by additional growth. Yet it seems to carry on down the post-industrial generations and all efforts to eliminate it (particularly in the USA, with the 'great society') seem to run up against some mechanism of the system which seems to reproduce it functionally at each stage of development, like a kind of drag on growth, a kind of mechanism indispensable to the general wealth. Should we believe Galbraith when he imputes this inexplicable residual poverty to the dysfunctions of the system (the priority accorded to military and other wasteful expenditure, a lagging of public services behind private consumption, etc.) or should we *turn* his argument *around* and conclude that *growth, in its very dynamic, is based on this disequilibrium*? Galbraith is very contradictory on this: all his analyses tend to demonstrate in a sense *how its defects are functionally implicated in the system of growth*, yet he recoils before the logical conclusions which would challenge the system itself and recasts everything in a liberal perspective.

Generally, the idealists do not go beyond this paradoxical affirmation: in spite of everything, and by a *devilish* inversion of its aims (which, as everyone knows, cannot but be *beneficent*), growth produces, reproduces and restores social inequality, privileges, disequilibria, etc. They will admit, for example, as Galbraith does in *The Affluent Society*, that, ultimately, it is an increase in production which takes over the re-distributive role ('As there comes to be more and more . . . so there will in the end be enough for everyone' – these principles, based on the physics of fluids, are *never* true in a social relations context, where, as we shall see below, things work in precisely the opposite way). Moreover, from these principles, Galbraith derives an argument for the under-privileged, to the effect that even those on the bottom rung of the ladder have more to gain from an accelerated growth of production than from any other form of redistribution. But this is all specious: for, if growth grants *everyone* access to an income and a volume of goods which are higher in absolute terms, what is sociologically characteristic is the *process of distortion* which sets in at the very heart of growth. It is the *rate of distortion* which subtly structures growth and gives it its true meaning. It is so much easier to content oneself with the spectacular disappearance of a particular extreme form of penury or certain *secondary* inequalities, to assess affluence by statistics and *general* quantities, by *absolute* increa-ses and *gross* national products, than to analyse it in terms of structures! Structurally, it is the rate of distortion which is significant. It is that rate which, at an international level, marks the growing distance between the underdeveloped countries and the overdeveloped nations, and also, within those nations, the lower incomes falling further behind the higher, failing industries losing ground to the high-technology sectors, rural areas losing out to urban, industrial areas, etc. Chronic inflation allows this relative pauperization to be masked, by revising all nominal values upwards, whereas the calculation of the relative functions and averages would show up instances of partial decline at the bottom of the scale, and, at any event, a structural distortion throughout. There is no point constantly arguing that this is temporary or conjunctural when one sees the whole logic of the system sustaining it and the system indeed depending upon it for the fulfilment of its aims. At best, we can say the system stabilizes around a certain rate of distortion or, in other words, stabilizes, *whatever the absolute volume of wealth*, at a point which includes a *systematic* inequality.

The only way, in fact, to escape the idealist dead-end of this gloomy listing of dysfunctions is to admit that there is a *systematic logic* at work here. It is also the only way of getting beyond the false problematic of abundance and scarcity which, like votes of confidence in parliamentary circles, functions to stifle all discussion.

There is not in fact – and never has been – any 'affluent society', any more than there is an 'indigent society', since every society of whatever kind and *whatever the volume of goods produced or available wealth* is geared both to a *structural excess* and a *structural penury*. The excess may be the portion set aside for the gods or for sacrifice; it may be sumptuary expenditure, surplus value, economic profit or prestige budgets. It is, at any rate, that luxury levy which defines both the wealth of a society and its social structure, since it is always the prerogative of a privileged minority and its function is precisely to reproduce caste or class privilege. At the sociological level there is no equilibrium. Equilibrium is the ideal fantasy of economists which is contradicted, if not by the very logic of society as a condition, then at least by all known forms of social organization. Every society produces differentiation, social discrimination, and that structural organization is based on the use and distribution of wealth (among other things). The fact that a society enters upon a phase of growth, as our industrial society has done, changes nothing in this process. Quite the contrary, indeed, in a certain way the capitalist system (and the productivist system in general) has been the culmination of that functional unlevelling, that disequilibrium, by rationalizing it and generalizing it in all respects. The spirals of growth are arrayed around the same structural axis. As soon as the fiction of GDP is abandoned as the criterion of affluence, we have to admit that *growth neither takes us further from, nor brings us closer to, affluence. It is logically separated from it by the whole social structure* which is, here, the determining instance. A certain type of social relations and social contradictions, a certain type of 'inequality', which used to perpetuate itself in the absence of economic progress, is today reproduced in and through growth.[1]

This means that we must take another view of growth. We shall no longer say with the enthusiasts: 'Growth produces affluence and therefore equality.' Nor shall we take the extreme opposite view: 'Growth produces inequality.' Overturning the false problem of whether growth is egalitarian or inegalitarian, we shall say that it is **growth itself which is a function of inequality**. It is the need of the inegalitarian social order – the social structure of privilege – to maintain itself that produces and reproduces growth as its strategic element. To put it yet another way, the internal autonomy of (technological, economic) growth is weak and secondary by comparison with that determination by the social structure.

Growth society is, overall, the product of a compromise between egalitarian democratic principles, which for support within that society can draw on the myths of Affluence and Well-Being, and the fundamental imperative of maintaining an order of privilege and domination.

That society is not founded on technological progress. It is that mechanistic view which fuels the naïve illusion of future affluence. It is, rather, this contradictory dual determination which underpins the possibility of technological progress. It is this determination too which governs the emergence in our contemporary societies of certain egalitarian, democratic, 'progressive' processes. But it must be recognized that these only emerge there in *homoeopathic doses*, drip-fed out by the system to ensure its survival. In this systematic process, equality itself is a (secondary and derived) function of inequality. As is growth. The tendency for incomes to be equalized, for example (for it is chiefly at this level that the egalitarian myth operates), is necessary to the internalization of growth processes – an internalization which, as we have seen, contributes tactically to the reproduction of the social order, which is a structure of privilege and class power. All this points to the few symptoms of democratization as being *alibis* essential to the viability of the system.

These few symptoms are, moreover, themselves superficial and suspect. Galbraith rejoices at the decline in importance of inequality as an economic (and, hence, social) problem – not that it has disappeared, as he says, but because wealth no longer brings with it the fundamental advantages (power, enjoyment, prestige, distinction) it once implied. The power of property-owners and stockholders is at an end; it is now experts and organized technicians who exercise power, if not indeed intellectuals and scientists! The conspicuous consumption of the great capitalists, the 'Citizen Kanes', is over, and there are no great fortunes any more. Indeed, the rich feel almost duty-bound to underconsume. In short, without wishing to do so, Galbraith clearly shows that if there is equality (if poverty and wealth are no longer a problem), it is precisely because equality no longer has any real importance. Things have moved on; the criteria of value are now elsewhere. Social discrimination, power and so on – those things which remain *the key factors* – have been shifted away from income or wealth pure and simple. It is of little consequence, in these conditions, if all incomes are in the end equal; the system can even afford the luxury of making a great step in that direction, *for the fundamental determination of 'inequality' is no longer to be found there*. Knowledge, culture, the structures of responsibility and decision-making, and influence are all criteria which, though still largely associated with wealth and level of income, have to a great extent relegated these latter – together with external marks of status – in the order of the social determinants of value, in the hierarchy of criteria of 'power'. Galbraith, for example, confuses the 'underconsumption' of the rich with the abolition of criteria of prestige based on money. Now, admittedly, the rich man who drives a 2CV no longer bedazzles. What he does is more subtle: he super-differentiates himself, super-distinguishes himself by his *manner* of consuming, by style. He maintains his privilege absolutely by moving from conspicuous to discreet (super-conspicuous) consumption, by moving from quantitative ostentation to distinction, from money to culture.

In fact, even this argument, which we might term the thesis of the 'tendency of the rate of economic privilege to fall', is not certain. For money always transmutes itself into hierarchical privilege, into a privilege of power and culture. We may accept that it is no longer decisive (has it ever been?). What Galbraith and the others fail to see is that the very fact that (economic) inequality is no longer a problem in itself constitutes a problem. Registering a little too hastily the abatement of the 'iron law' in the economic field, they then go no further, and fail to produce a broader theory of this 'iron law' or to see how it shifts from the field of incomes and 'consumption' – henceforth blessed by Affluence – to a much more general social field where, functioning more subtly, it makes itself all the more irreversible.

The Industrial System and Poverty

When one examines the problem of the industrial system *objectively* in its entirety, cutting through all the liturgy of growth and affluence, one sees that all the possible positions boil down to two fundamental options:

1 The Galbraith option (shared by so many others). This magical-idealist position consists in expelling from the system all the negative phenomena – dysfunctions, nuisances, poverty – on the grounds that these are admittedly deplorable but accidental, residual and eventually remediable. In this way, the enchanted orbit of growth is preserved.
2 The view that the system survives on disequilibrium and structural penury, that its logic is totally ambivalent, and that it is so not merely conjuncturally but structurally. The system only sustains itself by producing wealth **and** poverty, by producing as many dissatisfactions as satisfactions, as much nuisance as 'progress'. Its only logic is to survive and its strategy in this regard is to keep human society out of kilter, in perpetual deficit. We know the system has traditionally and powerfully drawn on the aid of *war* to survive and to revive. Today the mechanisms and functions of war have been integrated into the economic system and the mechanisms of daily life.

If one accepts this structural paradox of growth, from which the contradictions and paradoxes of affluence derive, then it is naïve and mystificatory to confuse the logical processes of social underdevelopment with the poor, the 20 per cent of 'underprivileged', the individuals 'thrown on the scrapheap'. Those processes cannot be located in real persons, in real places, in real groups. By the same token, they cannot be eliminated by the billions of dollars which have been thrown at the lower classes, or by the massive redistribution programmes to 'dispel poverty' and provide equal life-chances (all this being got up as the 'new frontier',[2] a social ideal to tug at the heart strings). We have to acknowledge at times that the 'great societists' themselves believe in all this, their bewilderment at the failure of their 'unremitting, generous' efforts being only the more comical for that fact.

If poverty and nuisance cannot be eliminated, this is because they are anywhere but in the poor neighbourhoods. They are not in the slums or shanty-towns, but in the socio-economic structure. Yet this is precisely what has to be concealed, what must not be said, and indeed billions of dollars are spent on hiding the fact (in the same way, heavy medical and pharmaceutical expenditure may be necessary to avoid admitting that a problem is not what it appears to be, and may, for example, be psychological in nature – the well-known process of 'denial'). A society, like an individual, may ruin itself in this way, trying to escape analysis. Now, it is true here that analysis would be lethal for the system itself. So the sacrifice of useless millions in the struggle against what is merely the *visible phantom* of poverty is not too high a price to pay if it means that the myth of growth is preserved. We have to go even further and acknowledge that *this real poverty is a myth* – and one in which the myth of growth glories, pretending to battle fiercely against it and yet keeping it alive all the same as its secret goals require.

Having said this, we should not believe that it is because they are *deliberately* bloodthirsty and odious that the industrial or capitalist systems continually regenerate poverty or identify with the arms race. Moralistic analysis (which neither liberals nor Marxists escape) is always a mistake. If the system could find an equilibrium or survive on foundations other than unemployment, underdevelopment and military expenditure, it would do so. And on occasion it does. When it can safely maintain its power by way of beneficial social effects, by way of 'affluence', it does not fail to do so. It is not opposed on principle to the social 'spin-offs' of progress. It takes both nuclear power and the well-being of citizens as its objective, simultaneously and without distinction: the point is that, in its eyes, the two are ultimately equal as contents and its final goal lies elsewhere.

The simple fact is that, at the strategic level, it turns out that military expenditures (for example) are more reliable, easier to monitor and more effective in achieving the survival and goals of the system as a whole than education – as is also the case with motor cars rather than hospitals, colour televisions rather than playgrounds, etc. But that negative discrimination does not apply to public services as such. Things are much more serious than this: *the system knows only the conditions of its survival, it knows nothing of social and individual contents*. That should forearm us against a number of (typically social-reformist) illusions: the illusions which involve a belief that one can change the system by modifying its contents (transferring military expenditures to education etc.). Moreover, the paradox is that all these social demands are, slowly but surely, taken up and realized by the system itself, thus slipping through the fingers of those who turn them into a political platform. Consumption, information, communication, culture, affluence – all these things are today set in place, discovered and organized by the system itself, as new *productive forces*, for its greater glory. It too is changing over (relatively) from a violent to a non-violent structure: it is substituting affluence and consumption for exploitation and war. But it will win no affection for this, since it is not actually changing, but merely obeying its own laws.

The New Segregations

Not only affluence, but nuisance too has been taken up into the social logic. The ascendancy of the urban and industrial milieu is producing new examples of shortage: shortages of space and time, fresh air, greenery, water, silence. Certain goods, which were once free and abundantly available, are becoming luxuries accessible only to the privileged, while manufactured goods or services are offered on a mass scale.

The relative homogenization at the level of essential goods is thus being accompanied by a 'slippage' of values and a new hierarchy of utilities. The distortion and inequality are not reduced; they are *transferred elsewhere*. Everyday consumer objects are becoming less and less expressive of social rank. And incomes themselves, in so far as the great disparities are being reduced, are losing their value as a distinctive criterion. It is even possible that consumption (taken in the sense of expenditure, of the purchase and possession of visible objects) will gradually concede to other criteria and other types of behaviour the pre-eminent role it currently plays in the variable geometry of status. Ultimately, *it will become the prerogative of everyone when it no longer has any meaning*.

We are already seeing the social hierarchy being registered in more subtle criteria: type of work and responsibility, level of education and culture (the *way* of consuming everyday goods may itself be a kind of 'scarce commodity'), participation in decision-making. Knowledge and power are, or are going to become, the two great scarce commodities of our affluent societies.

But these abstract criteria do not prevent us, even today, from reading a growing discrimination in other concrete signs. Segregation by place of residence is not new, but, being increasingly linked to a consciously induced shortage and chronic speculation, it is tending to become decisive, in terms of both geographical segregation (town centres and outskirts, residential zones, rich ghettos, dormitory suburbs, etc.) and habitable space (the inside and outside of the dwelling, the addition of a 'second home', etc.). Objects are less important today than space and the social marking of space. Habitat thus perhaps has an *opposite* function to that of other consumables. The latter have a homogenizing function, the former a differentiating function in terms of space and location.

Nature, space, clean air, silence – it is the incidence of the pursuit of these scarce commodities and their high price which we read in the differential indices of expenditure between two categories at opposite ends of the social spectrum. The difference in expenditure between workers and senior managers on essential goods is 100:135, but it is 100:245 on household equipment, 100:305 on transport and 100:390 on leisure. One should not see these figures as showing a quantitative graduation within a homogeneous space of consumption, but see, through them, the social *discrimination* attaching to the *quality* of goods sought after.

There is much talk of the right to health, to space, to beauty, to holidays, to knowledge and to culture. And, as these new rights emerge, so ministries emerge with them, such as the Ministries of Health, or of Leisure. And why not add Beauty and Clean Air? This whole phenomenon, which seems to express a general individual and collective advance, rewarded in the end with embodiment in institutions, is ambiguous in its meaning and one might, as it were, see it as representing quite the opposite: *there is no right to space until there no longer is space for everyone*, and until space and silence are the privilege of some at the expense of others. Just as there was no 'right to property' until there was no longer land for everyone and there was no right to work until work became, within the framework of the division of labour, an exchangeable commodity, i.e. one which no longer belonged specifically to individuals. We might ask whether the 'right to leisure' does not, similarly, mean that leisure too has reached the stage of technical and social division which work did before it and has thus, in fact, come to an end.

The appearance of these new social rights, brandished as slogans and emblazoned on the democratic banner of the affluent society, is in fact symptomatic, therefore, of the elements concerned acquiring the status of distinctive signs and class (or caste) privileges. *The 'right to clean air' signifies the loss of clean air as a natural good, its transition to commodity status and its inegalitarian social redistribution.* One should not mistake for objective social progress (something being entered as a right in the tables of the law) what is simply the advance of the capitalist system – i.e. the progressive transformation of all concrete and natural values into productive forms, i.e. into sources

1   of economic profit;
2   of social privilege.

A Class Institution

Consumption no more homogenizes the social body than the educational system homogenizes cultural opportunities. It even highlights the disparities within it. One is tempted to regard consumption and the growing participation in the same(?) goods and the same(?) products, both material and cultural, as a corrective to social disparities, social hierarchy and the ever increasing level of discrimination where power and responsibilities are concerned. In fact, the ideology of consumption, like that of education (i.e. the representation one has of a total equality before the electric razor or the car, like the representation one has of a total equality before writing and reading), does indeed play this role. Everyone today can read and write; everyone has (or will have) the same washing machine and buys the same paperbacks. But this equality is entirely formal: though bearing on what is most concrete, it is in fact abstract. And it is, by contrast, on this homogeneous abstract base, on this foundation of the *abstract democracy of spelling or the TV set*, that the real system of discrimination is able to operate – and to operate all the more effectively.

In actual fact, it is not even true that consumer products, the signs of this social institution, establish this primary democratic platform: for, in themselves, and taken individually (the car, the razor, etc.), they have no meaning: it is their constellation, their configuration, the relation to these objects and their overall social 'perspective' which alone have a meaning. And that meaning is always a distinctive one. They themselves, in their materiality as signs (their subtle differences), reflect that structural determination. Like education, they obey the same social logic as other institutions, even in the inverted image they give of that logic.

Consumption, like the education system, is a class institution: not only is there inequality before objects in the economic sense (the purchase, choice and use of objects are governed by purchasing power and by educational level, which is itself dependent upon class background, etc.) – in short, not everyone has the same objects, just as not everyone has the same educational chances – but, more deeply, there is radical discrimination in the sense that only some people achieve mastery of an autonomous, rational logic of the elements of the environment (functional use, aesthetic organization, cultural accomplishment). Such people do not really deal with objects and do not, strictly speaking, 'consume', whilst the others are condemned to a magical economy, to the valorization of objects as such, and of all other things as objects (ideas, leisure, knowledge, culture): *this fetishistic logic is, strictly, the ideology of consumption.*

Similarly, for those who do not have the key to them – that is to say, the code which admits one to their legitimate, rational and effective use – knowledge and culture are merely the occasion of a sharper, subtler cultural segregation, since knowledge and culture merely appear in their eyes, and in the use they make of them, as a supplementary mana, a reserve of magic power, instead of being the opposite: a learning process and an objective training.[3]

A Salvational Dimension

By their number, redundancy, superfluity and formal extravagance, by the play of fashion and all that exceeds pure and simple function in them, objects merely *simulate the social essence* – **status** – that grace of predestination which is only ever bestowed by birth to a few and which the majority, having opposite destinies, can never attain. This hereditary legitimacy (whether of blood or of culture) is at the very heart of the concept of status, the key concept in the whole dynamics of social mobility. Underlying all aspirations, there is this ideal end of a status by birth, a status of grace and excellence. And status also haunts the environment of objects. It is status which arouses this frenzy, this berserk world of knick-knacks, gadgets, **fetishes**, all of which seek to mark out a value for all eternity and prove *salvation by works, since salvation by grace is unattainable*. Hence the very particular prestige of the ancient object, which is a sign of heredity, of innate value, of irreversible grace.

It is a class logic which imposes salvation by objects. That is a *salvation by works*, which, in its 'democratic' nature, stands opposed to the aristocratic principle of salvation by grace and election. Now, in the universal consensus, salvation by grace always wins out over salvation by works. This is to some degree what we see among the lower and middle classes, where 'proving oneself by objects' – salvation by consumption – in its endless process of moral demonstration, battles despairingly to attain a status of personal grace, of god-givenness and predestination. That remains, nonetheless, the preserve of the upper classes, who prove their excellence elsewhere, in the display of their culture and the exercise of their power.

Differentiation and Growth Society

All this leads us, then, beyond the Metaphysics of Needs and Affluence, to a genuine analysis of the *social logic* of consumption. That logic is by no means that of the individual appropriation of the *use-value* of goods and services – a logic of unequal abundance, some having rightful access to the miracle, others merely to the by-products of the miracle. It is a logic not of satisfaction, but of the production and manipulation of social signifiers. The process of consumption may be analysed within this perspective from two basic angles:

1   As a *process of signification and communication*, based on a code into which consumption practices fit and from which they derive their meaning. Consumption here is a system of exchange, and the equivalent of a language. Structural analysis is the appropriate approach at this level. We shall come back to this below.

2   As a *process of classification and social differentiation* in which sign/ objects are ordered not now merely as significant differences in a code

but as status values in a hierarchy. Here consumption can be submitted to a strategic analysis which determines its specific importance in the distribution of status values (overlapping with other social signifiers: knowledge, power, culture, etc.).

The principle of analysis remains as follows: you never consume the object in itself (in its use-value); you are always manipulating objects (in the broadest sense) as signs which distinguish you either by affiliating you to your own group taken as an ideal reference or by marking you off from your group by reference to a group of higher status.

Yet, this process of status differentiation, which is a fundamental social process by which everyone *takes their place within society*, has a lived aspect and a structural aspect, the one conscious, the other unconscious, the one ethical (the morality of social standing, of status rivalry, of the ladder of prestige), the other structural. One is permanently governed by a code whose rules and meaning-constraints – like those of language – are, for the most part, beyond the grasp of individuals.

The consumer experiences his distinctive behaviours as freedom, as aspiration, as choice. His experience is not one of being *forced to be different*, of obeying a code. To differentiate oneself is always, by the same token, to bring into play the total order of differences, which is, from the first, the product of the total society and inevitably exceeds the scope of the individual. In the very act of scoring his points in the order of differences, each individual maintains that order, and therefore condemns himself only ever to occupy a relative position within it. Each individual experiences his differential social gains as absolute gains; he does not experience the structural constraint which means that positions change, but the order of differences remains.

Yet it is this *constraint of relativity* which is crucial, in so far as it is with reference to this that the differential occupation of positions *will never end*. It alone can account for the fundamental character of consumption, its **unlimited** character, a dimension which cannot be explained by any theory of needs and satisfaction, since, if the calculation were made in terms of a calorific or energy balance sheet or of use-values, a saturation point would very soon be reached. But we very clearly see the opposite happening: an acceleration of the rate of consumption, increased pressure on demand, which means that the gap between a giant-scale productivity and an even more frantic propensity to consume is, in fact, growing wider (meanwhile, affluence, understood as the harmonious matching of the two, recedes indefinitely). This can only be explained if we radically abandon the individual logic of satisfaction and accord the social logic of differentiation the decisive importance it deserves. And if we distinguish that logic of difference from mere conscious determinations of prestige, since these latter are still *satisfactions*, the consumption of *positive differences*, whereas the sign or mark of distinction is always both a positive **and** a negative difference – this is why it refers on indefinitely to other signs and impels the consumer on to definitive dissatisfaction.[4]

The alarm of economists and other idealist theorists of well-being at the clear inability of the consumption system to stabilize – at its uncontrolled, runaway character – is always very instructive. It is characteristic of their way of seeing things in terms of increases in goods and incomes – and never in terms of relation and differentiation by signs. Thus Gervasi writes: 'Growth is accompanied by the constant introduction of new products as the rise in incomes expands the scope for consumption.' 'The rising trend of incomes brings not only a wave of new products, but also a proliferation of different qualities for the same product.' (Why? What is the logical relation?) 'The rise in incomes leads to a progressive improvement in quality.' We have here again the same implicit thesis: 'The more you earn, the more you want, and better', this being true of everyone individually, without distinction, each person seeking a rational optimum of well-being.

Very generally, moreover, the field of consumption is a homogeneous one for them (with, at most, some disparities of income or 'cultural' disparities in it), which fans out statistically around an average type: the 'consumer'. This is a view induced by the conception of American society as an immense middle class – and European sociology has now, largely, fallen in with that view. In fact, the field of consumption is a *structured social field*, where not only goods, but needs themselves, like the various cultural characteristics, pass from a key group, a leading elite, to the other social categories as these 'rise' relatively on the social ladder. There is no 'mass of consumers' and no need emerges spontaneously from the grassroots consumer: needs have no chance of appearing in the 'standard package' of needs if they have not already been part of the 'select package'. The *path of needs*, like the path of objects and goods, is thus first socially selective: needs and satisfactions trickle down in accordance with an absolute principle, a kind of social categorical imperative which is the maintenance of distance and of differentiation by signs. It is this law which conditions all introduction of new objects as distinctive social material. It is this law of the 'top-down' replenishment of distinctive material which runs through the whole world of consumption, not the rise in incomes, which runs in the opposite direction (from the bottom up, towards total homogeneity).

No product has any chance of being mass-produced, no need has any chance of being satisfied on a mass scale unless it has already ceased to form part of the higher model and has been replaced by some other distinctive good or need – such that the distance is preserved. Popularization occurs only as a function of selective innovation at the top. And that process occurs, of course, as a function of the 'falling rate of distinction' of objects and goods in a growth society. Here again some preconceptions are in need of revision: popularization has its own mechanics (the mass media, etc.), but it has no logic of its own regarding content. It is within the upper echelons of society, as a reaction against the loss of earlier distinctive markers, that innovation takes place, in order to restore social distance. As a result, the needs of the middle and lower classes are always, like objects, subject to a certain backwardness; they lag temporally and culturally behind the needs of the upper classes. This is a not insignificant form of *segregation* in so-called democratic society.

One of the contradictions of growth is that it produces goods and needs at the same time, but does not produce them at the same rate – the rate of production of goods being dependent on industrial and economic productivity, the rate of production of needs on the logic of social differentiation. Now, the upward and irreversible mobility of the needs 'set free' by growth (i.e. *produced* by the industrial system as it obeys its internal logical constraints)[5] has its own dynamic, which is different from the dynamic of the production of the material and cultural goods supposedly meant to satisfy those needs. Beyond a certain level of urban socialization, status competition and psychological 'take-off', aspiration is irreversible and unlimited, and develops to a rhythm of accelerated socio-differentiation and generalized interrelativity. Hence the specific problems linked to this 'differential' dynamic of consumption. If aspirations were simply concurrent with productivity, subordinate to it, there would be no problem. In fact, by their very own logic, which is a logic of difference, they constitute an uncontrollable variable. They are not just another variable in the economic calculation – a socio-cultural variable of situation or context – but a crucial structural variable which governs all others.

We must, admittedly, accept (as the various studies on this point, particularly on cultural needs, have done) a certain *sociological inertia* of needs. In other words, a certain indexing of needs and aspirations to the social position achieved (and not in the least, as conditioning theorists believe, to the goods on offer). Once again at this level, we find the same processes which are those of social mobility. A certain 'realism' means that people in a particular social situation never have aspirations much beyond what they can reasonably hope to attain. By having aspirations *a little* beyond their objective chances, they internalize the official norms of a growth society. By having aspirations which are *little* beyond, they internalize the real norms of expansion of that society (Malthusian even in its expansion) which are always short of what is possible. The less one has, the lower one's aspirations (at least up to a certain threshold, where total unrealism takes over to compensate for destitution). Thus, *the very process of the production of aspirations is inegalitarian*, since resignation at the bottom end of the social scale and freer aspirations at the top compound the inequality of objective possibilities of satisfaction. Here again, however, the problem must be seen in the round: it is quite possible that strictly consumer aspirations (material and cultural) – which, for their part, display a much greater degree of elasticity than professional or cultural aspirations – in fact *compensate* for the serious underachievement of certain classes in terms of social mobility. The compulsion to consume might be said to compensate for failure to rise up the vertical social ladder. At the same time as expressing a status demand, the aspirations to 'overconsume' (on the part of the lower classes in particular) might be seen as expressing the felt failure of that demand.

The fact remains that needs and aspirations, activated by social differentiation and demands for status, tend in a growth society always to progress a little more quickly than available goods or objective chances. Moreover, the industrial system itself, which presupposes the growth of needs, also presupposes *a perpetual excess of needs* over the supply of goods (in the same way as it speculates on a reserve of unemployment to maximize the profit it extracts from labour power: we meet here once again the deep-level analogy between needs and pro-ductive forces).[6] Speculating upon this discrepancy between goods and needs, the system does, however, verge on a contradiction in that growth not only implies the growth of needs and a certain disequilibrium between goods and needs, but further implies *the growth of that very disequilibrium* between the growth of needs and the growth of productiv-ity. Hence the 'psychological pauperization' and the chronic, latent state of crisis, which is itself functionally linked to growth, but which can lead to a point of breakdown, an explosive contradiction.

Confronting the growth of needs and the growth of production means bringing out the decisive 'intermediate' variable that is differentiation. Hence, it is the increasing differentiation of products and the increasing differentiation of the social demand for prestige that must be seen in their interrelations.[7] Now, the former is limited, whereas the latter is not. There are no limits to man's 'needs' as a social being (i.e. as a being productive of *meaning* and relative to others in *value*). The quantitative intake of food is limited, the digestive system is limited, but the cultural system of food is, for its part, indefinite. And it is, moreover, a relatively contingent system. The strategic value of advertising – and also its trick – is precisely this: that it targets everyone *in their relation to others*, in their hankerings after reified social prestige. It is never addressed to a lone individual, but is aimed at human beings in their differential relations and, even when it seems to tap into their 'deep' motivations, it always does so in *spectacular* fashion. That is to say, it always calls in their friends and relations, the group, and society, all hierarchically ordered within the process of reading and interpretation, the process of 'setting-off' or 'showing-off' [*faire-valoir*] which it sets in train.

In a small group, needs, like competition, can doubtless stabilize. There is less of an escalation in the signifiers of status and the stuff of distinction. We can see this in traditional societies or micro-groups. But, in a society of industrial and urban concentration such as our own, where people are crowded together at much greater levels of density, the demand for differentiation grows even more quickly than material productivity. When the whole social world becomes urbanized, when communication becomes total, 'needs' grow exponentially – not from the growth of *appetite*, but from *competition*.

That escalation, that differential 'chain reaction', sanctioned by the total dictatorship of *fashion*, has the urban space as its locus. (And, reciprocally, the process reinforces urban concentration by rapid acculturation of the rural or marginal areas. It is, therefore, irreversible. Any vague desire to halt it is naïve.) Human density in itself exerts a fascination. But the *language of cities* is competition itself. Motives, desires, encounters, stimuli, the endless judgements of others, continual eroticization, information, the appeals of advertising: all these things make up a kind of abstract destiny of collective participation, set against a real background of generalized competition.

Just as industrial concentration results in an ever increased production of goods, so urban concentration results in a limitless promotion of needs. Now, though the two types of concentration are contemporaneous, they nonetheless have their own dynamics, as we have seen, and their results do not coincide. Urban concentration (and hence differentiation) outstrips productivity. That is the basis of urban alienation. A neurotic equilibrium does, however, establish itself in the end, somewhat to the advantage of the more coherent order of production – the proliferation of needs washing back over the order of products, and becoming integrated into it after a fashion.

All this defines *the growth society as the opposite of an affluent society.* Thanks to this constant tension between competitive needs and production, thanks to this *shortage-based* tension, to this 'psychological pauperization', the order of production manages only to give rise to – and only to 'satisfy' – the needs appropriate to it. In the growth-based order, there are, by this logic, no autonomous needs and there cannot be any. *There are only the needs of growth.* There is no place for individual goals in the system; there is room only for the goals of the system. All the dysfunctions pointed out by Galbraith, Bertrand de Jouvenel, etc., are *logical*. It is reasonably clear that cars and motorways are a need of the system, but so is the university training of middle managers. Hence the 'democratization' of the university is as much a systemic need as car production.[8] Because the system produces only for its own needs, it is all the readier systematically to hide behind the alibi of individual needs. Hence the gigantic growth of private consumption by comparison with public services (Galbraith). This is no accident. The cult of individual spontaneity and the naturalness of needs is, by its nature, father to the productivist option. Even the most 'rational' needs (education, culture, health, transport, leisure), cut off from their real collective significance, are taken up, in the same way as the incidental needs deriving from growth, into the systematic future perspectives of that growth.

Furthermore, it is in an even deeper sense that growth society is the opposite of an affluent society. Before being a society productive of goods, it is in fact a society productive of privileges. Now, there is a necessary, sociologically definable relationship between *privilege* and *penury*. There could not (in any society whatever) be privilege without penury. The two are structurally linked. Growth is, therefore, by its social *logic*, paradoxically defined by the reproduction of a structural penury. That penury no longer has the same sense as primary penury (a dearth of *goods*): that could be regarded as provisional and it is, in part, overcome in our societies, but the structural penury which substitutes for it is definitive since it is *systematized* as a booster function and power strategy in the very logic of the order of growth.

In conclusion, we shall state that there is, at any event, a logical contradiction between the ideological hypothesis of growth society, which is social homogenization at the highest level, and its concrete social logic, based on a structural differentiation – this logically contradictory whole forming the basis of an overall strategy.

And, lastly, we shall once again stress the major illusion, the cardinal myth of this false affluent society: the illusion of distribution on the idealist pattern of 'communicating vessels'. The flow of goods and products does not find its level like the sea. Social inertia, unlike natural inertia, does not lead to a state of distortion, disparity and privilege. Growth is not democracy. Profusion is a function of discrimination. How could it be the corrective to it?

The Palaeolithic, or the First Affluent Society

We must abandon the received idea we have of an affluent society as a society in which all material (and cultural) needs are easily met, for that leaves all social logic out of account. We should rather espouse the notion recently propounded by Marshall Sahlins in his article on the first affluent society, that it is our industrial and productivist societies which, unlike certain primitive societies, are *dominated by scarcity*, by the obsession with scarcity characteristic of the market economy.[9] The more one produces, the more clearly does one show up, amidst plenty, how irremediably far off is that final point which affluence would represent, defined as an equilibrium between human production and human gōals. Since what is satisfied in a growth society, and increasingly satisfied as productivity grows, are the very needs of the order of production, not the 'needs' of man (the whole system depends indeed on these being misrecognized), it is clear that affluence recedes indefinitely: more precisely, it is irrevocably rejected and the organized reign of scarcity (structural penury) preferred.

For Sahlins, it was the hunter-gatherers (the primitive nomadic tribes of Australia, the Kalahari, etc.) who, in spite of their absolute 'poverty', knew true affluence. The primitive people of those societies have no personal possessions; they are not obsessed by their objects, which they throw away as and when they need to in order to be able to move about more easily. They have no apparatus of production, or 'work': they hunt and gather 'at their leisure', as we might say, and share everything within the group. They are entirely prodigal: they consume everything immediately, make no economic calculations and amass no stores. The hunter-gatherer has nothing of that bourgeois invention, *economic man*, about him. He is ignorant of the basic principles of Political Economy. And, indeed, he never exploits human energies, natural resources or the effective economic possibilities to the full. He sleeps a lot. He has a trust – and this is what characterizes his economic system – in the wealth of natural resources, whereas our system is characterized (ever more so with technical advance) by despair at the insufficiency of human means, by a radical, catastrophic anxiety which is the deep effect of the market economy and generalized competition.

The *collective* 'improvidence' and 'prodigality' characteristic of primitive societies are the sign of *real* affluence. We have only the *signs* of affluence. Beneath a gigantic apparatus of production, we anxiously eye the *signs* of poverty and scarcity. But poverty consists, says Sahlins, neither in a small quantity of goods, nor simply in a relation between ends and means: it is, above all, a *relation between human beings*. The basis for the confidence of primitive peoples and for the fact that, within hunger, they live a life of plenty, is ultimately the transparency and reciprocity of social relations. It is the fact that no monopolization whatever of nature, the soil, the instruments or products of 'labour' intervenes to obstruct exchange and institute scarcity. There is among them no accumulation, which is always the source of power. In the economy of the gift and symbolic exchange, a small and always finite quantity of goods is sufficient to create general wealth since those goods pass constantly from one person to the other. Wealth has its basis not in goods, but in the concrete exchange between persons. It is, therefore, unlimited since the cycle of exchange is endless, even among a limited number of individuals, with each moment of the exchange cycle adding to the value of the object exchanged. It is this concrete and relational dialectic which we find inverted, as a *dialectic of penury* and unlimited need, in the process of competition and differentiation characteristic of our civilized, industrial societies. Where, in primitive exchange, every relationship adds to the social wealth, in our 'differential' societies every social relationship adds to individual lack, since every thing possessed is relativized in relation to others (in primitive exchange, it is *valorized* by the very relationship with others).

It is not, therefore, paradoxical to argue that in our 'affluent' societies abundance is *lost* and that it will not be restored by an interminable increase in productivity, by unleashing new productive forces. Since the structural definition of abundance and wealth lies in social organization, only a revolution of the social organization and of social relations could bring those things about. Will we return, one day, beyond the market economy, to prodigality? Instead of prodigality, we have 'consumption', forced consumption in perpetuity, twin sister to scarcity. It was social logic which brought primitive peoples the 'first' (and only) affluent society. It is our social logic which condemns us to luxurious and spectacular penury.

5

Towards a Theory of Consumption

The Autopsy of *Homo oeconomicus*

A fairy story: 'Once upon a time there was a Man who lived in Scarcity. After many adventures and a long journey through Economic Science, he met the Affluent Society. They married and had lots of needs.' 'The beauty of the economic man,' as A.N. Whitehead remarked, 'was that we knew exactly what he was after.'[1] That human fossil of the Golden Age, born, in the modern era, from the happy union of Human Nature and Human Rights, is endowed with a heightened sense of formal rationality, which leads him to:

1 seek his own happiness without the slightest hesitation;
2 prefer objects which will provide him with the greatest satisfactions.

The whole discourse, lay and academic, on consumption is articulated upon this sequence, which is the mythological sequence of a folk-tale: a Man 'endowed' with wants or needs which 'lead' him towards objects which 'give' him satisfaction. Since man is, nonetheless, never satisfied (he is, indeed, criticized for this), the same story begins over and over again, with the sterile self-evidence of old fables.

Some react with perplexity: 'Needs are the most stubbornly unknown of all the unknowns with which economic science deals' (Knight). But this doubt does not stop the litany on needs being faithfully recited by all the proponents of the anthropological disciplines from Marx to Galbraith, from Robinson Crusoe to Chombart de Lauwe. For economists, the key term is 'utility': the desire for a specific good for purposes of consumption or, in other words, the destruction of its utility. Need is therefore already given its object [*finalisé*] by the available goods; preferences are orientated by the particular spread of products offered on the market: this is, basically, *effective demand*. For the psychologist, the key idea is 'motivation', a slightly more complex theory, less 'object-oriented' and more 'instinct-oriented', of a kind of pre-existent, ill-defined necessity. For sociologists and psycho-sociologists who come last in line, there is a 'socio-cultural' dimension here. The anthropological postulate of an *individual* endowed with needs and inclined by nature to satisfy them is not questioned, nor is that of the consumer as a free, conscious being who is presumed to know what he wants (sociologists are wary of 'deep motivations'), but on the basis of this idealist postulate it is accepted that there is a 'social dynamic' of needs. Models of competition and conformity are brought in ('keeping up with the Joneses') drawn from the group context or from grand 'cultural models' relating to society at large or to history.

Roughly speaking, three positions can be identified: for Marshall, needs are interdependent and rational; for Galbraith (we shall come back to him), choices are imposed by persuasion; for Gervasi (and others), needs are interdependent and are the product of a learning process (rather than a rational calculation).

Gervasi: 'Choices are not made at random, but are socially controlled and reflect the cultural model within which they are made. It is not just any old goods which are produced or consumed: they must have some meaning with regard to a system of values.' This leads into a view of consumption in terms of integration: 'The goal of the economy is not the maximization of production *for the individual*, but the maximization of production linked in with the value system of the society' (Parsons). Duesenberry will claim, in this same vein, that the only choice is, in fact, to vary one's possessions as a function of one's position on the hierarchical ladder. Ultimately, it is the difference of choices between one society and another and the similarity of choices within the same society which force us to consider consumer behaviour as a social phenomenon. There is an appreciable difference between this view and that of the economists: their 'rational' choice has here become conformist choice, the choice of conformity. Needs are directed not so much towards objects as towards values, and their satisfaction initially has the sense of *signing up to those values*. The fundamental, unconscious, automatic choice of the consumer is to accept the style of life of a particular society (it is, therefore, no longer a choice(!) and the theory of the autonomy and sovereignty of the consumer is refuted).

This sociology culminates in the notion of the 'standard package', defined by Riesman as the set of goods and services which forms more or less the baseline heritage of the average American. Rising regularly, indexed to the national standard of living, it is an ideal minimum of a statistical kind, a standard model of middle-class life. Exceeded by some, only dreamt of by others, it is an *idea* in which the American way of life is encapsulated.[2] Here again, the 'standard package' refers not so much to the materiality of goods (TV, bathroom, car, etc.) as to *the ideal of conformity*.

All this sociology does not advance us very much. Apart from the fact that the notion of conformity has never been anything but a cover for an immense tautology (in this case: the average American defined by the 'standard package', which is itself defined by the statistical average of goods consumed. Or, to put it sociologically, a particular individual is a member of a particular group because he consumes particular goods, and he consumes particular goods because he is a member of a particular group). The postulate of formal rationality we have seen at work among economists is simply transferred here to the relation between the individual and the group. Conformity and satisfaction are analogous: they involve the same matching-up of a subject to objects, or a subject to a group – *these terms being posited as separate entities* – by means of a logical principle of equivalence. The concepts of 'need' and 'norm' are the expressions in the respective cases of this miraculous match-up.

Between the 'utility' of the economists and the 'conformity' of the sociologists, there is the same difference as Galbraith establishes between the pursuit of profit, the pecuniary motivation characteristic of the 'traditional' capitalist system, and the behaviour of identification and adaptation specific to the era of organization and the technostructure. The basic question which results, both for the psycho-sociologists of conformity and for Galbraith, and which (with good reason) does not arise for the economists – for whom the consumer remains an individual ideally free in his final, rational calculation – is that of the *conditioning of needs*.

Since Packard's *The Hidden Persuaders* and Dichter's *The Strategy of Desire* (not to mention a number of other works), the conditioning of needs (by advertising in particular) has become the favourite theme in the discussion of the consumer society. The celebration of affluence and the great lament over 'artificial' or 'alienated' needs are the two central strands in a single mass culture – and even in the social-scientific ideology on the question. This latter is generally rooted in an old moral and social philosophy deriving from the humanist tradition. In the case of Galbraith, it is based on more rigorous economic and political thinking. We shall therefore concentrate here on two of his works: *The Affluent Society* and *The New Industrial State*.

Summarizing his position, we may say that the basic problem of contemporary capitalism is no longer the contradiction between 'profit maximization' and the 'rationalization of production' (from the point of view of the entrepreneur), but that between a potentially unlimited productivity (at the level of the technostructure) and the need to dispose of the product. It becomes vital for the system in this phase to control not just the apparatus of production, but consumer demand; to control not just prices, but what will be demanded at those prices. The 'general effect' – either prior to the act of production (surveys, market research) or subsequent to it (advertising, marketing, packaging) – is to 'shift the locus of decision in the purchase of goods from the consumer where it is beyond control to the firm where it is subject to control'.[3] More generally, 'the accommodation of the market behaviour of the individual, as well as of social attitudes in general, to the needs of producers and the goals of the technostructure is an inherent feature of the system [it would be more appropriate to say: a *logical* feature]. It becomes increasingly important with the growth of the industrial system.'[4] This is what Galbraith calls the 'revised sequence', as opposed to the 'accepted sequence', where the initiative is supposed to lie with the consumer and to impact back, through the market, on the manufacturers. In this new case, by contrast, the manufacturers control market behaviour, and guide and model social attitudes and needs. This is, at least tendentially, the total dictatorship of the order of production.

This 'revised sequence' destroys the fundamental myth of the 'accepted sequence' (it has at least that critical value): namely, that it is the individual who exercises power in the economic system. That emphasis on the power of the individual contributed largely to legitimating organization: all the dysfunctions, nuisances and inherent contradictions of the order of production are justified since they extend the scope of consumer sovereignty. It is clear, by contrast, that the whole economic and psycho-sociological apparatus of market research, motivational studies, etc., which, it is claimed, ensures that real demand and the deep wants of the consumer govern the market, exists solely to stimulate that demand in order to create further outlets for products while constantly masking this objective process by staging its opposite. 'Man only became an object of science for man when automobiles became harder to sell than to manufacture.'

So Galbraith everywhere denounces the boosting of demand by those 'artificial accelerators' the technostructure deploys in its imperialist expansion, accelerators which render any stabilization of demand impossible.[5] Income, prestige purchases and surplus labour form a frantic vicious circle, the infernal round of consumption based on the celebration of so-called 'psychological' needs. These are differentiated from 'physiological' needs by apparently being based on 'discretionary income' and freedom of choice; they can thus be ruthlessly manipulated. Advertising clearly plays a crucial role here (this, too, has become a conventional idea). It seems attuned to the needs of the individual and to products. In fact, says Galbraith, it is attuned to the industrial system: 'It appears to place a significance on products only in so far as it is important for the system, and it upholds the importance and prestige of the technostructure from the social point of view.' Through advertising, the system appropriates social objectives for its own gain, and imposes its own goals as social objectives: 'What's good for General Motors . . .'.

Once again, one can only agree with Galbraith (and others) that the freedom and sovereignty of the consumer are mystification pure and simple. This carefully sustained mystique (preserved first and foremost by economists) of individual satisfaction and choice, which is the culmination of a whole civilization of 'freedom', is the very ideology of the industrial system, justifying its arbitrary power and all the collective nuisances it generates: dirt, pollution, deculturation. In fact, the consumer is sovereign in a jungle of ugliness where *freedom of choice has been forced upon him.* The revised sequence (that is to say, the *system of* consumption) thus ideologically complements and continues the work of the *electoral system*. The drugstore and the polling booth, the loci of individual freedom, are also the system's two mammary glands.

We have set out at length this analysis of the 'technostructural' conditioning of needs and consumption because it is all-powerful today, because it constitutes, thematized as it is in every way in the pseudo-philosophy of 'alienation', a genuine collective representation which is itself part of consumption. But it is open to some fundamental objections, all of which relate to its idealist anthropological postulates. For Galbraith, the needs of the individual can be stabilized. There is in the *nature* of Man something like an *economic principle* which would make him impose limits on his objectives and needs and, at the same time, on his efforts, were it not for the action of 'artificial accelerators'. In short, a tendency to a – not now maximal, but 'harmonious' – satisfaction, a satisfaction that is balanced at the individual level and which – rather than getting caught up in the vicious circle of excessive gratifications described above – should be able to articulate itself on a social organization of collective needs which is also harmonious. All this is completely utopian.

1 On the principle of 'authentic' or 'artificial' satisfactions, Galbraith rails against the 'specious' reasoning of the economists: 'There is no proof that an expensive woman obtains the same satisfaction from yet another gown as does a hungry man from a hamburger. But there is no proof that she does not. Since it cannot be proven that she does not, her desire, it is held, must be accorded equal standing with that of a poor man for meat.'[6] 'Absurd,' says Galbraith. But, it is not absurd at all (here the classical economists are almost right to disagree with him – but, in fact, they take their stand in establishing this equivalence on the terrain of effective demand and thus sidestep all the problems). It is nonetheless true that, from the point of view of the consumer's own satisfaction, there is no basis on which to decide what is 'factitious' and what is not. The enjoyment of TV or of a second home is experienced as 'true' freedom; no one experiences these things as an alienation. Only an intellectual can say such a thing, from the depths of his moralizing idealism, but this at most marks him out as being, for his part, an alienated moralist.

2 On the 'economic principle', Galbraith says: 'What is called economic development consists in no small part in devising strategies to overcome the tendency of men to place limits on their objectives as regards income and thus on their efforts.'[7] And he cites the example of Filipino workers in California: 'The pressure of debt, and the pressure on each to emulate the most extravagant, quickly converted these happy and easygoing people into a modern and reliable work force.'[8] And all the underdeveloped countries, where the appearance of Western gadgets is the most reliable spur to economic growth. This theory, which we might term the theory of 'pressurizing' or economic training in consumption, linked to pressurized economic growth, is seductive. It shows

up forced acculturation to the processes of consumption as the *logical next stage* in the development of the industrial system, following on from the nineteenth century when workers were trained in the processes of industrial production (timekeeping, disciplined action).[9] Having said this, we would have to explain *why* consumers 'take' the bait, why they are vulnerable to this strategy. It is too easy to appeal to a 'happy and easygoing' nature and to impute a mechanical responsibility to the system. There is no more a 'natural' tendency to be easygoing than there is to pressurized working. What Galbraith does not see – and this forces him to present individuals as mere passive victims of the system – is the whole social logic of differentiation, the distinguishing processes of class or caste which are fundamental to the social structure and are given free rein in 'democratic' society. In short, there is a whole sociological dimension of difference, status, etc., lacking here, in consequence of which all needs are reorganized around an *objective* social demand for signs and differences, a dimension no longer grounding consumption as a function of 'harmonious' individual satisfaction (which might thus be limited in terms of the ideal norms of 'nature'), but as an unlimited social activity. We shall come back to this point later.

3   'Needs are in reality the fruits of production,' says Galbraith, not realizing just how right he is. For, beneath its demystified, lucid air, this thesis, as he understands it, is merely a more subtle version of the natural 'authenticity' of certain needs, and bewitchment by the 'artificial'. Galbraith means that, without the productivist system, a great number of needs would not exist. He means that by producing particular goods and services, companies at the same time produce all the means of suggestion tailored to gaining acceptance for them and therefore, ultimately, 'produce' the needs which correspond to them. There is a serious psychological lacuna in this conception. Needs are closely specified in advance here in relation to *finite objects*. The need is simply a need for a *particular* object, and the consumer's psyche is, ultimately, just a shop-window or a catalogue. It is true also that, taking this simplistic view of human beings, one cannot but arrive at a crushing psychological reduction in which empirical needs are mirror-reflections of empirical objects. Now, at this level, the conditioning thesis is false. We know how consumers resist particular precise injunctions, how they rove over the gamut of objects with which they might fulfil their 'needs', how advertising is not all-powerful and sometimes induces opposite reactions, and what substitutions there can be between one object and another to meet the same 'need' etc. In short, at the empirical level, a whole complicated strategy, psychological and sociological, cuts across the strategy of production.

The truth is, not that 'needs are the fruits of production', but that **the system of needs** is **the product of the system of production**. This is quite different. By system of needs, we mean that needs are not produced one by one, in relation to the respective objects, but are produced as *consumption power*, as an overall propensity within the more general framework of the productive forces. It is in this sense that the techno-structure may be said to be extending its grasp. The order of production does not 'capture' the order of enjoyment (strictly speaking, such an idea is meaningless) for its own ends. It *denies* the order of enjoyment and supplants it, while reorganizing everything into a system of productive forces. Over the history of the industrial system, we may trace the following *genealogy of consumption*:

1   The order of production produces the machine/productive force, a technical system radically different from the traditional tool.
2   It produces capital/rationalized productive force, a rational system of investment and circulation, radically different from 'wealth' and from earlier modes of exchange.
3   It produces waged labour power, an abstract, systematized product-ive force, radically different from concrete labour and the traditional 'workmanship'.
4   And so it produces needs, the **system** of needs, demand/productive force as a rationalized, integrated, controlled whole, complementary to the three others in a process of total control of the productive forces and production processes. Needs as a system are also radically different from enjoyment and satisfaction. They are produced as *system elements*, not as *a relationship of an individual to an object* (just as labour power no longer has anything to do with – and even denies – the worker's relation to the product of his labour, and just as exchange-value no longer has anything to do with concrete, personal exchange, or the commodity form with real goods, etc.).

This is what Galbraith – and with him all the 'alienists' of consumption – fail to see, as they persist in demonstrating that *man's relation to objects, man's relation to himself is rigged*, bamboozled, manipulated – consuming this myth as he consumes objects – because, accepting the timeless postulate of a free, conscious subject (in order to have this resurface at the end of history in a happy ending), they cannot but attribute all the dysfunctions they uncover to a diabolical power – here the techno-structure, armed with advertising, public relations and motivational research. This is magical thinking if ever there were such a thing. They do not see that needs, taken one by one, are *nothing* and that there is only a system of needs, or rather that needs are only *the most advanced form of the rational systematization of the productive forces at the individual level*, where 'consumption' takes over *logically* and necessarily from production.

This may clear up a number of mysteries which are inexplicable to our pious 'alienists'. They deplore the fact, for example, that, though we are in the 'age of affluence', the puritan ethic has not been abandoned, that the old moral and self-denying Malthusianism has not been replaced by a modern mentality based on enjoyment. The whole of Dichter's *Strategy of Desire* is aimed at getting around and subverting these old mental structures 'from below'. And it is true: there has been no revolution of mores and the puritan ideology is still in force. In the analysis of leisure we shall see how it pervades all apparently hedonistic practices. We may assert that the puritan ethic, with all it implies in terms of sublimation, transcending of self and repression (in a word, in terms of morality), *haunts* consumption and needs. It is that ethic which drives it from the inside and gives it this compulsive, unlimited character. And the puritan ideology is itself reactivated by the process of consumption: this is indeed what makes the latter the powerful factor of integration and social control we know it to be. Now, all this remains paradoxical and inexplicable from the point of view of consumption-as-enjoyment. By contrast, all is clear if we accept that needs and consumption are in fact an *organized extension of the productive forces*: there is then nothing surprising about the fact that they should also fall under the productivist and puritan ethic which was the dominant morality of the industrial age. The generalized integration of the individual 'private' level (needs, feelings, aspirations, drives) as productive forces cannot but be accompanied by a generalized extension at this level of the patterns of repression, sublimation, concentration, systematization, rationalization – and, of course, alienation! – which for centuries, but particularly since the nineteenth century, have governed the construction of the industrial system.

Shifting Objects – Shifting Needs

Until now the whole analysis of consumption has been based on the naïve anthropology of *Homo oeconomicus*, rather than *Homo psychooeconomicus*. Within the ideological extension of classical political economy, it has been a theory of needs, objects (in the broadest sense) and satisfactions. Or, rather, it has not been a theory, but an immense tautology: 'I buy this because I need it' is equivalent to the fire which burns because of its phlogistic essence. We have shown elsewhere to what degree all this empiricist/finalist thinking (the individual taken as end, and his conscious representation taken as the logic of events) was of the same order as the magical speculation of primitive peoples (and ethnologists) around the notion of mana.[10] No theory of consumption is possible at this level: the spontaneously self-evident, like analytical thinking in terms of needs, will never produce anything but a consumed reflection of consumption.

This rationalist mythology of needs and satisfactions is as naïve and helpless as traditional medicine is when faced with hysterical or psychosomatic symptoms. Let us explain this point: outside the field of its objective function, where it is irreplaceable, outside the field of its denotation, the object becomes substitutable in a more or less unlimited way within the field of connotations, where it assumes sign-value. Thus the washing machine *serves* as an appliance and *acts* as an element of prestige, comfort, etc. It is strictly this latter field which is the field of consumption. All kinds of other objects may be substituted here for the washing machine as signifying element. In the logic of signs, as in that of symbols, objects are no longer linked in any sense to a *definite* function or need. Precisely because they are responding here to something quite different, which is either the social logic or the logic of desire, for which they function as a shifting and unconscious field of signification.

Objects and needs are here substitutable, within reason, like the symptoms of hysterical or psychosomatic conversion. They obey the same logic of slippage, transference, limitless and apparently arbitrary convertibility. When an illness is *organic*, there is a necessary relation between symptom and organ (similarly, when taken as an appliance or tool, there is a necessary relation between the object and its function). In hysterical or psychosomatic conversion, the symptom is, like the sign, (relatively) arbitrary: there is a chain of somatic signifiers – migraine, bowel disorder, lumbago, throat infection, general fatigue – along which the symptom 'wanders', just as there is a long sequence of signs/objects or symbols/objects over which wander not needs (which are always linked to the rational finality of the object), but desire and a further determination which is that of the unconscious social logic.

If we pin the need down to a particular spot, if, that is, we *satisfy* it by taking it literally, by taking it as it presents itself, as the need for a *particular* object, then we make the same mistake as we would in applying a traditional remedy to the organ where the symptom is located. As soon as it is cured at this one point, it will resurface at another.

The world of objects and needs might thus be seen as a world of *generalized hysteria*. Just as, in conversion, all the body's organs and functions become a gigantic paradigm for the symptom to work its way through, in consumption objects become a vast paradigm for another language to work through, for something other to speak. And we might say that this evanescence, this continual mobility to the point where it becomes impossible to define an objective specificity of the need (just as it is impossible in hysteria to define an objective specificity of the illness for the good reason that it does not exist), this flight from one signifier to another is merely the superficial reality of a *desire* which is, for its part, insatiable because it is based on lack. And that it is this forever unquenchable desire which signifies itself locally in successive objects and needs.

Sociologically – in the face of the endless, naïve confusion at the unstoppable advance and boundless renewal of needs, which is in fact irreconcilable with the rationalist theory that a satisfied need creates a state of equilibrium and resolution of tensions – we may advance the hypothesis that, if one admits that need is never so much the need for a particular object as the 'need' for difference (*the desire for the* social *meaning*), then it will be clear that there can never be any *achieved* satisfaction, or therefore any *definition* of need.[11]

To the shifting nature of desire must be added, then (though is there a metaphorical relation between the two?), the shifting nature of differential significations. Between the two, individual, finite needs only assume meaning as successive foci. It is in their very substitution that they signify, yet simultaneously veil, the true spheres of signification – the spheres of lack and difference – which overflow them on all sides.

Denial of Enjoyment

The 'craving' for objects is 'objectless' (Riesman). Consumer behaviour, which is apparently focused on, and orientated towards, objects and enjoyment [*jouissance*], in fact conduces to quite other goals: that of the metaphorical or displaced expression of desire, that of production, through differential signs, of a social code of values. It is not, then, the individual function of interest across a corpus of objects which is determinant, but the immediately social function of exchange, of communication, of distribution of values across a corpus of signs.

The truth of consumption is that it is not a function of enjoyment, but a *function of production* and, hence, like all material production, not an individual function, but *an immediately and totally collective one*. Without overturning the traditional conception in this way, no theoretical analysis is possible: whatever approach one takes, one falls back into the phenomenology of enjoyment.

Consumption is a system which secures the ordering of signs and the integration of the group: it is therefore both a morality (a system of ideological values) and a communication system, a structure of exchange. It is on this basis, and on the fact that this social function and structural organization far surpass individuals and impose themselves upon them by way of an unconscious social constraint, that we can found a theoretical hypothesis that is neither a mere reciting of figures nor a descriptive metaphysics.

According to this hypothesis, paradoxical as it may seem, consumption is defined as *exclusive of enjoyment*. As social logic, the consumption system establishes itself on the basis of a denial of enjoyment. Enjoyment no longer appears there at all as finality, as rational end, but as the individual rationalization of a process whose ends lie elsewhere. Enjoyment would define consumption *for oneself*, as something autonomous and final. But consumption is never that. Enjoyment is enjoyment for one's own benefit, but consuming is something one never does alone (this is the illusion of the consumer, meticulously sustained by the whole of the *ideological* discourse on consumption). One enters, rather, into a generalized system of exchange and production of coded values where, in spite of themselves, all consumers are involved with all others.

In this sense, consumption is an order of significations, *like language*, or like the kinship system in primitive society.

A Structural Analysis?

Let us recall here the Lévi-Straussian principle: what confers on consumption its character of being a social fact is not what it apparently preserves of nature (satisfaction, enjoyment/pleasure), but the essential procedure by which it breaks with nature (what defines it as a code, an institution, a system of organization). Just as the kinship system is in the last instance based not on consanguinity and filiation, on a natural datum, but on an arbitrary classification arrangement, so the system of consumption is in the last instance based not on need and enjoyment but on a code of signs (signs/objects) and differences.

Marriage rules are so many ways of providing for the circulation of women within the social group or, in other words, so many ways of replacing a system of consanguineous relations of a biological order by a sociological system of alliance. Marriage rules and kinship systems may thus be regarded as a kind of language or, in other words, as a set of operations aimed at ensuring a certain type of communication between individuals and groups. It is the same with consumption: there, too, a bio-functional, bio-economic system of goods and products (the biological level of need and subsistence) is supplanted by a sociological system of signs (the level of consumption proper). And the basic function of the regulated circulation of objects and goods is the same as it is with women or words: ensuring a certain type of communication.

We shall come back to the differences between these various types of 'language': they have to do essentially with the mode of production of the values exchanged and the type of division of labour attaching to them. Clearly, goods are something produced, which women are not, and they are produced in a different way from words. The fact remains that, at the distribution level, goods and objects – like words and (in the past) women – form a global, arbitrary, coherent system of signs, a *cultural* system which, for the contingent world of needs and enjoyment, for the natural and biological order, substitutes a social order of values and classification.

This is not to say that there are no needs or no natural utility, etc. The point is, rather, that consumption, as a concept specific to contemporary society, is not to be defined at that level. For needs and the like are valid for all societies. What is sociologically significant for us, and which marks out our age as an age of consumption, is precisely the generalized reorganization of this primary level into a system of signs which reveals itself to be one of the specific modes, and perhaps *the* specific mode, of transition from nature to culture in our era.

The circulation, purchase, sale, appropriation of differentiated goods and signs/objects today constitute our language, our code, the code by which the entire society *communicates* and converses. Such is the structure of consumption, its language [*langue*], by comparison with which individual needs and pleasures [*jouissances*] are merely speech effects.

The Fun System or Enforced Enjoyment

One of the strongest proofs that the principle and finality of consumption is not enjoyment or pleasure is that that is now something which is forced upon us, something institutionalized, not as a right or a pleasure, but as the *duty* of the citizen.

The puritan regarded himself, his own person, as a business to be made to prosper for the greater glory of God. His 'personal' qualities, his 'character', which he spent his life producing, were for him a capital to be invested opportunely, to be managed without speculation or waste. Conversely, but in the same way, consumerist man [*l'homme-consommateur*] regards *enjoyment as an obligation*; he sees himself as *an enjoyment and satisfaction business*. He sees it as his duty to be happy, loving, adulating/adulated, charming/charmed, participative, euphoric and dynamic. This is the principle of maximizing existence by multiplying contacts and relationships, by intense use of signs and objects, by systematic exploitation of all the potentialities of enjoyment.

There is no question for the consumer, for the modern citizen, of evading this enforced happiness and enjoyment, which is the equivalent in the new ethics of the traditional imperative to labour and produce. Modern man spends less and less of his life in production within work and more and more of it in the *production* and continual innovation of his own needs and well-being. He must constantly see to it that all his potentialities, all his consumer capacities are mobilized. If he forgets to do so, he will be gently and insistently reminded that he has no right not to be happy. It is not, then, true that he is passive. He is engaged in – has to engage in – continual activity. If not, he would run the risk of being content with what he has and becoming asocial.

Hence the revival of a *universal curiosity* (a concept to be explored further) in respect of cookery, culture, science, religion, sexuality, etc. 'Try Jesus!' runs an American slogan. You have to try *everything*, for consumerist man is haunted by the fear of 'missing' something, some form of enjoyment or other. You never know whether a particular encounter, a particular experience (Christmas in the Canaries, eel in whisky, the Prado, LSD, Japanese-style love-making) will not elicit some 'sensation'. It is no longer desire, or even 'taste', or a specific inclination that are at stake, but a generalized curiosity, driven by a vague sense of unease – it is the 'fun morality' or the imperative to enjoy oneself, to exploit to the full one's potential for thrills, pleasure or gratification.

Consumption as the Emergence and Control of New Productive Forces

Consumption is, therefore, merely an *apparently* anomic sector, because it is not, according to the Durkheimian definition, governed by formal rules and seems open to the immoderation and individual contingency of needs. It is not at all, as is generally imagined (this is why economic 'science' is, ultimately, reluctant to discuss it), a marginal sector of indeterminacy where the individual, elsewhere constantly constrained by social rules, might at last – being left to himself in the 'private' sphere – recover a margin of freedom and personal leeway. Consumption is an active, collective behaviour: it is something enforced, a morality, an institution. It is a whole system of values, with all that expression implies in terms of group integration and social control functions.

The consumer society is also the society of learning to consume, of social training in consumption. That is to say, there is a new and specific mode of *socialization* related to the emergence of new productive forces and the monopoly restructuring of a high-productivity economic system.

Credit plays a crucial role here, even if it only partially affects spending budgets. It is an exemplary idea because, in the guise of gratification, ease of access to affluence and a hedonist mentality 'freed from the old taboos of saving, etc.', credit is in fact a systematic socio-economic training in enforced saving and economic calculation for generations of consumers who would otherwise, in a life of subsistence, have escaped demand planning and would not have been exploitable as consumption power. Credit is a disciplinary process of the extortion of savings and the regulation of demand, just as wage labour was a rational process of extortion of labour power and increases in productivity. The example quoted by Galbraith of the Puerto Ricans who have been turned from the passive, easygoing people they once were into a modern labour force by being motivated to consume is striking evidence of the tactical value of regulated, enforced, instructed, stimulated consumption within the modern socio-economic order. And this is achieved, as Marc Alexandre shows in his article 'La société de consommation', by the *mental* training of the masses through credit (with the discipline and budgetary constraints it imposes) in economic foresight, investment and 'basic' capitalist behaviour.[12] The rational and disciplinary ethics which was, according to Weber, at the origins of modern productivist capitalism, in this way invests a whole area which had previously eluded it.

It is difficult to grasp the extent to which the current training in systematic, organized consumption is *the equivalent and extension, in the twentieth century, of the great nineteenth-century-long process of the training of rural populations for industrial work*. The same process of rationalization of productive forces which took place in the nineteenth century in the sector of *production* reaches its culmination in the twentieth in that of *consumption*. The industrial system, having socialized the masses as labour power, had much further to go to complete its own project [*s'accomplir*] and socialize them (that is, control them) as consumption power. The small savers or anarchic consumers of the pre-war age, who were free to consume or not, no longer have any place in this system.

The whole ideology of consumption is there to persuade us that we have entered a new era and that a decisive human 'Revolution' separates the painful, heroic Age of Production from the euphoric Age of Consumption, where justice is at last done to Man and his desires. Nothing could be further from the truth. Production and consumption are part of *one and the same process of expanded reproduction of the productive forces and their control*. This imperative, which is that of the system, passes into daily mentalities, ethics and ideology – and here is the great trick – in its *inverted* form: in the form of the liberation of needs, individual self-fulfilment, enjoyment and affluence, etc. The themes of Spending, Enjoyment and Non-Calculation ('Buy now, pay later') have taken over from the 'puritan' themes of Saving, Work, and Heritage. But this is merely the semblance of a Human Revolution: in fact, it is an internal substitution, within the framework of a general process and a system which remain in all essentials unchanged, of a new system of values for an old one which has become (relatively) ineffective. What could become a new finality has become, when emptied of its real content, an enforced mediation of the reproduction of the system.

The needs and satisfactions of consumers are productive forces that have now been constrained and rationalized like the others (labour power, etc.). From all the angles we have (as yet barely) explored, consumption has thus appeared to us, by contrast with the ideology through which we experience it, as a dimension of constraint:

1   it is dominated by the *constraint of signification* at the level of structural analysis;
2   and by the *constraint of production* and of the production cycle in the strategic (socio-economico-political) analysis.

Affluence and consumption are not, then, achieved Utopia. They are a new objective situation, governed by the same basic processes, but overdetermined by a new morality – the whole corresponding to a *new* sphere of productive forces in process of controlled integration into the *same* expanded system. In this sense, there is no objective 'Progress' (nor, *a fortiori*, has there been any 'Revolution'): we have here quite simply the same thing and something else. This results in the fact, which is indeed perceptible in everyday life, of the total *ambiguity* of Affluence and Consumption: they are always lived as *myth* (the assumption of happiness beyond history and morality) and *endured as an objective process of adaptation* to a new type of collective behaviour.

On consumption as a civic constraint, Eisenhower stated in 1958: 'In a free society, government best encourages economic growth when it encourages the *efforts* of individuals and private groups. The government will never spend money as profitably as an individual tax-payer would have were he freed from the burden of taxation.' It is as though consumption, while not being a direct impost, might effectively succeed taxation as a social levy. 'With nine million dollars of tax cuts,' adds *Time* magazine, 'consumers went to two million retail stores in search of prosperity . . . They realized that they could increase economic growth by replacing their fans with air-conditioners. They *secured the boom* of 1954 by purchasing five million miniaturized television sets, a million and a half electric carving knives etc.' In short, they performed their civic duty. 'Thrift is un-American,' said Whyte.

On needs as productive forces – the equivalent of the 'reserves of labour' of the heroic age – take this advertisement for cinema advertising: 'Thanks to its giant screens, cinema enables you to present your product *in situ*: colours, shapes, packaging. The 2,500 cinemas in our advertising network have a weekly audience of three and a half million. 67% of that audience are between 15 and 35. They are consumers *at the height of their needs* who want, and are able, to buy.' They are, precisely, people at the height of their (labour) powers.

The Logistical Function of the Individual

'The individual serves the industrial system not by supplying it with savings and the resulting capital; he serves it by consuming its products. On no other matter, religious, political, or moral, is he so elaborately and skilfully and expensively instructed,' writes Galbraith.[13]

The system needs people as workers (wage labour), as savers (taxes, loans, etc.), but increasingly it needs them *as consumers*. The productivity of labour is increasingly a matter for technology and organization and investment is increasingly left to companies themselves (cf. Paul Fabra, 'Les superbénéfices et la monopolisation de l'épargne par les grandes entreprises', *Le Monde*, 26 June 1969). *Where the individual as such is required and is practically irreplaceable today is as a consumer.* We may therefore predict that the heyday of the system of individualist values is just around the corner, that system whose centre of gravity is currently shifting from the individual entrepreneur and saver, those figureheads of competitive capitalism, to the individual consumer, broadening out at the same time to the totality of individuals – keeping step in this regard with the extension of the techno-bureaucratic structures.

During the competitive stage, capitalism sustained itself after a fashion with a hybrid system of individualistic and altruistic values. The fiction of an altruistic social morality (inherited from the whole of traditional spirituality) was there to smooth over the antagonism of social relations. The 'moral law' was the product of individual antagonisms, just as the 'law of the market' was that of competitive processes: it preserved the fiction of an equilibrium. Individual salvation for the community of all Christians, and individual rights limited only by the rights of others, were long-held beliefs. They are impossible today. Just as the 'free market' has virtually disappeared, to be replaced by bureaucratic, state monopoly control, so altruistic ideology is no longer sufficient to restore a minimum of social integration. No other collective ideology has arisen to take over from these values. Only the state's collective constraint is there to halt the exacerbation of individualisms. Hence the deep contradiction between political and civil society in the 'consumer society': the system is forced to produce more and more consumer individualism, which it is at the same time forced to repress ever more harshly. This can only be resolved by an added dose of altruistic ideology (itself bureaucratized: 'social lubrication' by solicitude, redistribution, gifts, hand-outs, wholesale propaganda for charitableness and human relations).[14] Since this dose of altruistic ideology itself forms part of the system of consumption, it is not capable on its own of helping it attain equilibrium.

Consumption is, therefore, a powerful element of social control (by the atomization of consuming individuals), but by that very fact it brings with it a need for ever greater *bureaucratic constraint* on the processes of consumption – which will as a consequence be exalted more and more energetically as the *realm of freedom*. There is no escaping from this circle.

The automobile and traffic provide the classic example of all these contradictions: unlimited promotion of individual consumption sits alongside desperate calls for collective responsibility and social morality and increasingly severe constraints. The paradox is as follows: one cannot both repeat to the individual that 'the level of consumption is the just measure of social merit' and demand of him another kind of social responsibility since, in his individual consumption efforts, he is already taking on that social responsibility fully. Once again, consumption is *social labour*. The consumer is required and mobilized as *worker* at this level too (perhaps as much today as he is at the level of 'production'). One should not, then, ask the 'consumption worker' to sacrifice his wages (his individual satisfactions) for the good of the collectivity. Somewhere in their social subconscious, the millions of consumers have a kind of practical intuition of this new status as alienated worker. They spontaneously interpret the call for public solidarity as mystification, and their tenacious resistance on this level is merely a reflex of *political defence*. The 'fanatical egoism' of the consumer is also the subconscious rough sense of being, in spite of all the emotional rhetoric on affluence and well-being, the new exploited subject of modern times. The fact that this resistance and this 'egoism' lead the system into irresolvable contradictions to which it responds only by reinforced constraints merely confirms that consumption is a gigantic *political* field, the analysis of which – after that of production and alongside it – remains to be carried out.

The whole discourse on consumption aims to make the consumer Universal Man, to make him the general, ideal and definitive embodiment of the Human Race and to turn consumption into the beginnings of a 'human liberation' that is to be achieved instead of, and in spite of, the failure of political and social liberation. But the consumer has nothing of a universal being about him: he is himself a political and social being, a productive force and, as such, he breathes new life into some basic *historical* problems: of ownership of the means of consumption (not the means of production), of economic responsibility (responsibility for the *content* of production), etc. There is here a potential for deep crises and new contradictions.

The *Ego consumans*

Nowhere – or hardly anywhere – up to now have these contradictions surfaced consciously, apart from a few strikes by American housewives and the sporadic destruction of consumer goods (May 1968 and the 'No bra day', when American women publicly burned their bras). And it has to be said that everything is stacked against this happening. 'What does the consumer represent in the modern world? Nothing. What could he be? Everything, or almost everything. Because he remains alone next to millions of other solitary individuals, he is at the mercy of every vested interest' (*Le Coopérateur*, 1965). And it must be said that individualist interest plays a large part in this (even though we have seen that there are contradictions latent within it). Because it affects a collective sector, the sector of social labour, exploitation by *dispossession* (of labour power) reveals itself generative of solidarity (beyond a certain threshold). It leads to a (relative) class consciousness. The managed *possession* of consumer goods and objects is individualizing, atomizing and de-historicizing. As a producer, by the very fact of the division of labour, the worker presupposes others: exploitation is the exploitation of all. As a consumer, man becomes solitary again, or cellular – at best, he becomes *gregarious* (watching TV with the family, part of the crowd at the stadium or the cinema, etc.). The structures of consumption are both very fluid and closed. Can one imagine car drivers organizing against road tax? Or collective action being mounted against television? Every one of millions of TV viewers may be opposed to advertising, but it will still be broadcast. The fact is that consumption is orchestrated initially as a speaking to oneself [*un discours à soi-même*], and it tends to play itself out, with its satisfactions and disappointments, in this minimal exchange. The consumer object isolates. The private sphere has no concrete negativity because it is enfolded in on its objects, which have none. It is structured from the outside by the system of production whose strategy (no longer ideological at this level, but always political) . . . whose strategy of desire invests in this instance the materiality of our existence, its monotony and its distractions. Or, alternatively, as we have seen, the consumer object produces distinction(s), produces status stratification. If, in this case, it no longer isolates, it differentiates. It *collectively assigns* consumers to a code, without, however, arousing any *collective solidarity* (in fact, it does the opposite).

Overall, then, consumers as such are lacking in consciousness and unorganized, as was often the case with workers in the early nineteenth century. It is as such that they are everywhere celebrated, praised, hymned by 'right-thinking' writers as 'Public Opinion', that mystical, providential, *sovereign* reality. Just as 'the People' is glorified by Democracy provided that it remains the people (and does not intervene on the political and social stage), so consumers are recognized as enjoying sovereignty (Katona speaks of the 'powerful consumer') so long as they do not attempt to exercise it on the social stage. The People are the workers, provided they are unorganized. The Public and Public Opinion are the consumers, provided they content themselves with consuming.

6

Personalization or the Smallest Marginal Difference

To Be or Not to Be Myself

There is no woman, however *demanding*, who cannot satisfy the tastes and *desires of her personality* with a Mercedes-Benz! From the hue of the leather, the trim and the colour of the bodywork to the hubcaps and the thousand and one comforts offered by the fittings, *standard or optional*. As for men, though mainly concerned with the technical qualities and performance of a car, they will willingly fulfil their wives' desires, since they will be equally proud to be complimented on their good taste. You can choose your Mercedes-Benz from 76 different colour styles and 697 selections of interior décor.

To have *found* your personality, to be able to assert it, is to discover the pleasure of being *truly* yourself. It often takes *very little* to achieve this. After a great deal of searching, I realized that a *little light tint* in my hair was enough to create perfect harmony with my complexion and my eyes. I found this blonde tone in the Récital range of rinses . . . And this Récital blonde, which is *so natural*, has not changed me. I am *more than ever* myself.

These two pieces (there are so many one could have chosen) were taken from *Le Monde* and a minor women's weekly respectively. The prestige and social status evoked within them are worlds apart: between the magnificent Mercedes 300 SL and the 'little light tint' of the Récital shampoo there is an enormous social gulf, and the women represented in the two pieces doubtless never meet (except perhaps at the Club Méditerranée – who knows?). They are at opposite ends of the social scale, but united by the same constraint of differentiation, *personalization*. The one is 'A', the other 'non-A', but the pattern of 'personal' value is the same for both, and for all of us beating a path through the 'personalized' jungle of 'optional' merchandise, desperately seeking the foundation cream that will reveal the naturalness of our face, the little touch that will show up our deep individual bent, the difference which will make us ourselves.

All the contradictions involved in this theme, which is basic to consumption, can be felt in the desperate gymnastics performed by the language in which it is expressed, in the constant attempt to achieve an impossible, magical synthesis. If you *are* someone, can you 'find' your personality? And where are *you* while this personality is haunting you? If you are yourself, do you have to be so 'truly'? There again, if you have a false 'self' for a double, is a little light tint sufficient to restore the miraculous unity of one's being? What does this 'so' natural blonde mean? Is it natural or isn't it? And if I am myself, how can I be so 'more than ever'? Wasn't I entirely myself yesterday? Can I raise myself to the second power? Can I represent an added value to myself, appreciating as a company's assets appreciate? One could find thousands of examples of this illogicality, of this internal contradiction eating away at all that relates to the personality today. '*But*,' as Riesman writes, '*the product now in demand is neither a staple nor a machine; it is a personality.*' The high point of this magical litany of personalization is achieved with the following injunction:

Personalize your own home yourself!

This 'over-reflexive' expression (personalizing oneself . . . in person etc.!) tells the real story. What all this rhetoric says, while floundering about unable to say it, is precisely that *there is no one there – no person*. The 'person' as absolute value, with its indestructible features and specific force, forged by the whole of the Western tradition as the organizing myth of the Subject – the person with its passions, its will, its character (or banality) – is absent, dead, swept out of our functional universe. And it is this absent person, this lost instance which is going to 'personalize' itself. It is this lost being which is going to reconstitute itself *in abstracto*, by force of signs, in the expanded range of differences, in the Mercedes, in the little light tint, in a thousand other signs, incorporated and arrayed to re-create a *synthetic individuality* and, at bottom, to shine forth in the most total anonymity, since difference is by definition that which has no name.

The Industrial Production of Differences

Advertising as a whole has no *meaning*. It merely conveys significations. Its significations (and the behaviours they call forth) are never *personal*: they are all differential; they are all marginal and combinatorial. In other words, they are of the order of *the industrial production of differences* – and this might, I believe, serve as the most cogent definition of the *system of consumption*.

The real differences which characterized persons made them *contradictory* beings. Differences of the 'personalizing' type no longer set individuals one against another; these differences are all arrayed hierarchically on an indefinite scale and converge in *models*, on the basis of which they are subtly produced and reproduced. As a result, to differentiate oneself is precisely to affiliate to a model, to label oneself by reference to an abstract model, to a combinatorial pattern of fashion, and therefore to relinquish any real difference, any *singularity*, since these can only arise in concrete, conflictual relations with others and the world. This is the miracle and the tragedy of differentiation. In this way, the whole process of consumption is governed by the production of artificially diversified models (like brands of soap powder), where the trend to monopoly is the same as in the other sectors of production. There is *monopoly concentration of the production of differences*.

This is an absurd formula: monopoly and difference are logically incompatible. If they can be combined, it is precisely because the differences are not differences and, instead of marking a person out as someone singular, they mark rather his conformity with a code, his integration into a sliding scale of values.

There is in 'personalization' something similar to that 'naturalization' effect we constantly meet in the environment – the effect which consists in restoring nature as sign after it has been eliminated in reality. Thus, for example, a forest is cut down to build a group of buildings, which are then given the name 'Park Estate' and a few trees are planted to create a 'natural' feel. The 'naturalness' which haunts the whole of advertising is, similarly, a 'cosmetic' effect: 'Use Ultra-Beauty cosmetics for the smooth, even, lasting look in which your complexion has that *natural* bloom you dream of!' . . . 'I'm certain my wife doesn't use make-up!' . . . 'This veil of make-up, invisible and yet present.' Similarly, the 'functionalization' of an object is a coherent abstraction which superimposes itself upon – and everywhere substitutes for – its objective function ('functionality' is not use-value, it is sign-value).

The logic of personalization is the same: it is contemporaneous with naturalization, functionalization, culturalization, etc. The general process can be defined historically: it is industrial monopoly concentration which, *abolishing the real differences* between human beings, homogenizing persons and products, *simultaneously ushers in the reign of differentiation*. Things are much the same here as with religious or social movements: it is upon the *ebbing* of their original impulse that churches or institutions are built. Here, too, *it is upon the loss of differences that the cult of difference is founded*.[1]

Modern monopoly production is never just the production of goods; it is always also the (monopoly) production of relations, and of differences. Thus, a deep logical collusion links the mega-corporation and the micro-consumer, the monopoly structure of production and the 'individualistic' structure of consumption, since the 'consumed' difference in which the individual revels is also one of the key sectors of generalized production. At the same time, under the sign of monopoly, there is very great homogeneity today between the various contents of production/consumption: goods, products, services, relations and differences. All these things, once distinct, are now produced in the same way, and are thus equally fated to be consumed.

There is also in the combinatorial personality an echo of the combinatorial culture we spoke of above. Just as that consisted in a collective realignment, through the mass media, to the lowest common culture (LCC), so personalization consists in a daily realignment to the smallest marginal difference (SMD): seeking out the little qualitative differences by which style and status are indicated. For example, smoke a Kent:

> The actor smokes one before going on stage, the rally driver before clipping on his helmet, the painter before signing his canvas, the young boss before saying 'no' to his main shareholder[!] . . . The moment it ceases to smoulder in the ashtray, the action is on – precise, calculated, unstoppable.

Or smoke a Marlboro, like the journalist 'with two million readers awaiting his editorial'. You have a classy girl and an Alfa-Romeo 2600 Sprint? Just add 'Green Water' cologne and the trinity is complete: your status as a true aristocrat of the post-industrial age is secure. Or put the same earthenware tiles in your kitchen as Françoise Hardy or the same built-in gas hob as Brigitte Bardot. Or use a toaster which makes you initialled toast, or put charcoal *'aux herbes de Provence'* in your barbecue. Of course, the 'marginal' differences themselves are part of a subtle hierarchy. From the highly select bank, with its Louis XVI-style safes reserved for 800 choice clients (Americans who must keep at least 25,000 dollars in their current accounts) to the managing director's desk which is antique or *Premier Empire* (for senior managers, opulent functional suffices), from the arrogant prestige of *nouveau riche* villas to the non-chalance of high-class clothing, all these marginal differences mark out the most rigorous social discrimination, in accordance with a general law of the distribution of distinctive matter (and against that law – even more than against the criminal law – ignorance is no defence). Not everything is permitted, and violations of this code of differences, which, though it is a shifting one, is no less a *ritual* for all that, are punished. As can be seen in the amusing story of the commercial traveller who bought the same Mercedes as his boss and was fired. He appealed against his dismissal and was granted compensation by a tribunal, but the employer did not take him back. All men are equal before objects as use-value, but they are by no means equal before objects as signs and differences, which are profoundly hierarchical.

Metaconsumption

It is important to grasp that this personalization, this pursuit of status and social standing, are all based on signs. That is to say, they are based not on objects or goods as such, but on *differences*. Only in this way can we understand the paradox of 'underconsumption' or 'inconspicuous consumption', i.e. the paradox of prestigious super-differentiation, which is no longer displayed in *ostentation* (Veblen's 'conspicuous consumption'), but in discretion, sobriety and self-effacement. These latter merely represent a further degree of luxury, an added element of ostentation which goes over into its opposite and, hence, a *more subtle difference*. Differentiation may then take the form of the rejection of objects, the rejection of 'consumption', and yet this still remains the very ultimate in consumption.

> If you're wealthy and middle-class, don't go to the Quatre-Saisons. Leave the Quatre-Saisons to the young couples panicking over the funds they haven't got, the students, the secretaries, the salesgirls, the workers sick of living in squalor . . . Leave it to all those who want nice furniture because ugliness is wearisome, but want simple furniture too because they hate pretentious flats.

Who is going to answer this perverse invitation? Some wealthy middle-class individual, perhaps, or some intellectual anxious to seem a man of the people. At the level of signs, there is no absolute wealth or poverty, nor any opposition between the *signs* of wealth and the *signs* of poverty: they are merely sharps and flats on the keyboard of differences. 'Ladies, come to X for the most windswept look you can find!' . . . 'This simple dress leaves not a hint of *haute couture*.'

There is also a full-blown syndrome of anti-consumption, a very 'modern' phenomenon which is, at bottom, a *metaconsumption* and acts as a cultural indicator of class. The middle classes tend rather towards conspicuous consumption. They are, in this regard, heirs to the great capitalist dinosaurs of the nineteenth and early twentieth centuries. This is where they are culturally *naïve*. Needless to say, there is a whole class strategy behind this:

> One of the few restrictions on the consumption of the mobile person is the resistance of the upper class to the *arrivistes* by exercise of the strategy of conspicuous underconsumption; in this way the already arrived attempt to impose their own limits on those who would become their peers.[2]

This phenomenon, in its many and varied forms, is a crucial one for the interpretation of our society, since one might be taken in by this formal reversal of signs and mistake what is merely a change in the form of the distance between classes as an effect of democratization. It is on the basis of luxury that the lost simplicity is consumed. And this same effect is met at all levels: it is on the basis of the bourgeois condition that intellectual 'slumming' and 'proletarianism' are consumed, just as, in another sphere, it is on the basis of a lost heroic past that contemporary Americans go on package tours to prospect for gold in the rivers of the West: this 'exorcism' of opposite effects, of lost realities, of contradictory terms is everywhere the sign of an effect of consumption and over-consumption which, in every case, fits into a logic of distinction.

It is crucial to grasp this social logic of differentiation as fundamental to the analysis and to see that the exploitation of objects as differential, as signs – the level which alone specifically defines consumption – is precisely established upon the relegation of their use-value (and the 'needs' attaching to it).

> Preferences in the consumption field are not viewed as a development of the human ability to relate oneself discriminatingly to cultural objects. For the objects are hardly given meaning in private and personal values when they are so heavily used as counters in a preferential method of relating oneself to others. The cultural objects, whatever their nature, are mementos that some-how remain unhumanized by the force of a genuinely fetishistic attachment.[3]

This factor (the priority of differential value), which Riesman applies to 'cultural' objects (though there is in this regard no difference between 'cultural objects' and 'material objects'), can be seen illustrated in an almost experimental way by the example of a mining town in the Quebec taiga, where, as the reporter tells us, in spite of the proximity of the forest and the almost total uselessness of a car, every family nonetheless has its automobile outside its door:

> This vehicle, washed and polished, and occasionally taken out for a run of a few miles on the local bypass (there are no other roads) is a symbol of the American standard of living, the sign that one belongs to mechanical civilization.

(and the author compares these magnificent limousines with a totally useless bicycle found in the Senegalese bush outside the house of a black former NCO who had returned to live in his village). Even more strikingly, the same demonstrative, ostentatious reflex leads well-off executives to have summer cottages built in a 10-mile radius around the town. In this spacious, airy town, with its salubrious climate and open to nature on all sides, what could be more useless than a 'place in the country'! What we see at work here, then, is prestigious differentiation in the pure state, and we see to what extent the 'objective' reasons for owning an automobile or a second home merely provide a cover for a more fundamental determination.

Distinction or Conformism?

The logic of differentiation is not generally made a principle of analysis by traditional sociology. That sociology identifies a 'need of the individual to differentiate himself' as one more element in the repertoire of individual needs, which it sees as alternating with the opposite need to conform. The two coexist happily at the psycho-sociological descriptive level, in the most total illogicality and absence of theory – a state of affairs dubbed 'dialectic of equality and distinction' or 'dialectic of conformism and originality', etc. This is to confuse everything. It has to be recognized that consumption is not ordered around an individual with his *personal* needs, which are then subsequently indexed, according to demands of prestige or conformity, to a group context. There is, *first*, a structural logic of differentiation, which produces individuals as *personalized*, that is to say, as different one from another, but in terms of general models and a code, to which, in the very act of particularizing themselves, they *conform*. The singularity/conformism schema, regarded in terms of the individual, is not essential: it is merely the level of life-experience. The basic logic is that of *differentiation/personalization, viewed in terms of the code*. In other words, conformity is not status equalization, the *conscious* homogenization of the group (each individual aligning himself with the others), but the fact of having the same code in common, of sharing the same signs which make all the members of that

group different from a particular other group. It is the difference from
the other group which creates the *parity* (rather than the conformity) of
the members of a group. Consensus is established differentially, and the
effect of conformity is merely the result of this. This is a crucial point,
since it entails that all sociological analysis (particularly where consumption is concerned) is to be shifted from the phenomenal study of prestige,
'imitation' and the superficial field of the conscious social dynamic
towards the analysis of codes, structural relations, and systems of
signs and distinctive material – that is to say, towards a *theory* of the
unconscious field of social logic.

Thus, the function of this system of differentiation goes far beyond the
satisfaction of needs of prestige. If we accept a hypothesis we advanced
earlier, we can see that the system never operates in terms of *real*
(singular, irreducible) differences between *persons*. What grounds it as a
system is precisely the fact that it eliminates the specific content, the
(necessarily *different*) specificity of each human being, and substitutes the
differential form, which can be industrialized and commercialized as a
distinguishing sign. It eliminates all original qualities and retains only
the schema generative of distinctions and the systematic production of
that schema. At this level, differences are no longer exclusive: not only
do they logically imply one another in the combinatory of fashion (in the
same way as there is 'play' between different colours), but, in sociological terms, it is *the exchange of differences which clinches group integration*.
Differences coded in this way, far from dividing individuals, become
rather *the matter of exchange*. This is a fundamental point, through which
consumption is defined: not any longer (1) as a functional practice of
objects – possession, etc., or (2) as a mere individual or group prestige
function, but (3) as a system of communication and exchange, as a code
of signs continually being sent, received and reinvented – as *language*.

In the past, differences of birth, blood and religion were not exchanged: they were not differences of fashion, but essential distinctions.
They were not 'consumed'. Current differences (of clothing, ideology,
and even sex) are exchanged within a vast consortium of consumption.
This is a socialized exchange of signs. And if everything can be exchanged in this way, in the form of signs, this is not by virtue of some
'liberalization' of mores, but because differences are systematically produced in accordance with an order which integrates them all as identify-
ing signs and, being substitutable one for another, there is no more
tension or contradiction between them than there is between high and
low or left and right.

So, in Riesman, we see the members of the peer group socializing
preferences, exchanging evaluations and, by their continual competition,
ensuring the internal reciprocity and narcissistic cohesion of the group.
They come together (Latin *competere*) in the group through 'competition',
or rather through what, being filtered through the code of fashion, is no

longer open and violent competition – such as that of the market or a physical struggle – but *a ludic abstraction of competition.*

Code and Revolution

It will be easier now to grasp the crucial ideological function of the system of consumption in the current socio-political order. That ideological function can be deduced from the definition of consumption as the establishment of a generalized code of differential values and from the function of the system of exchange and communication which we have just determined.

Modern (capitalist, productivist, post-industrial) social systems do not, to any great extent, base their social control, the ideological regulation of the economic and political contradictions by which they are riven, on the great egalitarian and democratic principles, on that whole system of ideological and cultural values that is broadcast to all corners of the earth and is operative everywhere. Even when seriously internalized through schooling and socialization, these conscious egalitarian values – of law and justice, etc. – remain relatively fragile, and would never be up to the task of integrating a society whose objective reality they too visibly contradict. Let us say that at this ideological level, contradictions can always break out again. But the system can count much more effectively on an *unconscious* mechanism of integration and regulation. And this, unlike equality, consists precisely in involving individuals in a system of *differences*, in a *code of signs*. Such is culture, such is language, such is 'consumption' in the deepest sense of the term. What is politically effective is the creation not of a situation in which contradiction is replaced by equality and equilibrium, but of one in which contradiction is replaced by **difference**. The solution to social contradiction is not equalization, but differentiation. No revolution is possible at the level of a code – or, alternatively, revolutions take place every day at that level, but they are 'fashion revolutions', which are harmless and foil the other kind.

Here again, the proponents of the classical analysis are wrong in their interpretation of the ideological role of consumption. It is not by heaping comfort, satisfaction and social standing on individuals that consumption is able to defuse virulent social tension (that idea is linked to the naïve theory of needs and can only lead to the absurd hope of making people ever more destitute in order to have them rebel). It is, rather, by *training them in the unconscious discipline of a code*, and competitive cooperation at the level of that code; it is not by creating more creature comforts, but by getting them to play by the *rules* of the game. This is how consumption can on its own substitute for all ideologies and, in the long run, take over alone the role of integrating the whole of society, as hierarchical or religious rituals did in primitive societies.

The Structural Models

'What mother has not dreamt of a washing machine specially designed for her alone?' asks an advert. And, indeed, what mother has not? Millions, then, have dreamt of the *same* washing machine, specially designed for each of them alone.

'The body you dream of is **your own**.' This admirable tautology, which self-evidently resolves down to an argument for a particular kind of bra, brings together all the paradoxes of 'personalized' narcissism. It is by coming close to your *reference* ideal, by being 'truly yourself', that you most fully obey the collective imperative and most closely coincide with a particular 'imposed' model. Fiendish trick or the dialectic of mass culture?

We shall see how consumer society conceives itself as, precisely, a society of consumption and reflects itself narcissistically in its image. This process spreads right down to each individual, remaining all the while a collective function, and this explains why it is in no way incompatible with conformism. Indeed, the opposite is true, as the two examples above well illustrate. The narcissism of the individual in consumer society *is not an enjoyment of singularity*; it is *a refraction of collective features*. However, it is always presented as narcissistic investment of 'oneself' through smallest marginal differences (SMDs).

The individual is everywhere invited, primarily, to enjoy **himself**, to indulge himself. The understanding is that it is by pleasing oneself that one is likely to please others. Ultimately, perhaps, self-indulgence and self-seduction may totally supplant the objective aim of seduction. The enterprise of seduction turns round upon itself in a kind of perfect 'consumption', but its referent remains, nonetheless, the instance of the other. Put simply, pleasing has become an enterprise in which the person to be pleased is merely a secondary consideration. Like the repetition of the brand name in advertising.

This invitation to self-indulgence is mainly directed at women. But the pressure is exerted on *women* through the myth of *Woman*. Woman as collective and cultural model of self-indulgence. Évelyne Sullerot puts this well:

> Woman is sold to women . . . while doing what she believes is preening herself, scenting herself, clothing herself, in a word 'creating' herself, she is, in fact, consuming herself.

And this falls in with the logic of the system: not just one's relationship with others, but also one's relation to oneself becomes a *consumed* relation. Though this should not be confused, once again, with the fact of being pleasing to oneself on the strength of genuine qualities – of beauty, charm, taste, etc. That is something quite different; in that case, there is no consumption, but a spontaneous and natural relation. Consumption is always defined by the substitution for this spontaneous relation of a relation mediated by signs. If woman does, in fact, consume *herself*, this is because her relation to herself is objectivized and fuelled by signs, signs which make up the feminine model, which constitutes the real object of consumption. It is that model women consume when they 'personalize' themselves. Ultimately, women 'can reasonably trust in neither the sparkle of their eyes, nor the softness of their skin: those things, which are theirs, bring them no certainty' (Bredin, *La Nef*). There is a great difference between *having self-worth* [*valoir*] by dint of natural qualities and *showing oneself off to best advantage* [*se faire valoir*] by sub-scribing to a model and conforming to a ready-made code. What we have in this latter case is a *functional femininity* in which all the natural values of beauty, charm and sensuality give way to the *exponential* values of (artificially achieved) naturalness, eroticism, 'figure' and expressive-ness.

Like violence,[4] the forms of seduction and narcissism are laid down in advance by *models* produced industrially by the mass media and com-posed of *identifiable* signs (if all girls are to think they are Brigitte Bardot, then they must stand out from the crowd by virtue of their hair, their mouths or a particular feature of clothing – that is to say, necessarily the same thing for all of them). Everyone finds his or her own personality in living up to these models.

The Masculine and the Feminine Models

Functional femininity has its counterpart in functional masculinity or virility. The models are, quite naturally, arranged in twos. They are the product not of the *differentiated* nature of the sexes, but of the differential logic of the system. The relation of the Masculine and the Feminine to *real* men and women is relatively arbitrary. Increasingly today, men and women play equally on the two registers in creating their significations, but, for their part, the terms of the signifying opposition only derive validity from their distinction. These two models are not descriptive: they *govern* consumption.

The masculine model is the model of particularity [*exigence*] and choice. All masculine advertising stresses the rule of *choice*, in terms of rigour and inflexible attention, as a matter of 'professional ethics'. The modern man of quality is *particular* or *demanding*. He will countenance no failing and he neglects no detail. He is a 'select' individual, though he is not so passively or by natural grace, but by practising selectivity (the fact that that selectivity is orchestrated by others is a quite separate matter). There is no question of letting himself go or indulging himself; his aim is to achieve distinction. Knowing how to choose and not to let one's standards slip are equivalent to the military and puritan virtues: intrans-igence, decisiveness, valour. These virtues will be possessed by the least young dandy who buys his clothes from Romoli or Cardin. The mascu-line model is, then, a model of competitive or selective virtue. Much more deeply, choice – as a sign of belonging to the elect (he who chooses, who *knows how to* choose, is chosen, is one of the elect) – is the counterpart in our societies to the rite of *challenge* and competition in primitive ones: it confers status.

In the feminine model, women are, much rather, enjoined to take pleasure themselves. It is not, in this case, selectivity and particularity, but self-indulgence and narcissistic concern for one's own welfare which are indispensable. At bottom, men are still being invited to play soldiers, and women to play dolls with themselves.

Even at the level of modern advertising, the two models – the masculine and the feminine – are always segregated, then, and masculine hierarchical pre-eminence still survives (it is here, in the models, that the *fixity of the value system* can be read: the hybridity of 'real' behaviour matters little in this regard, since the deep mentality is shaped by the models – and the masculine/feminine opposition, like that between manual and intellectual labour, has not changed).

We have, then, to retranslate this structural opposition into the language of social supremacy.

1   The masculine choice is 'agonistic': it is, by analogy with the challenge, the noble behaviour *par excellence*. It is honour which is in play, or *Bewährung* (proving oneself), an ascetic and aristocratic virtue.

2   By contrast, what is perpetuated in the feminine model is the *derived* value, the vicarious value (Veblen writes of 'vicarious status' and 'vicarious consumption'). Women are only called on to gratify themselves in order the better to be able to enter as objects into the masculine competition (enjoying themselves in order to be the more enjoyable). They never enter into direct competition (except with other women over men). If a woman is beautiful – that is to say, if the woman is a woman – she will be chosen. If the man is a man, he will choose his wife among other objects/signs (**his** car, **his** wife, **his** eau de toilette). Under cover of self-gratification, woman (the feminine model) is consigned to the performance of proxy 'services'. She is not autonomously determined.

This status, shown up at the narcissistic level in advertising, has quite other – and equally real – aspects at the level of productive activity. Woman, whose fate lies with the paraphernalia (household objects), fulfils not only an economic function, but a prestige function, deriving from the aristocratic or bourgeois idleness of women who, by that idleness, attested to the prestige of their masters: the housewife does not produce; she does not show up in the nation's accounts; she is not recorded as a *productive force*. She is, in fact, fated to be of value as a *force of prestige*, by her official uselessness, by her status as a 'kept' slave. She remains an attribute, reigning over those secondary attributes, the household objects.

Or, in the middle and upper classes, she devotes herself to 'cultural' activities. These are also unpaid, unaccounted and generally unaccountable. That is to say, they are activities involving no responsibility. She 'consumes' culture, though she does not even do this in her own right: it is decorative culture. Thus she is engaged in *cultural promotion*, which, in spite of all the democratic alibis, always falls in with this same requirement that it be useless. Ultimately, culture is simply a sumptuary side-effect of 'beauty' – culture and beauty being not so much values in themselves, activities carried on for their own sake, as evidence of superfluity, an 'alienated' social function (performed by proxy).

Once again, we are speaking here of differential *models*, which are not to be confused with real sexes, or with social categories. There is diffusion and contamination everywhere. Modern man (as we see everywhere in advertising) is also called on to indulge himself. The modern woman is called on to choose and to compete, to be 'particular' or 'demanding'. All this is, of course, in keeping with a society where the respective social, economic and sexual functions are *relatively* inter-mingled. However, the distinction between the masculine and feminine models remains, for its part, total (and, indeed, even the mixing of social and occupational tasks and roles is, in the end, a weak and marginal phenomenon). It is even possible that the structural and hierarch-ical opposition between the Masculine and the Feminine is growing stronger in certain respects. Thus, the appearance in advertisements (for Sélimaille knitwear) of Publicis's handsome young male nude marked the extreme point of contamination. This did not, however, change the distinct and antagonistic models one jot. What it did bring out was the emergence of a 'third', hermaphroditic model, everywhere linked to the emergence of adolescence and youth. This is a sexually ambiguous, narcissistic model, but one much closer to the feminine model of self-indulgence than the demanding masculine one.

Furthermore, what we are seeing very generally today is the *extension of the feminine model to the whole field of consumption*. What we have said of women in their relationship to prestige values, and of their 'proxy' status, goes, virtually and absolutely, for *Homo consumans* in general – men and women together. And it goes for all members of social cat-egories whose destinies lie more or less (increasingly, as the current political strategy has it) with 'paraphernalia', household objects and 'proxy' pleasures. Entire classes are thus fated, in the image of Woman (who, as Woman/Object remains emblematic of consumption), to *func-tion* as consumers. Their promotion to the rank of consumers might thus be said to seal their destiny as serfs. Though, as is not the case with the housewife, far from sinking into oblivion, their alienated activity is today boosting the national economic figures.

PART III
MASS MEDIA, SEX AND LEISURE

7

Mass-Media Culture

The 'Neo' – or Anachronistic Resurrection

As Marx said of Napoleon III, sometimes in history the same events occur twice: the first time with real historical import; the second merely as caricatural evocation of the event, as a grotesque avatar of it – sustained by a *legendary reference*. Cultural consumption may thus be defined as the time and place of the caricatural resurrection, the parodic evocation of what already no longer exists – of what is not so much 'consumed' as 'consummated' (completed, past and gone). The tourists who journey by coach to the far north to re-enact the Gold Rush, hiring Eskimo tunics and clubs to provide some local colour, are people who are consuming: they are consuming in ritual form something which was a historical event, and has been forcibly reactualized as legend. In history, this process is called restoration: it is a process of the denial of history and the anti-evolutionist resurrection of earlier models. Consumption, too, is thoroughly imbued with this anachronistic substance. In its service stations in winter, Esso offers you its log fire and barbecue kit. This is a characteristic example: it is the masters of petrol, the 'historical liquidators' of log fires and their entire symbolic value, who serve these back up to you as the Esso neo-log-fire. What is consumed here is the simultaneous, combined, collusive enjoyment of the automobile and the defunct prestige of everything whose death-knell the automobile sounded – these latter now resuscitated by the automobile! We ought not to see this as mere nostalgia: it is the historical and structural definition of consumption that, by way of this 'lived' level, it *exalts signs on the basis of a denial of things and the real*.

We have already seen how, through mass communications, the pathetic hypocrisy of the minor news item heightens with all the signs of catastrophe (deaths, murders, rapes, revolution) the tranquillity of daily life. But this same pathetic redundancy of signs is visible everywhere: the glorification of the very young and the very old, the front-page treatment for blue-blood weddings, the mass-media hymning of the body and sexuality – everywhere we see the historical disintegration of certain structures celebrating, as it were, under the sign of consumption, both their real disappearance and their caricatural resurrection. The family is dissolving? It is glorified. Children aren't children any more? Childhood is turned into something sacred. The old are alone, sidelined? A collective show of sympathy for the aged. And, even more clearly, the body is glorified precisely as its real possibilities are atrophying and it is increasingly harassed by the system of urban, professional and bureaucratic control and constraints.

Cultural Recycling

It is now one of the characteristic dimensions of our society, in so far as one's professional expertise, individual career path and social position are concerned, to engage in retraining – in what is known, in French, as *le recyclage*. It is now the case that everyone who does not wish to fall behind, be left on the shelf or lose their professional standing must 'update' their knowledge, their expertise – in short, their practical range of skills – on the labour market. This is a notion heard particularly in connection with technical staff and also, more recently, with teachers. It claims, therefore, to be scientific and based on the continual advance of knowledge (in the exact sciences, sales techniques, teaching methods, etc.), to which all individuals should normally adapt if they are to remain 'up to speed'. In fact, the term 'recycling' prompts a number of thoughts: it inevitably brings to mind the 'cycle' of fashion: in that field, too, everyone must be 'with-it' and must 'recycle themselves' – their clothes, their belongings, their cars – on a yearly, monthly or seasonal basis. If they do not, they are not true citizens of the consumer society. Now, it is clear that there is no continual progress in these fields: fashion is arbitrary, transient, cyclical, and adds nothing to the intrinsic qualities of the individual. It does, however, impose thoroughgoing constraints, and the sanction it wields is that of social success or banishment. We may ask ourselves whether the 'recycling of knowledge', under its scientific cover, does not conceal this same kind of accelerated, obligatory, arbitrary change as fashion, and does not bring into play at the level of knowledge and persons the same 'built-in obsolescence' as the cycle of production and fashion foists on material objects. In that case, we should have here not a rational process of the accumulation of scientific knowledge, but a non-rational social process of consumption, indissociable from all the others.

Medical recycling: the check-up. Bodily, muscular, physiological recycling: Le Président[1] for men; diets and beauty care for women; holidays for everyone. But we can (and *must*) extend this notion to much broader phenomena: the very 'rediscovery' of the body is a corporeal recycling; the 'rediscovery' of Nature, in the form of a countryside trimmed down to the dimensions of a mere sample, surrounded on all sides by the vast fabric of the city, carefully policed, and served up 'at room temperature' as parkland, nature reserve or background scenery for second homes, is, in fact, a recycling of Nature. That is to say, it is no longer an original, specific presence at all, standing in symbolic opposition to culture, but a *simulation*, a 'consommé' of the signs of nature set back in circulation – in short, nature *recycled*. If we have not yet reached this point everywhere, it is nonetheless the current trend. Whether we speak of countryside planning, conservation or environment, it is, in every case, a question of recycling a nature which is itself doomed. Like events, like knowledge, Nature is governed in this system by the *principle of being up-to-the-minute*. It *has to* change functionally, like fashion. It provides an *ambience* and is therefore subject to a replacement cycle. This is the same principle as is today invading the occupational field, where the values of science, technique, skill and competence are giving way to 'recycling' – that is to say, to the irresistible pressures of mobility, status and the career *profile*.[2]

This principle of organization governs all 'mass' culture today. What all the acculturated receive is not culture, but *cultural recycling*. (Ultimately, not even the truly 'cultured' escape this, or at least they will not.) They get to be 'in the know', to 'know what's going on'; they get to update their cultural rig-out on a monthly or yearly basis. They get to submit to that low-intensity constraint which is perpetually shifting like fashion and is the *absolute opposite* of culture conceived as:

1 an inherited legacy of works, thought and tradition;
2 a continuous dimension of theoretical and critical reflection – critical transcendence and symbolic function.

Both these dimensions are also denied by the cyclical subculture, made up of obsolescent cultural ingredients and signs, by the *up-to-the-minute* cultural *scene*, which runs from kinetic art to weekly encyclopaedias – recycled culture.

We can see that the problem of the consumption of culture is not, properly speaking, linked to cultural contents. Nor is it connected with the 'audience for culture' (the eternal false problem of the 'vulgarization' of art and culture to which both the practitioners of 'aristocratic' culture and the champions of 'mass' culture fall prey). The decisive factor is not whether millions or only a few thousand partake of a particular work, but that that work, like the car of the year, or nature in parklands, is condemned to be merely an ephemeral sign because it is produced, deliberately or otherwise, in what is today the universal dimension of production: the dimension of the cycle and recycling. Culture is no longer made to last. It keeps up its claim to universality, of course, and to being an ideal reference, doing so all the more strongly for the fact that it is losing its semantic substance (just as Nature was never glorified quite so much before it was everywhere laid waste). However, in its reality, and by its mode of production, it is subject to the same pressure to be 'up-to-the-minute' as material goods. And we must stress once again that this does not have to do with the *industrial dissemination* of culture. The fact that Van Gogh is exhibited in department stores or that Kierkegaard sells 200,000 copies is of no matter here. What affects the *meaning* of the works is the fact that *all significations have become cyclical*. In other words that, through the very system of communication, a particular mode of succession and alternation has been imposed upon them, a combinatorial modulation which is precisely that of hemlines and television pro-grammes (cf. below, 'Medium is Message'). And also the fact that, given this situation, culture, like the pseudo-event in 'public information', like the pseudo-object in advertising, can be produced (and virtually is produced) *out of the medium itself*, out of the code of reference. Here we find that same logical procedure we come upon in 'simulation models'[3] or see at work in gadgets, which are *merely a play on forms and technology*. Ultimately, there is no longer any difference between 'cultural creativity' (in kinetic art, etc.) and this ludic/technical play of combinations. And no difference between 'avant-garde creations' and 'mass culture' either. The latter tends to combine stereotyped themes and (ideological, folk-loric, sentimental, moral, historical) contents, while the former combines forms and modes of expression. But both play primarily on a code, and on a calculation of market share and amortization. Moreover, it is curious to see how the system of literary prizes, currently despised in the world of letters for its academic decrepitude (from a universal standpoint, it is, in fact, stupid to award a prize to *one book a year*), has gained a remarkable new lease of life from its adaptation to the functional cycle of modern culture. The regularity of these prizes, which in other ages was absurd, is now compatible with the present vogue for recycling, with the focus of cultural fashion on the present. In the past, these prizes marked out a book for posterity, and it was faintly ridiculous. Today, they mark out a book for topical interest, and it works. They have found their second wind.

The *Tirlipot* and the Quiz Machine, or the Lowest Common Culture (LCC)

The mechanics of the *tirlipot* game consist, in theory, in seeking out the definition of a verb by question-and-answer methods (*tirlipoter* [to 'whatsit'] is the equivalent of the 'thingamyjig', a floating signifier for which, by selective restitution, the specific signifier is to be substituted).[4] It is, then, in theory, an intellectual learning process. It is evident, however, that, with a few rare exceptions, the contestants are incapable of asking real questions: they find questioning, probing or analysing a nuisance. They start out from the answer (a particular verb which they have in mind) and deduce the question from it. This is, in fact, the interrogative form of the dictionary definition (e.g. 'is to *tirlipot* to put an end to something?' If the compère says 'Yes, in a way' or even, simply, 'Perhaps . . . what do you have in mind?', then the automatic reply comes back 'to finish' or 'complete'). What we have here is precisely the approach of the handyman trying one screw after another to see if they fit, a rudimentary exploratory method based on trial-and-error, with no rational investigation involved.

With *the quiz machine* we find the same principle. There is no learning. A minicomputer asks you questions, offering a range of five replies to each. You choose the right answer. Time counts. If you respond instantaneously, you get maximum points and are a 'champion'. This is not, therefore, thinking time, but reaction time. The machine does not bring intellectual processes into play, but merely immediate reaction mechanisms. You must not weigh up the proposed answers or deliberate: you have to *see* the right answer, register it like a stimulus on the same optomotor lines as the photo-electric cell. To know is to see (cf. the Riesmannian 'radar', which allows you to move about among other people, maintaining or cutting off the contact, immediately selecting positive and negative relationships). Most of all, there must be no analytical thinking: this is penalized by a lower points total due to the time wasted.

If these games do not have a learning function (as is always argued by the programme-makers and the mass-media ideologues), what in fact is their function? In *tirlipot*, it is clearly participation: the content is of no importance. For the contestant, it is the pleasure of occupying the airwaves for 20 seconds, long enough to have one's voice heard, to mingle that voice with the compère's, to hold his attention by striking up a brief dialogue with him and, through him, to strike up magical contact with that warm and anonymous multitude, the public. It is clear that most people are not at all disappointed when they get the answer wrong. They have had what they wanted: *communion* – or, rather, that modern, technical, aseptic form of communion that is *communication*, 'contact'. What marks out the consumer society is not, in fact, the much deplored absence of ceremonies – the radio game is a ceremony just as much as the mass or primitive sacrifice – but the fact that ceremonial communion is no longer achieved by way of bread and wine, which can be seen as flesh and blood, but through the mass media (which are not just the messages, but the whole broadcasting set-up, the network, the station, the receivers and, of course, the programme-makers and public). In other words, *communion is no longer achieved through a symbolic medium, but through a technical one*: this is what makes it communication.

What is shared, then, is no longer a 'culture', the living body, the actual presence of the group (everything which made up the symbolic and metabolic function of the ceremony and the feast), nor is it even knowledge in the proper sense of the term, but that strange corpus of signs and references, of recollections from schooldays and intellectual fashion signals known as 'mass culture', which we might term lowest common culture (LCC), the way one speaks of a lowest common denominator in mathematics. This is also akin to the 'standard package' which lays down the lowest common panoply of objects the average consumer must possess in order to accede to the title of citizen of this consumer society. The LCC lays down the lowest common panoply of 'right answers' the average individual is supposed to possess if he is to win his spurs as cultural citizen.

Mass communication excludes culture and knowledge. There is no question of real symbolic or didactic processes coming into play, since that would be to compromise the collective participation which is the meaning of the ceremony, a participation which can only be enacted through a *liturgy,* a formal code of signs meticulously voided of all meaning content.

We can see that the term 'culture' is potentially very misleading. This cultural 'consommé', this 'digest'/repertoire of coded questions/ answers, this LCC, is to culture what life insurance is to life: it is there to ward off its dangers, and, on the basis of the denial of a living culture, to glorify the ritualized signs of *culturalization.*

However, this LCC, which draws its sustenance from an automatized question-and-answer mechanism, has many affinities with the 'culture' of the schoolroom. Indeed, all these games have the archetype of the *examination* as their mainspring. And this is no accident. The examination is the pre-eminent form of social advancement. Everyone wants to take exams, even in bastardized, radiophonic form, because there is today something prestigious about being examined. The endless proliferation of these games contains within it, then, a powerful process of social integration: we can, ultimately, imagine a whole society integrated into these mass-media contests, the whole of social organization dependent on their sanction. There has already been one society in history which had a total system of selection and organization by examination: China under the Mandarins. But that system only affected an educated fringe. In this case, we should have entire masses mobilized in an endless game of double-or-quits, in which everyone would be securing or endangering his social destiny. In this way, we would be spared the archaic machinery of social control, the best system of integration having always been that of ritualized competition. We have not reached that point yet. For the moment, let us note the very great aspiration to be a part of the exam situation – a dual aspiration this, since everyone may be examined, but anyone can also slot into that situation as examiner, as judge (as a tiny fragment of that collective authority called the public). This is an oneiric duplication, phantasmic in the strictest sense: being both the one person and the other. But it is also a tactical operation of integration by delegation of power. What defines *mass* communication is, therefore, the combination of technical medium and LCC (*not the massive numbers of people* taking part). The quiz machine is also a mass medium, even if the game seems to be an individual one. In playing this machine, where intellectual dexterity registers as beeps and flashing lights – an admirable synthesis of knowledge and the household appliance – you are still being programmed by a collective agency. The computerized medium is merely a technical materialization of the collective medium, of that system of 'lowest common culture' signals which governs the participation of all in each and each in the same system.

Let us say, once again, that it is pointless and absurd to compare High Culture and Mass-Media Culture and to contrast their value. The one has a complex syntax, the other is a combinatory of elements which can always be broken down into stimulus–response and question-and-answer patterns. The latter is most vividly illustrated in the radio game. But, far beyond this ritual spectacle, this pattern governs the behaviour of the consumer in each of his acts, in his general conduct, which is organized as a series of responses to different stimuli. Tastes, preferences, needs, decisions: where both objects and relationships are concerned, the consumer is perpetually appealed to, 'questioned' and required to respond. Making a purchase is, in this context, akin to a radio quiz. It is today not so much an original act on the part of the individual aimed at concretely satisfying a need, as, primarily, *the response to a question* – a response which engages the individual in the collective ritual of consumption. It is a game to the extent that every object is always one among a range of variants, between which the individual is required to choose – the act of purchasing is a choosing, the determination of a preference – precisely as he or she must choose between the answers offered by the quiz game. It is in this sense that the purchaser *plays*, replying to a question which is never the direct one regarding the utility of the object, but the indirect one regarding the 'play' among the variants of the object. That 'play' and the choice which marks its successful conclusion characterize the purchaser/consumer as opposed to the traditional user.

Lowest Common Multiples (LCMs)

The lowest common culture (LCC) of the radio waves or the mass-circulation magazines today has an artistic subsidiary. This is the multiplication of artworks, for which the Bible – itself now multiplied and delivered to the masses in weekly instalments – provided the miraculous prototype in the celebrated multiplication of loaves and fishes beside the Sea of Galilee.

A great democratic wind has blown through the heavenly Jerusalem of culture and art. 'Contemporary art', from Rauschenberg to Picasso, from Vasarely to Chagall and on to younger artists, is holding its 'private view' at the Printemps department store (though, admittedly, it is doing so at the top of the building and not compromising the second-floor 'interior decoration' department with its harbour views and setting suns). The work of art is breaking out of the solitude in which it has for centuries been confined as unique object and privileged moment. Once upon a time, as everyone knows, galleries were sanctuaries. But the masses have now taken over from the solitary owner or the enlightened art-lover. And there is not simply industrial reproduction to delight the masses, but a work of art that is both unique and collective: the Multiple.

> In a happy initiative, under the aegis of the Prisunic department stores, Jacques Putman has just published a collection of original prints at a very affordable price (100 F). No one finds it odd any longer to acquire a lithograph or an etching *at the same time as a pair of stockings or a garden chair*. The second 'Prisunic Suite' has just gone on show at L'Oeil gallery. It is now on sale in the shops. This is not a promotion, nor yet a revolution[!]. The multiplication of images is a response to a multiplying public, which inevitably[!] leads to the creation of places to view those images. Experimental research no longer ends in enslavement to power and money: the art-loving benefactor is giving way to the *participating client* . . . Each numbered and signed print is made in an edition of 300 copies . . . A victory for the consumer society? Perhaps. But what matter, since quality is preserved? Those who will not understand contemporary art today are those who do not want to.

Art speculation, which was based on rarity value, is over. With the 'Unlimited Multiple', art moves into the industrial era (as it so happens, these Multiples, produced in limited editions, immediately give rise to a black market and 'alternative' speculation: the false ingenuousness of the producers and designers). The work of art in the pork butchers, the abstract in the factory . . . Don't say, 'What is Art?' any more; don't say, 'Art is too dear'; don't say, 'Art isn't for me': read *Les Muses*.

It would be too easy to say that a Picasso painting in a factory will never abolish the division of labour and that the multiplication of multiples, were that to be achieved, will never abolish social division and the transcendence of Culture. The illusion of the ideologues of the Multiple (let us not speak here of the conscious or subconscious speculators among both artists and dealers, though they are by far the largest group involved) and of cultural dissemination or promotion more generally is, nonetheless, an instructive one. Their noble effort to democratize culture or, where the designers are concerned, 'to create beautiful objects for the greatest number', visibly meets with failure – or with such commercial success that it becomes suspect as a result, which amounts to the same thing. But this contradiction is merely apparent: it exists because these fine souls stubbornly insist on *regarding Culture as a universal, while seeking, at the same time, to disseminate it in the form of finite objects* (whether unique or produced in their thousands). In so doing, they are merely delivering up to the logic of consumption (i.e. to the manipulation of signs) certain contents or symbolic activities which were not previously subject to that logic. Producing multiple works does not in itself imply any 'vulgarization' or 'loss of quality': what happens is that, as 'mass-produced' objects, works so produced become effectively objects of the same kind 'as the pair of stockings and the garden chair', and acquire their meaning in relation to those things. They no longer stand opposed, as *works* and as semantic substance – as *open* significations – to other *finite* objects. They have become finite objects themselves and are part of the package, the constellation of accessories by which the 'socio-cultural' standing of the average citizen is determined. This, at least, is what would happen in the best of cases, where everyone really did have access to them. For the moment, although they are not artworks any longer, these pseudo-works are nonetheless rare objects, economically or 'psychologically' inaccessible to most people and sustaining, as distinctive objects, a slightly expanded parallel Culture market.

It is perhaps more interesting – though the problem is the same – to look at what is consumed in the weekly instalment encyclopaedias, such as *La Bible*, *Les Muses*, *Alpha*, *Le Million* and in the mass-circulation musical and artistic publications, such as *Grands peintres* and *Grands musiciens*. We know that the audience for these publications is potentially very large, embracing all those in the middle classes who are educated to secondary or technical level (or whose children are so educated): white-collar workers, lower and middle managers.

To these recent large-scale publications we should also add those which, from *Science et vie* to *Historia* and the like, have long fed the demand for culture of the 'potentially upwardly mobile'. What do they want from this frequenting of science, history, music and encyclopaedic knowledge – that is to say, of established, legitimate disciplines, the contents of which – unlike what is broadcast by the mass media – have a specific value? Are they looking to learn something, to acquire a real grounding in culture, or do they want a mark of social advancement? Are they looking to culture as a practice or as a possession to be acquired; are they seeking knowledge or status? Is what we have here a 'package effect' once again, that effect which, as we have seen, marks out – as one sign among others – the object of consumption?

In the case of *Science et vie* (we draw in what follows on a readership survey of this magazine analysed by the Centre de sociologie européenne), the readers' demands are ambiguous: there is here a disguised, clandestine aspiration to acquire 'high-brow' culture by way of accession to technical culture. Reading *Science et vie* is the product of a compromise: an aspiration to elite culture is present, but so too is a defensive counter-motivation in the form of a rejection of elitism (in other words, there is both an aspiration to join the higher class and a reaffirmation of class position). More precisely, such reading functions *as a mark of membership*. But membership of what? The abstract community, the virtual collective of all those driven by the same ambiguous exigency, of all those who also read *Science et vie* (or *Les Muses*, etc.). This is an act of allegiance of a mythological order: the reader imagines a group whose presence he consumes *in abstracto* through his reading: an unreal, mass relationship, which is, quite precisely, the *mass communication effect*. An undifferentiated complicity which nonetheless constitutes the deeply experienced substance of that reading – embodying a value of recognition, of membership, of mythic participation (one can detect just this same process at work among the readers of the *Nouvel Observateur*: to read that magazine is to *affiliate oneself* to the readers of that magazine; it is to use a 'cultural' activity as a class emblem).

Naturally, most readers (we should perhaps say, most 'devotees') of these mass-circulation publications, which are the vehicles of a 'middle-brow' culture, will claim in good faith that they are concerned with their content and that their aim is knowledge. But this cultural 'use-value', this objective goal, is largely overdetermined by the sociological 'exchange-value'. It is that demand, indexed to increasingly intense status competition, which is met by the vast 'culturalized' material of periodicals, encyclopaedias and paperback editions. All this cultural substance may be said to be 'consumed', in so far as its content does not sustain an autonomous practice, but a rhetoric of social mobility, and in so far as it meets a demand which has *something other than culture* as its object or, rather, seeks culture only as a *coded element of social status*. There is here an inversion, and the strictly cultural content appears only as connotation, as a secondary function. We can say, then, that it is consumed in the same way as a washing machine becomes a consumer good at the point where it is no longer an implement but a luxury, prestige element. We know that, at that point, it no longer has any specific presence and many other objects could be substituted for it – culture being, precisely, one of them. Culture becomes an object of consumption in so far as, sliding towards another discourse, it becomes interchangeable and homogeneous with other objects (even if it remains hierarchically superior to them). And this is true not only of *Science et vie*, but also of 'high' culture, 'great' painting, and classical music, etc. All these things can be sold together at the drugstore or the newsagents. But it is not, strictly speaking, a question of the sales outlet, the size of the production run or the 'cultural level' of the audience. If all these things are sold and consumed together, that is because culture is subject to the same competitive demand for signs as any other category of objects and that it is *produced to meet that demand*

It is then subject to the same mode of appropriation as other messages, objects and images which make up the 'ambience' of our daily life: the mode of *'curiosity'*. This is not necessarily something frivolous or casual; there may be passionate curiosity, particularly among those categories of people in process of acculturation. But it presupposes succession, cycles, the pressure for changes of fashion. Thus, for the exclusive practice of culture as a symbolic system of meaning it substitutes a ludic and combinatorial practice of culture as a system of signs. 'Beethoven is fabulous!'

Ultimately, what individuals get from this 'culture' – which excludes both the autodidact, the marginal hero of traditional culture, and the cultured person, that embalmed humanistic flower on the verge of extinction – is cultural 'recycling', an aesthetic recycling which is one of the elements of the generalized 'personalization' of the individual, of cultural 'show' [*faire-valoir*] in competitive society and which is the equivalent, all other things being equal, of the setting-off or showing-off [*faire-valoir*] of the object by packaging. Industrial aesthetics – design – has no aim other than to restore to industrial objects – deeply affected by the division of labour and bearing the stamp of their functions – this 'aesthetic' homogeneity, this formal unity or playful dimension which might be said to connect them all in a kind of secondary 'environment' or 'ambience' function.

This is the work of those 'cultural designers' one now finds every-where: in a society where individuals are severely affected by the division of labour and the fragmentary nature of their work, they seek to 'redesign' them through 'culture', to integrate them into a single formal shell, to facilitate interaction in the name of the promotion of culture, to promote an ambience for people, as design does for objects. Moreover, we should not lose sight of the fact that this packaging, this cultural recycling is, like the 'beauty' industrial aesthetics bestows upon objects, 'undeniably a selling point', to quote Jacques Michel. 'It is an acknow-ledged fact today that a pleasant environment, created by harmony of shapes and colours and, of course, the quality of materials[!], has a beneficial effect on productivity.'[5] And it is true: acculturated people, like designed objects, are better integrated socially and professionally; they 'fit in' better and are more 'compatible'. One of the happiest hunting grounds of the functionalism of human relations is the promotion of culture: there 'human design' meets 'human engineering'.

We need a term which would be to culture what 'Aesthetics' (in the sense of industrial aesthetics, the functional rationalization of forms, the play of signs) is to beauty as a symbolic system. We have no word for this functionalized substance of messages, texts, images, classic master-pieces or cartoon strips, this coded 'creativity' and 'receptiveness', which have replaced inspiration and sensibility, this collective *managed* work on significations and communication, this 'industrial culturality', haunted pell-mell by the cultures of all ages, which we continue, for want of a better word, to call 'culture', though we do so at an enormous cost in misunderstandings, nurturing a constant dream – in the hyperfunction-alism of consumed culture – of the universal, of myths capable of deciphering our age without themselves being mythological 'spec-taculars', of an art which could decipher modernity without being abolished in it.

Kitsch

Alongside gadgetry, one of the other major categories of modern object is kitsch. The kitsch object is commonly understood as one of that great army of 'trashy' objects, made of plaster of Paris [*stuc*] or some such imitation material: that gallery of cheap junk – accessories, folksy knick-knacks, 'souvenirs', lampshades or fake African masks – which pro-liferates everywhere, with a preference for holiday resorts and places of leisure. Kitsch is the equivalent of the 'cliché' in speech. And this should tell us that, as in the case of the gadget, we are dealing with a *category* which is difficult to define, but which should not be confused with any particular *real* objects. Kitsch can be anywhere: in the detail of an object or in the plan of a new residential area, in an artificial flower or in a photo-novel. It can best be defined as a *pseudo-object* or, in other words, as a simulation, a copy, an imitation, a stereotype, as a dearth of real signification and a superabundance of signs, of allegorical references, disparate connotations, as a glorification of the detail and a saturation by details. There is, moreover, a close affinity between its internal organiza-tion (unconnected superabundance of signs) and its appearance on the market (proliferation of disparate objects, a mass-produced accumula-tion). Kitsch is a *cultural category*.

This proliferation of kitsch, which is produced by industrial reproduc-tion and the vulgarization at the level of objects of distinctive signs taken from all registers (the bygone, the 'neo', the exotic, the folksy, the futuristic) and from a disordered excess of 'ready-made' signs, has its basis, like 'mass culture', in the *sociological* reality of the consumer society. This is a mobile society: broad swathes of the population are moving up the social ladder, reaching a higher status and, at the same time, acceding to cultural demand, which is simply the need to manifest that status in signs. At all levels of society, the generations of parvenus want their package. There is no point, then, blaming the 'vulgarity' of the public or the 'cynical' tactics of the industrialists who wish to shift their wares. Though this aspect is important, it cannot *explain* the cancerous excrescence of the mass of 'pseudo-objects'. There has to be a demand, and that demand is a function of social mobility. There is no kitsch in a society without social mobility. In such a society, a limited range of luxury objects suffices as distinctive material for the privileged caste. Even the copy of a work of art still has 'authentic' value in the classical age. By contrast, it is the great periods of social mobility which see the object flourish in other guises: it is with the rising bourgeoisie of the Renaissance and the seventeenth century that preciosity and the baroque emerge. Though these are not the direct ancestors of kitsch, they already bear witness to the growth and fragmentation of distinctive material at a time of social pressure and relative hybridity of the upper classes. It is, however, mainly since the time of Louis-Philippe in France, the *Gründerjahre* in Germany (1870–90) and the end of the nineteenth century and the age of the department stores in all Western societies, that the universal knick-knack form has become one of the major manifestations of the object and one of the most fruitful branches of commerce. That era is unending, since our societies are now potentially in a phase of continual mobility.

Kitsch obviously reaffirms the value of the rare, precious, unique object (production of which can also become industrial). Kitsch and the 'authentic' object thus between them organize the world of consumption according to the logic of a distinctive material which is, today, always shifting and expanding. Kitsch has a weak distinctive value, but that weak value is linked to maximum statistical profitability: entire classes seize on it. This can be contrasted with the maximal distinctive quality of rare objects, which is connected with their limited supply. We are talking here not of beauty, but of distinctiveness, and this is a *sociological* function. In this sense, all objects can be classified hierarchically as values, depending on their statistical availability, on their more or less limited supply. This function defines at every moment, for a particular state of the social structure, the scope afforded to a particular social category to distinguish itself and mark its status through a particular category of objects or signs. When broader strata accede to a particular category of signs, the upper classes are obliged to distance themselves by other markers which are limited in number (either by their origin, such as paintings or authentic antiques, or systematically, such as luxury editions or custom-built cars). In this logic of distinction, kitsch is never innovative: it is defined by its derived and weak value. This weak valency is, in its turn, one of the reasons for its unlimited multiplication. *It multiplies in ever greater quantities*, whereas, at the top of the social ladder, 'classy' objects *become fewer in number by increasing in quality* and are revived by becoming rare.

This derivative function is once again linked to its 'aesthetic' or anti-aesthetic function. To the aesthetics of beauty and originality, kitsch opposes its *aesthetics of simulation*: it everywhere reproduces objects smaller or larger than life; it imitates materials (in plaster, plastic, etc.); it apes forms or combines them discordantly; *it repeats fashion* without having been part of the experience of fashion. In all this, it is all of a piece with the 'gimmicky' gadget in the technical world. That gadget is, similarly, a technological parody, an excrescence of useless functions, a continual *simulation* of function without any real, practical referent. This aesthetics of simulation is profoundly linked to kitsch's socially assigned function of translating social class aspirations and anticipations, of expressing the magical affiliation with a culture, with the forms, manners and markers of the upper class – an aesthetics of acculturation resulting in a subculture of objects.[6]

The Gadget and the Ludic

The machine was the emblem of industrial society. The gadget is the emblem of post-industrial society. No rigorous definition of the gadget exists. If, however, we agree to define the object of consumption by the relative disappearance of its objective function (as an implement) and a corresponding increase in its sign function, and if we accept that the object of consumption is characterized by a kind of *functional uselessness* (what is consumed is precisely something other than the 'useful'), then *the gadget is indeed the truth of the object in consumer society.* Hence, *anything can become a gadget* and everything potentially is one. The gadget might be said, then, to be defined by its potential uselessness and its ludic combinatorial value.[7] So both sew-on badges, which have had their hour of glory, and the 'Venusik', a perfectly 'pure' and useless cylinder of polished metal (its only possible use being as a paperweight, the function reserved for all absolutely useless objects!), are gadgets. 'Lovers of formal beauty and potential uselessness, the fabulous "Venusik" has arrived!'

But the typewriter which can write in 13 different character sets, 'depending on whether you are writing to your bank manager or your lawyer, a very important client or an old friend', is also a gadget – for where is 'objective' uselessness to begin? As are the inexpensive home-made trinkets and also the IBM dictation machine: 'Imagine a little machine (12cm × 15cm) you can have with you everywhere – in the office, at weekends and on your travels. You hold it in one hand and, with a flick of the thumb, whisper your decisions, dictate your directives, hail your victories. Everything you say is committed to its memory . . . Whether you are in Rome, Tokyo or New York, your secretary will not miss a single one of your syllables.' What could be more useful? What could be more useless? When technology is consigned to mental prac-tices of a magical type or to modish social practices, then the technical object itself becomes a mere gadget again.

In a car, are the chrome, the two-speed windscreen wipers and the electric windows gadgets? Yes and no: they do have some utility in terms of social prestige. The contemptuous connotation of the term comes quite simply from a *moral* perspective on the instrumental usefulness of objects: some are said to have a use, others not. By what criteria? There is no object, even the most marginal and decorative, that does not have some use, if only because, in having no use, it becomes once again a mark of distinction.[8] Conversely, there is no object which does not, in a sense, serve no precise purpose (or which cannot, in other words, serve a purpose other than its intended one). There is no way out of this, except to define a gadget as something which is explicitly intended for secondary functions. Thus, not only the chrome, but also the 'cockpit' and the whole car are gadgets if they are part of a logic of fashion and prestige or part of a fetishistic logic. And the systematics of objects means that this is the dominant tendency for all objects today.

The world of the pseudo-environment and the pseudo-object is one in which all 'functional' 'creators' revel. Take André Faye, 'technician of the art of living', who creates Louis XVI furniture, the stylish doors of which open to reveal the smooth, brilliant surface of a turntable or hi-fi speakers:

> His objects move, like Calder's mobiles: both everyday objects and real works of art can be designed on this basis. And when set in motion and coordinated with chromophonic projections, they come ever closer to the *total spectacle* to which he aspires . . . Cybernetic furniture, desks with variable geometry and orientation, a calligraphic Teletype machine . . . At long last a telephone fully built into the human body to enable you to call New York or answer Honolulu from the grounds of a mansion or beside a swimming pool.

All this, for Faye, represents 'a subjugation of technology to the art of living'. And it all irresistibly calls to mind the Concours Lépine.[9] What difference is there between the videophone desk and the cold-water-based heating system devised by some illustrious inventor? Yet, there is a difference. It is that the good old artisanal brainwave was a curious excrescence, the mildly unhinged poetry of a heroic technology. The gadget, by contrast, is part of a systematic logic which lays hold of the whole of daily life in the spectacular mode, and, as a consequence, casts a suspicion of artificiality, fakery and uselessness over the whole environment of objects, and, by extension, over the whole environment of human and social relations. In its broadest sense, the gadget attempts to move beyond the generalized crisis of *purpose* [*finalité*] and usefulness *in the ludic mode*. But it does not – and cannot – attain the symbolic freedom the toy has for the child. It is impoverished, a fashion effect, a kind of artificial accelerator of other objects; it is caught in a circuit where the useful and the symbolic resolve into a kind of combinatorial uselessness, as in those 'total' light shows, where the entertainment itself is a gimmick or, in other words, a social pseudo-event – a game without players. The pejorative resonance the terms 'gadgetry' and 'gimmickry' have acquired today ('a mere gadget', 'just gimmickry') no doubt reflects both a moral judgement and the anxiety generated by the generalized disappearance of use-value and the symbolic function.

But the reverse is also true. That is to say, the combinatorial 'new look' of the gadget can be opposed by – and this is the case for any object, even one which is itself a gadget – *the exaltedness of the new*. The period of newness is, in a sense, the sublime period of the object and may, in certain cases, attain the intensity, if not the quality, of the emotion of love. This phase is one of a symbolic discourse, in which fashion and reference to others have no part. It is in this mode of intense relation that the child experiences his objects and toys. And it is not the least of the charms, later, of a new car, book, gadget or item of clothing that they plunge us back into absolute childhood. This is the opposite logic to that of consumption.

The gadget is defined in fact by the way we act with it, which is not utilitarian or symbolic in character, but **ludic**. It is the ludic which increasingly governs our relations to objects, persons, culture, leisure and, at times, work, and also politics. It is the ludic which is becoming the dominant tone of our daily habitus, to the extent indeed that every-thing – objects, goods, relationships, services – is becoming gadgetry or gimmickry. The ludic represents a very particular type of investment: it is not economic (useless objects) and not symbolic (the gadget/object has no soul), but consists in a play with combinations, a combinatorial modulation: a play on the technical variants or potentialities of the object – in innovation *a playing with the rules of play*, in destruction a playing with life and death as the ultimate combination. Here, our domestic gadgets link up once again with slot machines, *tirlipots* and the other cultural radio games, the quiz machine in the drugstore, the car dash-board and the whole range of 'serious' technical apparatus which makes up the modern 'ambience' of work from the telephone to the computer – all those things we *play* with more or less consciously, fascinated as we are by the operation of machines, by childlike discovery and manipula-tion, by vague or passionate curiosity for the 'play' of mechanisms, the play of colours, the play of variants: this is the very soul of passionate play [*le jeu-passion*], but diffuse and generalized and hence less cogent, emptied of its pathos and become mere *curiosity* – something between indifference and fascination, which might be defined by its opposition to *passion*. Passion may be understood as a concrete relation to a *total person* or to some object taken as a person. It implies total investment and assumes an intense symbolic value. Whereas ludic curiosity is merely interest – albeit violent interest – in the *play of elements*.

Take the pinball machine. The player becomes absorbed in the machine's noise, jolts and flashing lights. He is playing with electricity. As he presses the controls, he has a sense of unleashing impulses and currents through a world of multi-coloured wires as complex as a nervous system. There is in his play an effect of magical participation in science. To grasp this, one has only to observe the crowd which gathers around the repair man in a café when he opens up the machine. No one understands the connections and circuits, but everyone accepts this strange world as an incontrovertible datum. There is nothing here of the relation of rider to horse, worker to tools or art-lover to work of art. The relation of man to object is strictly magical, which is to say that it is bewitched and manipulatory.

This ludic activity may give the appearance of being a passion. But it never is. It is consumption – in this case, abstract manipulation of lights, 'flippers' and electrical reaction times, in other cases, the abstract manip-ulation of marks of prestige in the variants of fashion. Consumption is combinatorial investment: it is exclusive of passion.

Pop: an Art of Consumption?

The logic of consumption, as we have seen, can be defined as a manipulation of signs. The symbolic values of creation and the symbolic relation of inwardness are absent from it: it is all in externals. The object loses its objective finality and its function; it becomes a term in a much greater combinatory, in sets of objects in which it has a merely relational value. Moreover, it loses its symbolic meaning, its millennial anthropomorphic status, and tends to peter out into a discourse of connotations which are also simply relative to one another within the framework of a totalitarian cultural system (that is to say, a system which is able to integrate all significations whatever their provenance).

We have based our argument here on the analysis of *everyday* objects. There is, however, another discourse on the object – the discourse of art. A history of the changing status of objects and their representation in art and literature would itself be revealing. After operating in the whole of traditional art as symbolic, decorative props, objects have ceased in the twentieth century to be indexed to moral and psychological values; they have ceased to live by proxy in the shadow of man and have begun to take on extraordinary importance as autonomous elements in an analysis of space (Cubism, etc.). They have as a result been fragmented, even to the point of abstraction. Having celebrated their parodic resurrection in Dada and Surrealism, which were then destructured and volatilized by the abstract, they are apparently now reconciled again with their image in neo-figuration and pop art. It is here that the question of their contemporary status arises: indeed it is forced upon us by their sudden elevation to the zenith of artistic figuration.

In short, is pop the form of art contemporaneous with the logic of signs and consumption we are speaking of, or is it merely an effect of fashion, and hence itself a pure object of consumption? There is no contradiction between the two. We may accept that pop art transposes an object-world, while at the same time simply issuing (by its own logic) in objects pure and simple. Advertising shares this same ambiguity.

Let us formulate the matter another way: the logic of consumption eliminates the traditional sublime status of artistic representation. There is, strictly, no longer any privileging of the essence or signification of the object over the image. The one is no longer the truth of the other: they coexist in the same physical and logical space, where they also 'operate' as signs (in their differential, reversible, combinatorial relation).[10] Whereas all art up to pop was based on a 'depth' vision of the world,[11] pop regards itself as homogeneous with this *immanent order of signs*: homogeneous with their industrial, mass production and hence with the artificial, manufactured character of the whole environment, homogeneous with the spatial saturation and simultaneous culturalized abstraction of this new order of things.

Does it succeed in 'rendering' this systematic secularization of objects, in 'rendering' this new sign-based [*signalétique*] environment, which is wholly in externals, so that nothing remains of the 'inner light' which gave all earlier painting its prestige? Is it an *art of the non-sacred*? That is to say, an art of pure manipulation? Is it itself a non-sacred art or, in other words, an art productive of objects, but not creative?

Some will say (including the pop artists themselves) that things are much simpler: they do what they do because they want to; basically, they enjoy doing it; they look around them and paint what they see; it is spontaneous realism, etc. This is mistaken. Pop signifies the end of perspective, the end of evocation, the end of testimony, the end of the creative act and, last but not least, the end of the subversion of the world and the curse of art. Its aim is not merely the immanence of the 'civilized' world, but its total integration into that world. There is in this a crazy ambition, the ambition of abolishing the splendours (and foundations) of a whole culture, the culture of transcendence. And there is in it perhaps quite simply also an ideology. Let us first remove two objections. First, that it is 'an American art' – in the objects it depicts (including the obsession with the Stars and Stripes), in its pragmatic, optimistic empirical practice, in the undeniably chauvinistic infatuation of certain of its backers and collectors who have 'identified' with it etc. Though the objection is a tendentious one, let us reply to it objectively. If all these things are *Americanism*, the pop artists, following their own logic, cannot but sign up to them. If manufactured objects 'speak American', that is because they have no other truth than that mythology which swamps them – and the only rigorous approach is to integrate this mythological discourse and integrate oneself into it. If the consumer society is trapped in its own mythology, if it has no critical perspective on itself, and if *that is precisely its definition*,[12] there can be no contemporary art which is not, in its very existence and practice, compromised by and complicit with that opaquely self-evident state of affairs. This is indeed why the pop artists paint objects in terms of their real appearance, since it is *in that way, as ready-made signs, 'fresh from the assembly line', that they function mythologically*. This is why they prefer to paint the brand names, slogans and acronyms these objects bear and, in the extreme case, may paint only those things (Robert Indiana). This is neither play nor 'realism': it is recognizing the obvious truth of the consumer society which is that the truth of objects and products is their *brand name*. If that is 'Americanism', then Americanism is the very logic of contemporary culture and one cannot fault the pop artists for pointing this up.

No more, indeed, can one criticize them for their commercial success and for accepting it unashamedly. The worst thing would be for them to claim some 'accursed' status and thus reinvest themselves with a sacred function. It is logical for an art which does not contradict the world of objects, but explores its system, to make itself part of that system. It is even the end of a hypocrisy and of a radical illogicality. As opposed to earlier painting (since the end of the nineteenth century), whose genius and transcendence did not prevent it from being a *signed* object and an object marketed in terms of its signature (the abstract expressionists pushed this conquering genius and shameful opportunism to its extreme), the pop artists reconcile the object of painting and the painting as object. Coherence or paradox? In its predilection for objects, its endless figuration of 'branded' objects and food products – and also in its commercial success – pop is the first art to explore its own status as 'signed' and 'consumed' art object.

Yet this logical enterprise, which one cannot but approve even in its extreme consequences (even where these contravene our traditional aesthetic *morality*), is accompanied by an ideology into which it is in some danger of sinking: an ideology of Nature, of 'Waking-Up' and authenticity reminiscent of the best moments of bourgeois spontaneity.

This 'radical empiricism', 'uncompromising positivism', and 'anti-teleologism' sometimes assumes a dangerously *initiatory* air.[13] Oldenburg writes:

> I drove around the city one day with Jimmy Dine. By chance we drove along Orchard Street, which is crowded with small stores on both sides. As we drove I remember having a vision of *The Store*. In my mind's eye, I saw a complete environment based on this theme. It seemed to me that I had discovered a new world. Everywhere I went I began wandering through the different stores *as if they were museums*. I saw the objects displayed in windows as precious works of art.

And Rosenquist:

> Then suddenly the ideas seemed to flow towards me through the window. All I had to do was seize them on the wing and start painting. Everything spontaneously fell into place – the idea, the composition, the images, the colors, everything started to work on its own.

As is clear from this, the pop artists are not to be outdone by previous generations so far as 'Inspiration' is concerned. Since Werther, this theme has underpinned the ideality of a *Nature* to which one only has to be faithful to achieve truth. One simply has to awaken or reveal that Nature. In John Cage, the musician who inspired Rauschenberg and Jasper Johns, we read: 'art should be an affirmation of life – not an attempt to bring order . . . but simply a way of *waking up* to the very life we are living, which is so excellent, once one gets one's mind, one's desires out of the way and lets it act of its own accord.' This assent to a revealed order – the universe of images and manufactured objects showing through ultimately as a *nature* – leads to mystico-realist professions of faith: 'A flag was just a flag, a number was simply a number' (Jasper Johns) or (Cage again): 'We must set about discovering a means to let sounds be themselves', which supposes an essence of the object, a level of absolute reality that is never that of the everyday environment and which, in relation to that environment, constitutes nothing short of a surreality. Wesselmann speaks in this way of the 'super-realism' of an ordinary kitchen.

In short, there is total confusion here and what we have is a kind of behaviourism composed of a juxtaposition of things seen (something like a consumer society impressionism), accompanied by a vague Zen or

Buddhist mysticism of the stripping away of the ego or superego to rediscover the 'id' of the surrounding world. There is also something distinctly American about this curious mixture!

But there is above all a serious ambiguity and incoherence here. For, by presenting the surrounding world not as what it is (first and foremost an artificial field of manipulable signs, a total cultural artifact, in which neither sensation nor vision are in play, but differential perception and the tactical play of significations), but as revealed nature, as essence, pop gives itself a dual connotation: on the one hand, it poses as the ideology of an integrated society (current society = nature = ideal society, though we have seen that this collusion forms part of its logic); on the other, it reinstates the whole *sacred process of art*, which destroys its own basic objective.

Pop lays claim to be the art of the banal (it is on these grounds that it calls itself 'pop(ular)' art), but what is the banal but a metaphysical category, a modern version of the category of the sublime? The object is banal only in its use, in the moment of its use (the 'working' radio in Wesselmann's installations). The object ceases to be banal as soon as it signifies. Now, we have seen that the 'truth' of the contemporary object is no longer to be used for something, but to signify, no longer to be manipulated as an instrument, but as a sign. And it is the success of pop, at its best, to show it to us as such.

Andy Warhol, who is the most radical in his approach, is also the artist who best sums up the theoretical contradiction in this art practice and the difficulties it has in envisaging its real object. He says: 'The canvas is an absolutely everyday object, like this chair or that poster' (as ever this desire to absorb art, to rehabilitate it, in which there is both American pragmatism – terroristic insistence on the useful, integrationist blackmail – and something like an echo of the mystique of sacrifice). He adds: 'Reality needs no intermediary, all you have to do is isolate it from the environment and put it on canvas.' Now, this is the whole question: the everydayness of this chair (or a particular hamburger, tail-fin or pin-up) is precisely its context and, specifically, the mass-produced context of all similar or almost similar chairs, etc. Everydayness is *difference in repetition*. By isolating the chair on the canvas, I remove all everydayness from it and, at the same time, deprive the canvas of its character of everyday object (in which respect, according to Warhol, it should absolutely resemble the chair). This is a familiar dead-end: art can neither be absorbed into everyday life (the canvas = the chair), nor can it grasp the everyday as such (the chair isolated on the canvas = the real chair). Immanence and transcendence are equally impossible: they are the two aspects of a single dream.

There is, in short, no essence of the everyday, of the banal, and thus no art of the everyday: this is a mystical aporia. If Warhol (and others) believe that there is, that is because they delude themselves about the very status of art and the artistic act – something far from uncommon among artists. Indeed, we find the same mystical nostalgia at the level of the productive act: 'I would like to be a machine,' says Andy Warhol, who does in fact paint with stencils, silk screens, etc. Now, there can be no worse arrogance for art than to pose as machine-like, no greater affectation on the part of the person who enjoys the status of creator, whether he wishes it or not, than to devote himself to serial automatism. Yet, one cannot accuse Warhol or the pop artists of bad faith: their logical demand runs up against a sociological and cultural status of art which they are powerless to change. It is this powerlessness that is expressed in their ideology. When *they* try to desacralize their practice, society simply sacralizes them the more. And we arrive at the situation where their attempt – the most radical yet – to secularize art, both in its themes and in its practice, leads to a glorification and unprecedented manifestation of the sacred in art. Quite simply, the pop artists forget that, for a painting to cease to be a sacred super-sign (a unique object, a signature, the object of a noble, magical commerce), it is not sufficient to change the content of the picture or the artist's intentions: it is the structures of the production of culture which decide the matter. Ultimately, only the rationalization of the art market, on the same basis as any other indus-trial market, could desacralize artworks and restore them to the status of everyday objects.[14] This is perhaps neither conceivable, nor possible, nor even desirable. Who knows? At any event, it is the limit state: once one has reached it, one either stops painting or continues at the cost of sliding back into the traditional mythology of artistic creation. It is along this fault line that classical pictorial values are rehabilitated: of an 'expres-sionist' kind in Oldenburg, fauvist and Matissian in Wesselmann, 'art nouveau' and akin to Japanese calligraphy in Lichtenstein, etc. But what do these 'legendary' resonances matter to us here? Of what consequence are these effects, which make it possible to say that 'this is still painting all the same'? The logic of pop lies elsewhere – not in an aesthetic computation or a metaphysics of the object.

One could define pop as a *game with* – and a manipulation of – the different levels of mental perception, a kind of mental Cubism that would seek to diffract objects not in terms of a spatial analytics, but in terms of the modalities of perception elaborated over the centuries by a whole culture on the basis of its intellectual and technical machinery: objective reality, image-as-reflection, drawn figuration, technical figura-tion (photography), abstract schematization, discursive utterance, etc. On the other hand, the use of the phonetic alphabet and industrial tech-niques have imposed patterns of division, splitting, abstraction and repetition (ethnographers report the bewilderment of primitive peoples when they discover several *absolutely* identical books: their whole vision of the world is overturned). We may see in these various modes the thousand figures of a *rhetoric of designation*, of recognition. And this is where pop art comes in: it works on the differences between these different levels or modes, and on the perception of those differences. For example, the screen print of a lynching is not an evocation of an event: it presupposes that the lynching has already been transformed into a news item, a journalistic sign, by way of mass communications – a sign taken up again at one further remove by the screen print. The same photograph repeated presupposes the single photograph and, beyond that, the real being whose reflection it is. And that real being might indeed figure in the work without exploding it: that would merely be one more combination.

Just as there is no order of reality in pop art, only levels of signification, so too there is no real space. The only space is that of the canvas, of the juxtaposition of the different sign-elements and the relationship between them. There is no real time either, the only time being that of the reading, the differential perception of the object and its image, of a particular image and the same image repeated, etc. This is the time necessary for *mental adjustment*, for *accommodation* to the image, to the artifact in its relation to the real object (we are speaking here not of a reminiscence, but of the perception of a *local*, *logical* difference). That reading will not be the search for connections and coherence either, but an onward movement, a registering of succession.

It is evident that the activity which pop imposes (taking it, once again, in its strictest ambition) is far removed from our 'aesthetic sense'. Pop is a 'cool' art: it demands not aesthetic ecstasy or affective or symbolic participation ('deep involvement'), but a kind of 'abstract involvement', a sort of *instrumental curiosity*. And this retains something of a child-like curiosity, a näive enchantment of discovery. And why not? One can also see pop as *images d'Épinal* or a book of hours of consumption, but one which particularly brings into play the intellectual reflexes of decoding and deciphering discussed above.

All in all, pop art is not a popular art. For the popular cultural ethos (if such a thing exists) is based precisely on an unambiguous realism, on linear narration (and not on the repetition or diffraction of levels), on allegory and the decorative (and this is not pop art, since these two categories refer to 'something other' which is essential), and on emotional participation linked to the varying fortunes of good and evil forces.[15] It is at a truly rudimentary level that pop art can be mistaken for a 'figurative' art: a colourful range of images, a näive chronicle of the consumer society, etc. It is true that Pop artists have been happy to claim that it is such. Their candour is immense, and their ambiguity too. As for their humour, or the humour ascribed to them, we are again on shifting ground. It might be instructive here to note the reactions of the public. In many, the works provoke a moral and obscene laugh (or hint of a laugh) – the canvases being indeed obscene to the classical gaze – followed by a derisive smile, which might be a judgement on either the objects painted or the painting itself. It is a smile which willingly enters into the game: 'This isn't very serious, but we aren't going to be scandalized by it. And, deep down, perhaps . . .' But these reactions are rather strained, amid some shameful dejection at not knowing quite what to make of it all. Even so, pop is both full of humour and humourless. Quite logically, it has nothing to do with subversive, aggressive humour, with the telescoping of surrealist objects. It is no longer a question of short-circuiting objects in their function, but one of juxtaposing them to analyse the relations between them. This approach is not terroristic.[16] At most it involves something akin to cultural alienation effects. In fact, something quite different is going on here. To return to the system we have been describing above, let us not forget that a *certain smile* is one of the *obligatory signs* of consumption: it no longer represents a humour, a critical distance, but is merely a reminder of that transcendent critical value which today is given material embodiment in the knowing wink. This false distance is present everywhere: in spy films, in Godard, in modern advertising, which uses it continually as a cultural allusion. It is not really clear in the end whether this 'cool' smile is the smile of humour or that of commercial complicity. This is also the case with pop, and its smile ultimately encapsulates all its ambiguity: it is not the smile of critical distance, but the smile of *collusion*.

The Orchestration of Messages

In TV, radio, press and advertising, we find a discontinuum of signs and messages in which all orders are equivalent. A radio sequence taken at random includes:

- an advert for Remington razors;
- a summary of the last fortnight's social unrest;
- an advert for Dunlop SP-Sport tyres;
- a debate on capital punishment;
- an advert for Lip watches;
- a report on the war in Biafra;
- an advert for Crio 'sunflower' washing powder.

In this litany, in which the drama of world history alternates with objects playing walk-on parts (the whole forming a kind of Prévert poem with alternating black and rose-tinted pages – the latter the advertising ones, of course), the periods of intensity are apparently the news reports. But these are also, paradoxically, the periods of neutrality and impersonality: the discourse about the world does not seek to generate concern. This tonal 'blankness' contrasts with the highly charged nature of the discourse on objects, with its cheery, elated note, its vibrato. All the pathos of reality, of unforeseen events, of persuasion is transferred to the object and its discourse. This careful balance between the discourse of 'news' [*information*] and the discourse of 'consumption', to the exclusive emotional advantage of the latter, tends to assign advertising a background function, to allot it the role of providing a repetitious, and therefore reassuring, backdrop of signs against which the vicissitudes of the world

are registered through an intermediary. Those vicissitudes, neutralized
by the editing, are then ripe, themselves, for simultaneous consumption. The radio news is not the hotch-potch it seems: its systematic
alternation imposes a single pattern of reception, which is a pattern of
consumption.

And this is not so much because the value accorded to the advertising
message by its tone suggests that, at bottom, world history is immaterial
and the only things worth getting excited about are consumer objects.
That is secondary. The real effect is more subtle: it is the imposition upon
us, by the systematic succession of messages, of the *equivalence* of history
and the minor news item, of the event and the spectacle, of information
and advertising *at the level of the sign*. It is not in the direct discourse of
advertising, but there that the real consumption effect is to be found.
It is in the segmenting – thanks to the technical media of TV and
radio – of the event and the world into discontinuous, successive, non-
contradictory messages – signs which can be juxtaposed and combined
with other signs within the abstract dimension of the programme. What
we consume, then, is not a particular spectacle or image in itself, but the
potential succession of all possible spectacles – and the certainty that the
law of succession and the segmenting of the schedules will mean that
there is no danger of anything emerging within them that is not one
spectacle or one sign among others.

Medium is Message

Here, and in this sense at least, we have to accept as a fundamental
feature of the analysis of consumption McLuhan's formula that 'the
medium is the message'. This means that the true message the media of
TV and radio deliver, the one which is decoded and 'consumed' deep
down and unconsciously, is not the manifest content of sounds and
images, but the constraining pattern – linked to the very technical
essence of those media – of the disarticulation of the real into successive
and equivalent signs: it is the *normal*, programmed, miraculous transition
from Vietnam to variety, on the basis of a total abstraction of both.

And there is something like a law of technological inertia which means
that the closer one gets to true documentary, to 'live coverage', and the
more closely the real is pursued with colour, depth and one technical
improvement after another, the greater does the real absence from the
world grow. And the more the 'truth' of TV or radio has to be recognized: that the primary function of each message is to refer to another
message. So Vietnam refers on to advertising, advertising to the TV
news, etc., the systematic juxtaposition of these things being the discursive mode of the medium, its message, its meaning. But we have to
recognize that, while speaking to and of itself in this way, the medium is
imposing a whole system of segmentation and interpretation of the
world upon us.

This technological process of mass communications delivers a certain kind of very imperative message: a *message-consumption message*, a message of segmentation and spectacularization, of misrecognition of the world and foregrounding of information as a commodity, of glorification of content as sign. In short, it performs a conditioning function (in the advertising sense of the term: in this sense, advertising is the 'mass' medium *par excellence*, and its schemata leave their stamp on all the other media) and a function of misrecognition.

This is true of all the media, even of the book medium, of 'literacy', which McLuhan makes one of the central linkages in his theory. He takes the view that the emergence of the printed book was a key turning-point in our civilization, not so much for the contents (ideological, informational, scientific, etc.) it passes down from one generation to another, as for the *basic constraint of systematization it exerts by virtue of its technical essence*. He takes the view that the book is, first and foremost, a *technical model*, and that the order of communication prevailing within it (visualized segmentation, letters, words, pages, etc.) is a more influential, more determining model in the long term than any particular symbol, idea or fantasy that makes up its manifest content: 'The effects of technology do not occur at the level of opinions or concepts, but alter sense ratios or patterns of perception steadily and without any resistance.'[17]

Self-evidently, most of the time, the content conceals from us the real function of the medium. It presents itself as a message, whereas the real message, with regard to which the manifest discourse is perhaps mere connotation, is the deep structural change (of scale, of model, of habitus) wrought in human relations. Crudely put, the 'message' of the railways is not the coal or the passengers it carries, but a vision of the world, the new status of urban areas, etc. The 'message' of TV is not the images it transmits, but the new modes of relating and perceiving it imposes, the alterations to traditional family and group structures. And we may go even further and say that, in the case of TV and the modern mass media, what is received, assimilated and 'consumed' is not so much a particular spectacle as the potentiality of all spectacles.

This, then, is the truth of the mass media: it is their function to neutralize the lived, unique, eventual character of the world and substitute for it a multiple universe of media which, as such, are homogeneous one with another, signifying each other reciprocally and referring back and forth to each other. In the extreme case, they each become the content of the others – and that is *the totalitarian 'message' of a consumer society*.

What the TV medium conveys by its technical organization is the idea (the ideology) of a world endlessly visualizable, endlessly segmentable and readable in images. It conveys the ideology of the *omnipotence of a system of reading over a world become a system of signs*. TV images present themselves as the metalanguage of an absent world. Just as the smallest technical object, the tiniest gadget, is a promise of a universal technical

Assumption, so images/signs are a presumption of an exhaustive imagining of the world, of a total assumption of the mode of reality into the image, which might be regarded as its memory, its universal decoding unit. Behind the 'consumption of images' looms the imperialism of a system of reading: increasingly, only what can be read (what *must* be read: the 'legendary') will tend to exist. And there will no longer be any question then of the truth of the world, or its history, but only of the internal coherence of the system of reading. Thus, on a confused, conflictual, contradictory world, each medium imposes its own more abstract, more coherent logic; it imposes itself – a medium – as message, to use McLuhan's expression. And it is the substance of the fragmented, filtered world, the world reinterpreted in terms of this simultaneously technical and 'legendary' code, that we 'consume' – the entire material of the world, the whole of culture industrially processed into finished products, into sign material, from which all eventual, cultural or political value has vanished.

If we regard the sign as the articulation of a signifier and a signified, we may specify two types of confusion. For the child, or the 'primitive', the signifier may fade in favour of the signified (as when the child mistakes its own image for a living being, or African TV viewers ask where the man who has just disappeared from the screen has gone). Conversely, in the self-centred image or the code-centred message, the signifier becomes its own signified, a circular confusion between the two arises to the signifier's advantage, and we see the abolition of the signified and the *tautology of the signifier*. This is what defines consumption, the systematic *consumption effect* at the level of the mass media. Instead of going out to the world via the mediation of the image, it is the image which circles back on itself via the world (it is the signifier which designates itself under cover of the signified).

We move from the message centred on the signified – a transitive message – to the message centred on the signifier. For example (in the case of TV), from events signified by the image to the consumption of the image as such – i.e. precisely as something different from those events, as spectacular – Brecht would say 'culinary' – substance, exhausting itself in the very time-span of its absorption, and never referring on beyond. Different too in the sense that it does not offer events to be either seen or understood in their (historical, social or cultural) specificity, but delivers them up, all without distinction reinterpreted in terms of the same code which is at once an *ideological structure* and a *technical structure* – i.e., in the case of TV, the ideological code of mass culture (a system of moral, social and political values) and the mode of segmentation, of articulation of the medium itself, which imposes a certain type of discursivity that neutralizes the multiple and shifting content of messages and substitutes its own imperative constraints of meaning. Unlike the manifest discourse of the images, this deep-level discursivity of the medium is decoded *unconsciously* by the viewer.

The Advertising Medium

In this sense, advertising is perhaps the most remarkable mass medium of our age. Just as, when it speaks of a particular object, it potentially glorifies all of them, and in referring to a particular object and brand it speaks in fact of the totality of objects and a world made up in its totality of objects and brands, so, in targeting each consumer, it is targeting them all, and in addressing each individual, it is addressing them all, thus simulating a *consumer totality*, retribalizing consumers in the McLuhanesque sense of the term, i.e. through a complicity, an immanent, immediate collusion at the level of the message, but above all at the level of the medium itself and the code. Every image, every advertisement imposes a consensus – that between all the individuals potentially called upon to decipher it, that is to say, called on, by decoding the message, to subscribe automatically to the code in which it has been couched.

It is not, then, its contents, its modes of distribution or its manifest (economic and psychological) objectives which give advertising its mass communication function; it is not its volume, or its real audience (though all these things are important and have a support function), but its very logic as an autonomized medium, i.e. as an object referring not to real objects, not to a real world or a referential dimension, but from *one sign to the other*, from *one object to the other*, from *one consumer to the other*. In the same way, books become means of mass communication if they link the person who reads them with all those who read them (reading a book is not, in that case, a matter of meaning content, but a pure and simple sign of cultural complicity), or if the book/object links up with others in the same collection, etc. One might analyse how language itself, a symbolic system, reverts to being a mass medium at the level of the brand name and the language of advertising. Mass communication is everywhere defined by this systematization at the level of the technical medium and the code, by the systematic production of messages not from the world, but from the medium itself.[18]

Pseudo-Event and Neo-Reality

We enter here the world of the pseudo-event, of pseudo-history and pseudo-culture which is discussed by Boorstin in *The Image*. By this he means a world of events, history, culture and ideas not produced from shifting, contradictory, real experience, but *produced as artifacts from elements of the code and the technical manipulation of the medium*. It is this, and nothing else, which defines all signification whatsoever as *consumable*. It is this generalization of the *substitution of the code for the referential dimension* which defines mass-media consumption.

The raw event is exchange: it is not material for exchange. It only becomes 'consumable' when filtered, fragmented and reworked by a whole industrial chain of production – the mass media – into a finished product, a material of combined, finite signs, analogous to the finished products of industrial production. This is the same operation make-up performs on the face: for real but discordant features, the systematic substitution of a network of abstract but coherent messages made up from technical elements and a code of imposed significations (the code of 'beauty').

We have to beware of interpreting this gigantic enterprise of production of the artificial and the cosmetic, of pseudo-objects and pseudo-events, which is invading our daily existence, as a denaturing or falsifying of an 'authentic' content. We can see from all that has just been said that the abduction of meaning, the depoliticization of politics, the deculturing of culture and the desexualization of the body in mass-media consumption occurs in a region far beyond the mere 'tendentious' reinterpretation of *content*. It is in the *form* that everything has changed: a neo-reality has everywhere been substituted for reality, a neo-reality entirely produced by combining elements of the code. Over the whole span of daily life, a vast *process of simulation* is taking place, similar in style to the 'simulation models' through which the operational and cybernetic sciences work. A model is 'built' by combining features or elements of reality, and an event, a structure or a future situation is 'played out on' those elements, and tactical conclusions are drawn from this with which to operate on reality. In a controlled scientific procedure, this can serve as an instrument of analysis. In mass communications, it assumes *force of reality*: reality itself is abolished, obliterated, in favour of this *neo-reality of the model*, which is given material force by the medium itself.

However, let us once again beware of language, which speaks automatically of the 'false', the 'pseudo' or the 'artificial'. And let us turn again, with Boorstin, to the subject of advertising in order to try to grasp this new logic, which is also a new practice and a new 'mentality'.

Beyond the True and the False

Advertising has a strategic position in this process. It is the reign of the pseudo-event *par excellence*. It turns the object into an event. In fact, it constructs it as such by eliminating its objective characteristics. It constructs it as a *model*, as a spectacular news item. 'Modern advertising began when the advertisement was no longer a spontaneous announcement and had become "made news" '[19] (it is in this way that advertising becomes homogeneous with 'news', which is itself subjected to the same labour of 'myth-making': advertising and 'news' thus constitute a single visual, written, phonic and mythic substance; they succeed each other and alternate in all the media in a way which seems *natural* to us – they give rise to the same curiosity and the same spectacular/ludic absorption).[20]

Journalists and advertisers are *mythic operators*: they present the object or the event as drama, as fiction. They 'offer it up reinterpreted' and might even, at a pinch, construct it deliberately. If we wish to judge objectively, then, we must apply the categories of myth to them: this latter is neither true nor false and the question is not whether one believes in it or not. That indeed gave rise to two false problems which are endlessly debated:

1   Do advertising executives believe in what they do? (If they did, they could be partly forgiven.)
2   Don't consumers ultimately believe in advertising? (If they did, they would be partly saved.)

So, Boorstin argues that advertisers should not be blamed, since the source of the persuasion and mystification was not so much their unscrupulousness as our pleasure at being deceived: it was not so much their desire to seduce, as our desire to be seduced. And he takes the example of Barnum, whose 'great discovery was not how easy it was to deceive the public, but rather, how much the public enjoyed being deceived'.[21] This is a seductive hypothesis, but a false one. This whole state of affairs is not based on some sort of reciprocal perversity, some cynical manipulation or collective masochism revolving around the true and the false. The truth is that advertising (like the other mass media) does not deceive us: *it is beyond the true and the false*, just as fashion is beyond ugliness and beauty and the modern object, in its sign function, is beyond usefulness and uselessness.

The problem of the 'veracity' of advertising should be posed as follows: if advertising men really 'lied', they would be easy to unmask. But they do not. And if they do not, this is not because they are too intelligent, but because 'the advertiser's art . . . consists largely of the art of making persuasive statements which are neither true nor false.'[22] For the good reason that there is no longer either any original or any real referential dimension and, like all myths and magic formulas, advertising is based on a different kind of *verification*, that of the self-fulfilling prophecy. 'The successful advertiser is the master of a new art: the art of making things true by saying they are so. He is a devotee of the technique of the self-fulfilling prophecy.'[23]

Advertising is prophetic language, in so far as it promotes not learning or understanding, but hope. What it says presupposes no anterior truth (that of the object's use-value), but an ulterior confirmation by the reality of the prophetic sign it sends out. This is how it achieves its end. It turns the object into a pseudo-event, which will become the real event of daily life through the consumer's endorsing its discourse. We can see that the true and the false are indiscernible here, just as they are in political opinion polls where we no longer know whether the real vote is simply ratifying the polls (and it is, then, no longer a real event, but merely a substitute for the polls which, from having been simulations that are *statistical indicators*, have become *determining* agents of reality) or whether the polls are reflecting public opinion. This is an inextricable tangle. Just as nature imitates art, so daily life ends up being the replica of the model.

The mode of 'self-fulfilling prophecy' is the tautological mode. Reality is no longer anything but the model speaking itself. So it is with magical formulas, so it is with simulations and so also with advertising which, among other styles of discourse, plays – for preference – on the tautological. Everything in that discourse is a 'metaphor' for one and the same thing: the brand. The expressions 'a better beer' (than what?), 'Lucky Strike, a toasted cigarette' (of course it's toasted; they all are!) merely refer back to a spiral of self-evidence. When Hertz ('the world no. 1 for car hire') says, at the end of a long advertisement, 'Be logical. If you did not find that little something more with us, we would not have reached the position we have today . . . And someone else perhaps would be placing this advertisement', what is this but pure tautology and circular argument? Everywhere, repetition itself functions as efficient causality in this way. Just as molecules are artificially synthesized in certain laboratories, so truth is 'artificially synthesized' here from efficient speech. 'Persil washes whitest' is not a sentence; it is Persil-speak. This and other advertising syntagms do not explain, do not offer any meaning, and are therefore neither true nor false, but they eliminate precisely both meaning and proof. They substitute an unadorned indicative, which is a repetitive imperative. And that tautology of discourse seeks, as in the magic formula, to induce tautological repetition *by the event*. The consumer, by his purchase, will merely ratify *the coming to pass of the myth*.

We might pursue the analysis of advertising discourse further in this direction, and we might also extend it to the various modern media. If we did so, we should see that everywhere, in a radical inversion of the traditional logic of signification and interpretation based on truth and falsehood, it is here the myth (or the model) which finds its event – by means of a production of speech which is now industrialized on the same basis as the production of material goods.

8

The Finest Consumer Object: The Body

In the consumer package, there is one object finer, more precious and more dazzling than any other – and even more laden with connotations than the automobile, in spite of the fact that that encapsulates them all. That object is the BODY. Its 'rediscovery', in a spirit of physical and sexual liberation, after a millennial age of puritanism; its omnipresence (specifically the omnipresence of the female body, a fact we shall have to try to explain) in advertising, fashion and mass culture; the hygienic, dietetic, therapeutic cult which surrounds it, the obsession with youth, elegance, virility/femininity, treatments and regimes, and the sacrificial practices attaching to it all bear witness to the fact that the body has today become an *object of salvation*. It has literally taken over that moral and ideological function from the soul.

Unremitting propaganda reminds us that, in the words of the old hymn, we have only one body and it has to be saved.[1] For centuries, there was a relentless effort to convince people they had no bodies (though they were never really convinced); today, there is a relentless effort to *convince them of their bodies*. There is something strange about this. Is not the body the most obvious of things? It seems not. The body is a *cultural* fact. Now, in any culture whatsoever, the mode of organization of the relation to the body reflects the mode of organization of the relation to things and of social relations. In a capitalist society, the general status of private property applies also to the body, to the way we operate socially with it and the mental representation we have of it. In the traditional order – in the case of the peasant, for example – there was no narcissistic investment or spectacular perception of his body, but an instrumental/magical vision, induced by the labour process and the relation to nature.

What we want to show is that the current structures of production/consumption induce in the subject a dual practice, linked to a split (but profoundly interdependent) representation of his/her own body: the representation of the body as **capital** and as **fetish** (or consumer object). In both cases, it is important that, far from the body being denied or left out of account, there is deliberate *investment in* it (in the two senses, economic and psychical, of the term).

The Secret Keys to Your Body

A fine example of this managed reappropriation of the body is provided by *Elle*, in an article entitled 'The secret keys to your body which unlock the door to complex-free living'.

'Your body is both your outer limit and your sixth sense,' the article begins, and it assumes a serious air by recounting the psycho-genesis of the appropriation of the body and its image: 'At around six months, you began to perceive, as yet very obscurely, that you had a distinct body.' After an allusion to the mirror-stage ('psychologists call this . . .') and a timid allusion to erogenous zones ('Freud says that . . .'), it comes to the central point: 'Are you at ease in your body?' Right away, in comes Brigitte Bardot (BB): she 'is at ease in her body'. 'Everything about her is beautiful: her neck, her back, particularly the small of the back . . . BB's secret? She really inhabits her body. She is like a little animal who precisely fills up her dress.' (Does she inhabit her body or her dress? Which of these, the body or the dress, is her second home? This is precisely the point: she wears her body like a dress, and this makes 'inhabiting' a fashion effect, a 'package' effect, and relates it to a ludic principle which is further reinforced by the 'little animal' reference.) If, in the past, it was 'the soul which clothed the body', today it is the skin which clothes it, though not the skin as irruption of nudity (and, hence, of desire), but as prestige garment and second home, as sign and as fashion reference (and therefore substitutable for the dress without change of meaning, as can be seen in the current exploitation of nudity in the theatre and elsewhere, where, in spite of the false sexual pathos, it appears as one more term in the fashion paradigm).

Let us return to our text. 'You have to be in touch with yourself, you have to learn to read your body' (if you don't, you are anti-BB).

> Lie on the ground and stretch out your arms. Now run the middle finger of your right hand very slowly along that invisible line which runs from the ring finger right along the arm to the crook of the elbow and the armpit. You'll find the same line on your legs. These are lines of sensitivity. This is your *carte du tendre*.[2] There are other lines of *tendresse*: along the spinal column, on the nape of the neck, the stomach, the shoulders . . . If you do not know them, then repression occurs in your body, as it does in your psyche . . . The territories of the body which your sensitivity does not inhabit, which your thinking does not visit, are ill-favoured areas . . . The circulation there is poor; there is a lack of muscle tone. Or, alternatively, cellulite[!] tends to settle there once and for all.

In other words: if you don't make your bodily devotions, if you sin by omission, you will be punished. Everything that ails you comes from being culpably irresponsible towards yourself (your own salvation). Quite apart from the atmosphere of singular moral terrorism which infuses this *carte du tendre* (and which equates with puritan terrorism, except that in this case it is no longer God punishing you, but your own body – a suddenly maleficent, repressive agency which takes its revenge if you are not gentle with it), one can see how this discourse, under the guise of reconciling everyone with their own body, does in fact reintroduce, between the subject and the objectivized body as threatening double, the same relations which are those of social life, the same determinations which are those of social relations: blackmail, repression, persecution syndrome, conjugal neurosis (the same women who read this will read a few pages further on that if they are not affectionate to their husbands, they will bear the responsibility for the failure of their marriages). Apart, then, from this latent terrorism, directed in *Elle* more particularly at women, what is interesting is the suggestion that one should revert back into one's own body and invest it narcissistically 'from the inside', not in any sense to get to know it in depth, but, by a wholly fetishistic and spectacular logic, to form it into a smoother, more perfect, more functional object for the outside world. This narcissistic relation – it is a *managed* narcissism, operating on the body as in colonized virgin 'territory', 'affectionately' [*tendrement*] exploring the body like a deposit to be mined in order to extract from it the visible signs of happiness, health, beauty, and the animality which triumphs in the marketplace of fashion – finds its mystical expression in the readers' confessions which follow: 'I was discovering my body. I could feel it in all its purity.' And, even better: 'It was as though I was being hugged by my body. I began to love it. And, loving it, I wanted to care for it with the same affection I felt for my children.' What is significant is this regressive involution of affectivity into the body-as-child, the body-as-trinket – inexhaustible metaphor of a penis cherished, cradled and . . . castrated. In this sense, the body, become the finest object of solicitude, monopolizes for itself all so-called normal affectivity (towards other real persons), without, however, taking on a value of its own, since, in this process of affective rerouting [*détournement*], any other object can, by the same fetishistic logic, play this role. The body is simply the finest of these psychically possessed, manipulated and consumed objects.

But the main thing is that this narcissistic reinvestment, orchestrated as a mystique of liberation and accomplishment, is in fact always simultaneously an investment of an efficient, competitive, economic type. The body 'reappropriated' in this way is reappropriated first to meet 'capitalist' objectives: in other words, where it is invested, it is invested in order to produce a yield. The body is not reappropriated for the autonomous ends of the subject, but in terms of a *normative* principle of enjoyment and hedonistic profitability, in terms of an enforced instrumentality that is indexed to the code and the norms of a society of production and managed consumption. In other words, one manages one's body; one handles it as one might handle an inheritance; one manipulates it as one of the many *signifiers of social status*. The woman who said she 'wanted to care for it with the same affection [she] felt for [her] children' immediately adds: 'I began to visit beauticians . . . The people who saw me after that crisis found me happier, better looking.' 'Recuperated' as an instrument of enjoyment and an indicator of prestige, the body is then subjected to a *labour of investment* (solicitude, obsession) which, once the myth of liberation that acts as cover is peeled away, doubtless represents a more profoundly alienated labour than the exploitation of the body as labour power.[3]

Functional Beauty

In this long process of sacralization of the body as exponential value, of the *functional* body – that is to say, the body which is no longer 'flesh' as in the religious conception, or labour power as in industrial logic, but is taken up again in its materiality (or its 'visible' ideality) as narcissistic cult object or element of social ritual and tactics – beauty and eroticism are two major leitmotivs.

They are inseparable and the two together institute this *new ethics of the relation to the body.* Though valid for both men and women, they are, nevertheless, differentiated into feminine and masculine poles. The two opposing models – the basic elements of which are largely interchangeable – might be termed **phryneism**[4] and **athleticism**. Still, the feminine model has a kind of priority: it is this model which, to some extent, functions as the template of this new ethics. And it is not by chance that it is in *Elle* that we find the type of material we have analysed above.[5]

For women, beauty has become an absolute, religious imperative. Being beautiful is no longer an effect of nature or a supplement to moral qualities. It is **the** basic, imperative quality of those who take the same care of their faces and figures as they do of their souls. It is a sign, at the level of the body, that one is a member of the elect, just as success is such a sign in business. And, indeed, in their respective magazines, beauty and success are accorded *the same mystical foundation*: for women, it is *sensitivity*, exploring and evoking 'from the inside' all the parts of the body; for the entrepreneur, it is the adequate *intuition* of all the possibilities of the market. A sign of election and salvation: the Protestant ethic is not far away here. And it is true that beauty is such an absolute imperative only because it is a form of capital.

Let us take this same logic a little further. The ethics of beauty, which is the very ethics of fashion, may be defined as the reduction of all concrete values – the 'use-values' of the body (energetic, gestural, sexual) – to a single functional 'exchange-value', which itself alone, in its abstraction, encapsulates the *idea* of the glorious, fulfilled body, the *idea* of desire and pleasure [*jouissance*], and of course thereby also denies and forgets them in their reality and in the end simply peters out into an exchange of signs. For beauty is nothing more than sign material being exchanged. It *functions* as sign-value. That is why we can say that the beauty imperative is one of the modalities of the functional imperative, this being valid for objects as much as it is for women (and men), the beautician every woman has become being the counterpart of the designer and stylist in the business sphere.

Moreover, if we look at the dominant principles of industrial aesthetics (functionalism), we can see that they apply generally to the charter for beauty: BB feeling 'at ease in her body' or 'precisely fill[ing] up her dress' is part of this same pattern of the 'harmonious marriage of function and form'.

Functional Eroticism

Alongside beauty, as we have just defined it, sexuality everywhere orientates the 'rediscovery' and *consumption* of the body today. The beauty imperative, which is an imperative of **turning** the body **to advantage** by way of narcissistic reinvestment, involves *the erotic as sexual foil*. We have clearly to distinguish the erotic as a generalized dimension of exchange in our societies from sexuality properly so called. We have to distinguish the erotic body – substrate of the exchanged signs of desire – from the body as site of fantasy and abode of desire. In the drive/body, the fantasy/body, the individual structure of desire predominates. In the 'eroticized' body, it is the social function of exchange which predominates. In this sense, the erotic imperative – which, like courtesy or so many other social rituals, is mediated by an instrumental code of signs – is merely (like the aesthetic imperative in beauty) a variant or metaphor of the functional imperative.

The *Elle* woman is 'hot' with that same heat, that same warmth one finds in modern furniture: it is an 'atmospheric' heat. It no longer comes from intimacy and sensuality, but from calculated sexual signification. Sensuality is heat. This sexuality, for its part, is *hot and cold*, like the play of warm and cold colours in a 'functional' interior. It has the same 'whiteness' as the enveloping forms of 'stylized', 'dressed-up' modern objects. But it is also not a 'frigidity', as has been suggested, since frigidity still implies a sexual resonance of violation. The fashion model is not frigid: she is an *abstraction*.

The fashion model's body is no longer an object of desire, but a functional object, a forum of signs in which fashion and the erotic are mingled. It is no longer a synthesis of gestures, even if fashion photography puts all its artistry into *re-creating* gesture and naturalness by a process of simulation.[6] It is no longer, strictly speaking, a body, but a *shape*.

This is where all modern censors are misled (or are content to be misled): the fact is that in advertising and fashion naked bodies (both women's and men's) refuse the status of flesh, of sex, of finality of desire, instrumentalizing rather the fragmented parts of the body in a gigantic process of *sublimation*, of denying the body in its very evocation.[7]

Just as the erotic is never in desire but in signs, so the functional beauty of the fashion models is never in their expressions but in their 'figures'. Irregularity or ugliness would bring out a meaning again: they are excluded. For beauty here is wholly in abstraction, in emptiness, in ecstatic absence and transparency. This disembodiment is ultimately encapsulated in the *gaze*. These fascinating/fascinated, sunken eyes, this objectless gaze – both oversignification of desire and total absence of desire – are beautiful in their empty erection, in the exaltation of their censorship. That is their functionality. Medusa eyes, eyes themselves turned to stone, pure signs. Thus, all along the unveiled, exalted body, in these spectacular eyes, eyes ringed by fashion, not by pleasure, it is the very meaning of the body, the truth of the body which vanishes in a hypnotic process. It is to this extent that the body – particularly the female body and, most particularly, the body of that absolute model, the fashion mannequin – constitutes itself as an object that is the equivalent to the other sexless and functional objects purveyed in advertising.

Pleasure Principle and Productive Force

Conversely, the least of objects, implicitly cathected on the pattern of the female body/object, is fetishized in this same way. Hence the generalized imbuing of the whole field of 'consumption' by eroticism. This is not *a* fashion in the lighter sense of the term; it is the specific, rigorous logic of *fashion*. Bodies and objects form a network of homogeneous signs which may, on the basis of the abstraction we have just discussed, exchange their significations (this is, properly speaking, their 'exchange-value') and 'show each other off [*se faire valoir*] mutually'.

This *homology between bodies and objects* takes us into the deep mechanisms of managed consumption. If the 'rediscovery of the body' is always the rediscovery of the body/object in the generalized context of other objects, one can see how easy, logical and necessary a transition there is from the functional appropriation of the body to the appropriation of goods and objects in shopping. And we know, indeed, to what extent the modern eroticism and aesthetics of the body are steeped in an environment teeming with products, gadgets and accessories in an atmosphere of total sophistication. From hygiene to make-up (not forgetting suntans, exercise and the many 'liberations' of fashion), the rediscovery of the body takes place initially through objects. It even seems that the only drive that is really liberated is the *drive to buy*. We may recall here the example of the woman who, having suddenly fallen madly in love with her body, dashes off to the beauty parlour. And there is also the more common, opposite case: all those women who go in for all the eaux de toilette, massages and treatments in the hope of 'rediscovering their bodies'. The theoretical equivalence between bodies and objects as signs is what in fact makes possible the magical equation: 'Buy – and you will be at ease in your body.'

This is where all the psycho-functionality analysed above assumes its full economic and ideological meaning. The body sells products. Beauty sells products. Eroticism sells products. And this is not the least of the reasons which, in the last instance, orientate the entire historical process of the 'liberation of the body'. It is the same with the body as it is with labour power. It *has to be* 'liberated, emancipated' to be able to be exploited rationally for productivist ends. Just as freedom to dispose of oneself and personal interest – the formal principles of the individual freedom of the worker – have to operate for labour power to be able to transform itself into the demand for wages and exchange-value, so the individual has to rediscover his body and invest it narcissistically – *the formal principle of pleasure* – for the force of desire to be able to transform itself into a demand for rationally manipulable objects/signs. *The individual has to take himself as object, as the finest of objects, as the most precious exchange material, for an economic process of profit generation to be established at the level of the deconstructed body, of deconstructed sexuality.*

Modern Strategy of the Body

However, this productivist objective, this economic process of profit generation, by which the social structures of production are generalized at the level of the body, is doubtless still secondary to the goals of integration and social control set in place by the whole mythological and psychological apparatus centred around the body.

In the history of ideologies, those relating to the body long had an offensive, critical value against the ideologies of the spiritualist, puritan, moralizing type which were centred on the soul or some other non-material principle. Since the Middle Ages, all heresies have been to some extent claims of the flesh, the advance resurrection of bodies against the rigid dogma of the Churches (this is the 'Adamical' tendency, which reappeared repeatedly, always to be condemned by orthodoxy). Since the eighteenth century, sensualist, empiricist, materialist philosophy has demolished the traditional spiritualist dogmas. It would be interesting to make a detailed analysis of the very long process of historical disintegration of that fundamental value called the soul, around which the whole individual scheme of salvation was organized and also, of course, the whole process of social integration. This long desacralization and secularization in favour of the body has run through the whole of the Western era: the values of the body have been subversive values, sources of the most acute ideological contradiction. But how do matters stand today when these values are largely uncontested and have gained acceptance as a new ethic (there is much to be said on this subject: we are now, rather, in a phase in which the puritan and hedonist ideologies are concertinaed, their themes intermingling at every level)? We can see that the body today, apparently triumphant, instead of still constituting a living, contradictory force, a force for 'demystification', has quite simply taken over from the soul as mythic instance, as dogma and as salvational scheme. Its 'discovery', which for many centuries represented a critique of the sacred, a call for greater freedom, truth and emancipation – in short a battling for humanity, against God – today occurs as an act of *resacralization*. The cult of the body no longer stands in contradiction to the cult of the soul: it is the successor to that cult and heir to its ideological function. As Norman O. Brown says in *Life against Death*: 'We must not be misled by the flat antinomy of the sacred and the secular, and interpret as "secularization" what is only a metamorphosis of the sacred.'[8]

The material evidence of the 'liberated' body (though, as we have seen, liberated as sign/object and censored in its subversive truth as desire, not only in athletic activity and hygiene, but also in eroticism) must not be allowed to deceive us here: it merely expresses the supplanting of an outdated ideology – that of the soul, which is inadequate for a developed productivist system and incapable now of ensuring ideological integration – by a more functional modern ideology which, in all essentials, preserves the individualistic value system and the social structures connected with it. And it even reinforces these, establishing them on an almost permanent basis, since it substitutes for the transcendence of the soul the total immanence, the spontaneous self-evidence of the body. Now, that self-evidence is false evidence. The body as instituted by modern mythology is no more material than the soul. Like the soul, it is an *idea* or, rather – since the term 'idea' does not mean much – it is a hypostasized part-object, a double privileged and invested as such. It has become, as the soul was in its time, the privileged substrate of objectivization – *the guiding myth of an ethic of consumption*. We can see how intimately the body is involved in the goals of production as (economic) support, as principle of the managed (psychological) integration of the individual, and as (political) strategy of social control.

Is the Body Feminine?

Let us come back to the question we set aside at the beginning of this chapter: that of the role which falls to woman and the female body as privileged vehicle of Beauty, Sexuality and managed Narcissism. For if it is clear that this process of reduction of the body to aesthetic/erotic exchange-value affects both the male and the female (we have suggested two terms for this, athleticism and phryneism, phryneism being defined roughly as the woman of *Elle* and the fashion magazines, masculine athleticism finding its wider model in the athleticism of the executive, a model presented everywhere in advertising, films, mass literature: bright eyes, broad shoulders, lithe muscles and a sports car. This athletic model also encompasses sexual athleticism: the high-ranking executive of the *Le Monde* small ads is also *Playboy* man. But in the end, however much of a

part is played by the masculine model[9] or the transitional, hermaphroditic models, the 'young' forming a kind of third sex, the site of a
'polymorphous, perverse sexuality'),[10] it is woman who orchestrates or
rather around whom is orchestrated this great Aesthetic/Erotic Myth. We
have to find an explanation for this which is not simply of the archetypal
sort along the lines: 'Sexuality is the sphere of Woman because she
represents Nature, etc.' Admittedly, in the historical era we are dealing
with here, woman has been confused with maleficent sexuality and
condemned as such. But that moral/sexual condemnation is entirely
underpinned by a *social* servitude: woman and the body have shared
the same servitude, the same relegation, throughout Western history. The
sexual definition of woman is *historical* in origin: the repression of
the body and the exploitation of woman were carried out in the same
spirit, every exploited (and therefore threatening) category having automatically to assume a sexual definition. Blacks are 'sexualized' for the
same reason, not because they might be said to be 'closer to Nature', but
because they are exploited and kept in serfdom. The repressed, sub-
limated sexuality of a whole civilization inevitably combines with the
category whose social repression and subjection form the very basis of
that culture.

Now, just as women and bodies were bound together in servitude, the
emancipation of woman and the emancipation of the body are logically
and historically linked (for related reasons, the emancipation of the
young is contemporaneous with them). But we can see that this simultaneous emancipation occurs *without the basic ideological confusion between
woman and sexuality being removed* – the legacy of puritanism still bears
down on us with all its force. Indeed, only now does it assume its full
scope since women, once *subjugated* as a sex, are today '**liberated**' as a
sex – to the extent that we see this almost irreversible confusion now
deepening in all its forms, since *it is in so far as she 'liberates' herself that
woman becomes more and more merged with her body*. But we have seen in
what conditions this takes place: it is, in fact, the apparently liberated
woman who merges with the apparently liberated body. We may say
both of women and the body – as we may say of young people and
all the categories whose emancipation constitutes the leitmotiv of modern democratic society – that all the things in whose name they are
'emancipated' (sexual freedom, eroticism, play, etc.) form themselves
into systems of '*tutelary*' values, 'irresponsible' values, simultaneously
orientating consumer behaviour and behaviours of social *relegation*, with
the very exaltation and excess of honour that surrounds them standing in
the way of real economic and social responsibility.

Women, young people and the body – the emergence of all of which
after thousands of years of servitude and forgetting in effect constitutes the most revolutionary potentiality – and, therefore, the most
fundamental risk for any social order whatever – are integrated and
recuperated as a 'myth of emancipation'. Women are given Woman to

consume, the young are given the Young and, in this formal and narcissistic emancipation, their real liberation is successfully averted. Or alternatively, by assigning Revolt to the Young ('Young = revolt'), two birds are killed with one stone: the revolt diffusely present throughout society is conjured away by allotting it to a particular category and that category is neutralized by confining it to a particular role – revolt. An admirable vicious circle of managed 'emancipation', which we also find applied in the case of women: by confusing women and sexual liberation, each is neutralized by the other. Women 'consume themselves' through sexual liberation, and sexual liberation 'is consumed' through women. There is no play on words here. One of the basic mechanisms of consumption is this formal autonomization of groups, classes and castes (and the individual) by and through the formal autonomization of systems of signs or roles.

There is no question here of denying the 'real' development of the status of women and young people as social categories: they are in fact freer; they vote, have rights, work more and work earlier. Similarly, it would be pointless to deny the objective importance now accorded to the body, to the care of it and its pleasures, to the 'added element of body and sexuality' which the average individual enjoys today. We are far from the 'ideal release' Rimbaud spoke of, but let us accept, nonetheless, that there is in all this a greater freedom of manoeuvre for, and a greater positive integration of, women and young people, and bodily problems. What we are saying is that this relative, concrete emancipation, because it is merely the emancipation of women, young people and the body *as categories* immediately indexed to a functional practice, is accompanied by a mythical transcendence or, rather, itself divides to produce a mythical transcendence, an *objectivization as myth*. The emancipation of some women (and – why not? – the relative emancipation of all) is merely to some extent the secondary gain, the spin-off from – and the cover for – that immense strategic operation which consists in *containing in the idea of woman and her body the whole social peril of sexual liberation*, in confining the peril of women's liberation to the *idea* of sexual liberation (in eroticism), in calling down on to the Woman/Object all the perils of the social liberation of women.[11]

The Medical Cult: 'Fitness'

The predominant relation to health is derived from the current way of relating to the body, which is not so much a relation to one's own body as to the functional, 'personalized' body. When it is mediated by an instrumental representation of the body, that relation can be defined as a general function of maintaining the body's equilibrium. When mediated by a representation of the body as prestige good, it becomes a functional status demand. It then enters into a competitive logic and expresses itself

in a virtually unlimited demand for medical, surgical and pharmaceutical services – a compulsive demand linked to the narcissistic investment
of the body/(part) object and a status demand linked to the processes of
personalization and social mobility; a demand which, at any event, bears
only a distant relation to that 'right to health' which is a modernist
extension of human rights, complementary to the rights to liberty and
property. Health today is not so much a biological imperative linked to
survival as a social imperative linked to status. It is not so much a basic
'value' as a form of prestige display. In the mystique of such display,
fitness stands next to beauty. Their signs are exchanged within the
framework of personalization, that anxious, perfectionist manipulation
of the sign function of the body. This corporeal syndrome of display,
which links narcissism and social prestige, can also be very clearly seen
in inverted form in the current very widespread fact, which must be
regarded as one of the essential elements of modern ethics, that any
loss of prestige, any social or psychological reversal is immediately
somatized.

It is, therefore, superficial to claim that the use of medicine (usage of
doctors) has been 'desacralized' and that because people go more often
and more freely to their doctors, because they use and abuse this
democratized social provision in a complex-free way (which is not true),
they are coming closer to an 'objective' practice of health and medicine.
'Democratically consumed' medicine has lost nothing of its sacredness
and its magical functionality. But it is clearly not that traditional functionality which attached, through the person of the priest-healer, the
sorcerer and the medicine-man, to operation on the *practical* body, on the
instrumental body threatened by outside hazards, such as still figures in
the 'uncultivated' peasant vision, in which the body is not interiorized as
a personal, 'personalized' value. In that vision, one does not achieve
one's salvation or mark one's status through one's body. It is, rather, a
tool of one's labour and mana, that is to say, efficient force. If it gets out
of sorts, the doctor restores the body's mana. This type of magic and the
corresponding status of the doctor is tending to disappear. But it is not
giving way, in the modern 'vision', to an objective representation of the
body. It is giving way to two complementary modalities: narcissistic
investment and prestige display: a 'psychical' dimension and a status
dimension. It is in these two directions that the status of the doctor and
of health is being reworked. And it is only now, through the 'rediscovery'
and the *individual* sacralization of the body, that *medicality is assuming its
full scope* (just as it was only with the mythic crystallization of the
'individual soul' that clericality as a transcendent institution really took
off).

Primitive 'religions' know no 'sacrament'; they are collective practices.
It was with the individualization of the principles of salvation (mainly in
Christian spirituality) that sacraments and the 'officiants' in charge of

them were established. It was with the even more thoroughgoing individualization of conscience that individual confession, the sacrament *par
excellence*, was instituted. Making all due allowance and wholly aware of
the dangers of the comparison, it seems to me to be the same with the
body and medicine: it is with generalized individual 'somatization' (in
the broadest, non-clinical sense of the term), with the body's becoming
an object of prestige and salvation and a fundamental value, that the
doctor becomes a 'confessor', a 'source of absolution' and an 'officiant',
and the medical profession settles into the overprivileged social status
which it currently enjoys.

All kinds of sacrificial behaviours of auto-solicitude and malign exorcism, of gratification and repression, converge more than ever on the
privatized, personalized body – a whole host of secondary, 'irrational'
purchases to no practical, therapeutic end. Much of this is consumption
which even transgresses economic imperatives (half of the money spent
on medicines is on non-prescription items, and this goes even for those
covered by the welfare system). What prompts such behaviour other
than the deep-seated belief that it has to cost you something (and it is
enough that it costs you something) for health to be yours *in exchange*?
This is ritual, sacrificial consumption rather than medication. Thus we
see a compulsive demand for medicines among the 'lower' classes and a
demand for the doctor among the better-off, but whether the doctor is
seen by the former as a dispenser of material signs and goods or by the
latter more as the 'psychoanalyst of the body', medicine and doctors
have a cultural *virtue* rather than a therapeutic function, and they are
consumed as 'virtual' mana. And that consumption takes place according to a thoroughly modern ethics which, by contrast with the traditional
form, which demanded that *the body should serve*, enjoins all individuals
to put themselves in the service of their own bodies (cf. the *Elle* article). One
has a duty to take care of oneself as one has to cultivate one's mind: it is,
in a sense, a mark of respectability. The modern woman is both the vestal
and the manager of her own body; she takes care to keep it beautiful and
competitive. The functional and the sacred are inextricably intermingled
here. And the doctor receives both the respect due to the expert and the
reverence due to the priest.

The Obsession with Slimness: The 'Figure'

The obsession with looking after one's figure can be understood in terms
of the same categorical imperative. There is in no sense, of course, any
natural affinity between beauty and slimness (one only has to glance at
other cultures to see this). Fat and obesity have also been regarded as
beautiful in other places and at other times. But *this* imperative, universal, democratic beauty inscribed as a right and a duty on the
pediment of consumer society, is *indissociable from slimness*. Beauty cannot

be fat or slim, heavy-limbed or slender as it could in a traditional definition based on the *harmony* of forms. It can only be slim and slender, according to its current definition as a combinatorial logic of signs, governed by the same algebraic economy as the functionality of objects or the elegance of a diagram. It even tends, somewhat, towards the scrawny and emaciated, on the lines of the models and mannequins that are simultaneously the negation of the flesh and the exaltation of fashion.

This may seem a strange state of affairs, for if we take as one definition of consumption that it is a generalization of the combinatorial processes of fashion, we know that fashion can play on anything, on opposite terms: it can play without distinction on the old and the new, the 'beautiful' and the 'ugly' (in their classical definitions), the moral and the immoral. *But it cannot play on the fat and the thin.* There is something akin to an absolute limit here. Might it be that in a society of overconsumption (of food), slenderness becomes a distinctive sign in itself? Even if slimness acts as such a sign in relation to all previous cultures and generations and to the peasant and 'lower' classes, we know there are no signs which are distinctive *in themselves*, but only opposing formal signs (old and new, long and short (skirts), etc.) which *follow one upon the other* as distinctive signs, and alternate in such a way as to bring fresh grist to the mill, without any one of these definitively squeezing out the other. Now, paradoxically, in the area of the 'figure', an area which is *par excellence* that of fashion, the fashion cycle no longer operates. There has to be something more fundamental than distinction. Something which *must* be linked to the very mode of complicity with our own bodies which we have seen being established in the contemporary era.

The 'liberation' of the body has the effect of constituting it as an object of solicitude. Now that solicitude, like everything which has to do with the body and the relation to the body, is *ambivalent*. It is never solely positive and overall, indeed, it is negative. The body is always 'liberated' as simultaneous object of this *dual solicitude*.[12] As a consequence, the immense process of solicitude of the 'gratifying' kind, a process we have described as the instituting of the body in its modern form, is accompanied by an equal and equally substantial investment of *repressive solicitude*.

It is this repressive solicitude which is expressed in all the modern collective obsessions relating to the body. Hygiene, in all its forms, with its fantasies of sterility, asepsis, prophylaxis or, by contrast, of promiscuity, contamination, pollution – tending to conjure away the 'organic' body and, in particular, the functions of excretion and secretion – aims at a negative definition of the body, by elimination, as though it were a smooth, faultless, sexless object, cut off from all external aggression and thereby protected from itself. The obsession with hygiene is not, however, the direct heir to puritan morality. That morality denied, reproved and repressed the body. In a more subtle way, contemporary ethics sanctifies it in its hygienic abstraction, in all its purity as a disincarnated signifier. But a signifier of what? Of forgotten, censored desire. This is why the (phobic, obsessional) hygienic compulsion is never far away. Overall, however, the preoccupation with hygiene founds a morality based not on pathos, but on play: it 'eludes' deep fantasies in favour of a superficial, cutaneous religion of the body. Taking care of, being 'loving' towards the body, that morality prevents any collusion between the body and desire. It is closer, all in all, to the sacrificial techniques of 'preparation' of the body, to the ludic techniques of control – not repression – of primitive societies, than it is to the repressive ethics of the puritan era.

Much more than in hygiene, it is in the ascetic practice of 'dieting' that the aggressive drive against the body is to be seen, a drive 'liberated' at the same time as the body itself. Ancient societies had their ritual fasting practices. As collective practices linked to the celebration of festivals (before or after – fasting before Communion – fasting in Advent – Lent after Mardi Gras), it was their function to siphon off all this diffuse aggressive drive against the body (the whole ambivalence of the relation to food and 'consumption') and channel it into collective observance. Now, these various institutions of fasting and mortification have fallen into disuse as so many archaisms incompatible with the total, democratic liberation of the body. Clearly, our consumer society can no longer bear any restrictive norm and even excludes such a norm on principle. However, in liberating the body in all its potentialities for satisfaction, it thought it was liberating a naturally pre-existing harmonious relationship between man and his body. It turns out that this was a *fantastic mistake*. The whole antagonistic aggressive drive liberated at the same time, now no longer canalized by social institutions, surges back today into the very heart of the universal solicitude for the body. It is that drive which fuels the veritable enterprise of self-repression now affecting one-third of the adult populations of the overdeveloped countries (and 50 per cent of women; an American study has shown that 300 adolescent girls out of 446 are on a diet). It is this drive which, above and beyond the (once again undeniable) determinations of fashion, is stoking up this irrepressible, irrational self-destructive frenzy in which beauty and elegance, which were the original goals, are now merely alibis for a daily, obsessive disciplinary exercise. In a total turnabout, the body becomes that menacing object which has to be watched over, reduced and mortified for 'aesthetic' ends, while one's eyes are kept riveted throughout on the skinny, emaciated models of *Vogue*, in whom one can decipher all the inverted aggressiveness of an affluent society towards its own body triumphalism, all the vehement denial of its own principles.

This meeting of beauty and repression in the cult of the figure (in which the body, in its materiality and sexuality, basically has no part any more, simply functioning now as the physical medium for two logics wholly removed from the logic of satisfaction: the *fashion imperative*, a principle of social organization, and the *death imperative*, a principle of psychical organization) is one of the great paradoxes of our 'civilization'. The mystique of the 'figure' and the fascination with slimness have such a profound impact only because they are forms of **violence**, because in them the body is literally *sacrificed* – both fixed in its perfection and violently vitalized as in sacrifice. All the contradictions of this society are encapsulated here, at the level of the body. 'With its remarkable action', Scandi-Sauna will bring you a slimmer waistline – better hips, thighs and ankles – a flat stomach – regenerated tissues – firmed-up flesh – smooth skin – a new figure. 'After three months of using Scandi-Sauna . . . I lost those extra pounds and, at the same time, acquired remarkable physical fitness and mental harmony.' In the USA, 'low-calorie foods', artificial sweeteners, fat-free butters and diets launched with great advertising campaigns make fortunes for their backers and manufacturers. It is estimated that 30 million Americans either are, or believe themselves to be, obese.

The Sex-Exchange Standard

Automatic sexualization of everyday essentials: 'Whether the article to be pitched out into commercial space is a brand of tyres or a new model of coffin, the aim is always to hit the potential client in the same spot: below the belt. Eroticism for the elite; pornography for the masses' (Jacques Sternberg, *Toi ma nuit*, Losfeld).

Naked theatre (Broadway: *Oh Calcutta!*): the authorities licensed the performances on condition that there were neither erections nor penetration on stage.

First pornography fair at Copenhagen – 'Sex 69': this was a 'fair' and not a festival, as the newspapers had reported. In other words, it was essentially a commercial event, designed to enable the manufacturers of pornographic material to conquer new markets. It seems that the Christiansborg leaders,[13] generously concerned to remove all mystery from this field – and, hence, much of its attraction – by bringing down the barriers, had underestimated the financial side of the business. A number of smart people, on the lookout for profitable investments, were not slow to grasp what an opportunity the intensive exploitation of this sector could represent for them, now that it was part of the open market. Having rapidly organized themselves, they are now, as a consequence, developing pornography into one of Denmark's most profitable industries (source: the press).

Not a millimetre of erogenous zone has been left unexploited (J.-F. Held). The talk everywhere is of 'sexual explosion', of the 'escalation of eroticism'. Sexuality is 'at the forefront' of consumer society, spectacularly overdetermining the entire signifying field of mass communications. All that is presented there has about it a conspicuous sexual vibrato.

Everything offered for consumption has a sexual coefficient. At the same time, of course, *it is sexuality itself which is offered for consumption*. Here again we have the same operation as we adverted to with regard to youth and revolt, women and sexuality: by indexing sexuality in an increasingly systematic way to commercialized and industrialized objects and messages, these latter are diverted from their objective rationality, while sexuality itself is diverted from its explosive finality. Social and sexual change thus tread well-beaten paths which have already been carefully explored by 'cultural' and promotional eroticism.

Admittedly, this explosion, this proliferation is contemporaneous with deep changes in the relations between the sexes and in individual relations to the body and sex. It is, even more, an expression of the real – and in many respects new-found – urgency of sexual problems. But it is not certain either that this sexual 'display' of modern society is not a gigantic cover for these very problems, or that, by giving them systematic 'official status', it does not lend them a deceptive appearance of 'freedom', which masks the profound contradictions involved.

We can sense that this eroticization is excessive and that there is meaning in the excessiveness. Is it merely the expression of a crisis of desublimation, of a relaxation of traditional taboos? In that case, we might imagine that once a certain saturation level had been reached, once the cravings of the heirs of puritanism had been satisfied, liberated sexuality would recover its equilibrium, having now detached itself, and achieved its independence, from the productivist, industrial spiral. One might also take the view that the escalation, once begun, will continue like that of GNP, the conquest of space or innovation in fashion and objects, *and for the same reasons* (J.-F. Held). In this perspective, sexuality is *once and for all part of the unlimited process of production and marginal differentiation*, because it is the very logic of that system which has 'liberated' it as *erotic system* and individual and collective consumption function.

Let us distance ourselves here from any kind of moral censorship: we are not speaking of 'corruption' and we know, in any case, that the worst sexual 'corruption' may be a sign of vitality, richness, emancipation: it is, in that case, revolutionary and marks the historical flowering of a new class conscious of its triumph. The Italian Renaissance was an age of this kind. Such sexuality is a mark of rejoicing. However, it is not this sexuality, but its spectre which resurfaces – as a sign of death – when a society is in decline. The decomposition of a class or a society always ends in the individual dispersal of its members and (among other things) in a veritable contagion of sexuality, both as individual motive and as social ambience. The end of the *ancien régime* was one such period. It seems that a seriously splintered collectivity, because it is cut off from its past and lacks any imagining of a future, re-enters an almost pure world of drives, mingling in the same feverish dissatisfaction the immediate determinations of profit and sex. The disturbance of social relations, and the precarious collusion and ferocious competition which create the ambience of the economic world, affect the nerves and the senses. Sexuality, ceasing to be a factor of cohesion and shared elation, becomes an individual frenzy for profit. Everyone is obsessed with it and thereby isolated. And, in a characteristic feature, as it is exacerbated, it also becomes *anxious* about itself. It is no longer shame, modesty or guilt, those marks of the centuries of puritanism, which weigh upon it: indeed, these gradually vanish as the official norms and prohibitions disappear. It is the individual agency of repression, internalized *censorship*, which penalizes this sexual liberation. Censorship is no longer socially instituted (religiously, morally, juridically) in formal opposition to sexuality; it now plunges deep into the individual unconscious and feeds on the same sources as sexuality. All the sexual gratifications which surround one now bear within them their own continual censorship. There is no longer any repression (or there is less); but censorship has become a function of everyday life.

'Nous implanterons une débauche inouïe' said Rimbaud in his 'Villes'.[14] But sexual liberation and the escalation of eroticism have nothing to do with the 'derangement of all the senses' [*dérèglement de tous les sens*].[15] The orchestrated derangement and muted anxiety with which it is imbued, far from 'changing life', merely make up a collective ambience in which sexuality in fact becomes a *private* affair, that is to say, one that is fiercely self-conscious, narcissistic and tired of itself – the very ideology of a system which it crowns in terms of mores and in which it is a *political* cog. For, above and beyond the advertisers, who 'play' the sexuality 'card' so as to sell more products, there is the existing social order, which 'plays the card of' sexual liberation (even if it condemns it morally) against the threatening dialectic of the totality.

Symbols and Fantasies in Advertising

This generalized censorship which defines *consumed* sexuality must not, above all, be confused with *moral* censorship. It does not penalize conscious sexual behaviours in the name of conscious imperatives. This is, indeed, a field in which apparent permissiveness is *de rigueur*; everything conspires towards it and even the perversions can be freely engaged in (these things are all relative, of course, but this is the general trend). The censorship which our society, in its sexual hyperaesthesia, sets in place is more subtle: *it operates at the level of fantasies themselves and the symbolic function*. This kind of censorship is unaffected by the campaigning measures used against traditional censorship: to use those today is to fight an enemy that is past and gone. And the weapons of the (still virulent) puritan forces, with their censorship and morality, are outdated too. The basic process is going on elsewhere, not at the conscious and manifest level of the seductive artifices – for good or ill –

of sex. There is a terrible naïvety about this, among both the decriers of sexual liberty and its defenders, on the right and on the left.

Let us take an example from an advertisement for Henriot champagne (J.-F. Held).

> A bottle and a rose. The rose flushes with colour, begins to open, approaches the screen, swells, becomes tumescent. The amplified sound of a beating heart fills the cinema, accelerates, grows fevered, wild. The cork begins to rise from the bottle slowly, inexorably. It grows in size, moves towards the camera, its brass binding wires breaking one after another. The heart beats and beats, the rose swells, the cork again – ah, and suddenly the heart stops, the cork flies off and the foaming champagne bubbles out over the neck of the bottle, the rose grows pale and closes, the tension subsides.

Let us recall also that advertisement for bathroom installations in which, with a great many contortions – and in ever greater close-up – a vamp simulates a mounting orgasm with taps and pipes and a whole battery of phallic, spermatic devices. And the thousands of similar examples in which there is all-out 'hidden persuasion' – so-called – that persuasion which 'so dangerously' manipulates our 'drives and fantasies' and no doubt has more impact in intellectual circles than on the imagination of consumers. Erotic advertising, so obsessive and guilt-inducing, stirs up such profound emotions in us. A naked blonde with black braces appears and, hey presto, the braces manufacturer is rich. And even though he points out that 'you only have to raise the most harmless umbrella towards the sky to turn it into a phallic symbol', Held does not question either the fact of its being a symbol, or the effectiveness of that symbol as such on effective demand. Further on, he compares two advertising projects for Weber lingerie: the manufacturers chose the first of these and they were right, he says, because, in the other, the

> swooning young man looks almost as though he has been slain. For women, the temptation to be dominant is great . . . but it is also a frightening temptation . . . If the sphinx-woman and her victim had become Weber's brand image, the ambiguous guilt of their possible clients would have been so great that they would have chosen less compromising brassières.

And so the analysts, all deliciously a-quiver, will turn their learned attentions to the fantasies in advertising, to the devouring orality in them, the anality or the phallic symbols – all these things directly plumbed into the consumer's unconscious, which was simply ready and waiting to be manipulated (that unconscious is, of course, assumed to be already there and given in advance, since Freud said so – a hidden essence, whose preferred fare is the symbol or the fantasy). There is the same vicious circularity between the unconscious and fantasies as there once was between subject and object at the level of consciousness. An unconscious stereotyped as an individual function and fantasies delivered as finished products by advertising agencies are indexed one to the other, defined one by the other. This is to elude all the real problems posed by the logic of the unconscious and the symbolic function by spectacularly materializing them in a mechanical process of signification and the efficacity of signs: 'There is the unconscious and then there are the fantasies which lock into it, and this miraculous combination sells products.' There is the same naïvety here as among the ethnologists who believed the myths related to them by native peoples and took them literally, along with the superstitious belief of those peoples in the magical efficacy of their myths and rites – all of which was done to maintain the ethnologists' own rationalist myth of the 'primitive mentality'. There are beginning to be doubts about the direct impact of advertising on sales. It is perhaps also time to cast equally radical doubt on this naïve fantasmic mechanics – which serves as an alibi for both advertisers and analysts.

Crudely put, the question is this: is there really any libido in all this? What is there that is sexual, libidinal in the eroticism deployed? Is advertising (and are the other mass-media systems) a genuine *'scene'* of fantasy? Is this *manifest* symbolic, fantasy content ultimately to be taken any more literally than the manifest content of dreams? And is the erotic injunction ultimately any more valid or symbolically effective than the direct commercial injunction is in the marketplace? What is really going on here?

In reality, one is faced with a mythology at one remove, which strives to pass off as *fantasy* what is merely *fantasmagoria*, to entrap individuals, by way of a rigged symbolics, with the *myth* of their individual unconscious, to make them invest it as a consumer function. People have to believe that they 'have' an unconscious, that that unconscious is there, projected into and objectivized in the 'erotic' symbolism of advertising, which serves as a proof that it exists, that they are right to believe in it and therefore to wish to come to terms with it, first at the level of the 'reading' of symbols, then by the acquisition of the goods designated by those symbols and supporting those 'fantasies'.

There are, in fact, neither symbols nor fantasies in this whole erotic shebang, and it is tilting at windmills to describe all this as a 'strategy of desire'. Even when there is not irony in the phallic or other messages, when they are not conveyed in an openly playful way, 'with a nod and a wink', we may safely take it that all the erotic material surrounding us is entirely *culturalized*. It is neither fantasmic nor symbolic material, but simply *atmospheric*. It is neither Desire nor the Unconscious speaking, but the psychoanalytic culture, or rather subculture, which has become banal and commonplace, has passed into ordinary commercial parlance. It is second-level affabulation; strictly speaking, it is *allegory*. Id (the Unconscious) does not speak there; what does speak merely refers on to psychoanalysis as it is established, integrated and 'recuperated' today in the cultural system. And it certainly does not refer to psychoanalysis as analytic practice, but to the sign function of psychoanalysis, as something culturalized, aestheticized, mass-mediafied. At any event, one should not confuse a formal and allegorical combinatory of mythologized themes with the discourse of the Unconscious, any more than the artificial log fire should be confused with the symbol of fire. There is no relation between that 'signified' fire and the poetic substance of fire analysed by Bachelard. That log fire is a cultural sign and nothing more; it has value merely as a cultural *reference*. Thus, the whole of advertising and modern erotics are made up of signs, not of meaning.

One must not be taken in by the escalation of the erotic in advertising (any more than by the escalation of 'irony', the play, the distancing and the 'counter-advertising' which, significantly, go along with it): all these contents are merely juxtaposed signs, all of which culminate in the super-sign that is the **brand name**, which is the only real message. Nowhere is there language – and certainly not the language of the Unconscious. This is why the 50 female bottoms priggishly arrayed by Airborne in its recent advert ('Ah, yes. They're all there . . . this is where we do all our initial research, examining every angle . . . for we believe, with Mme de Sévigné . . .', etc.) can be shown – and many others too. They don't offend against anything, nor do they awaken anything 'deep within us'. They are merely cultural connotations, a metalanguage of connotations: they speak the sexualist myth of a culture that is 'with-it'; they have nothing to do with real anality, which is precisely why they are inoffensive, and immediately consumable as images.

The real fantasy is not representable. If it *could* be represented, it would be unbearable. The advertisement for Gillette razor-blades showing two velvety female lips framed by a razor blade can only be viewed because it does not really express the – unbearable – fantasy of the castrating vagina to which it 'alludes', and because it is content simply to combine together signs emptied of their syntax, isolated signs, itemized signs, which trigger no unconscious associations (and which indeed systematically evade these), only 'cultural' ones. This is the Madame Tussaud's of symbols, a petrified forest of fantasies/signs which no longer have in them anything of the *work* of the drives.

All in all, then, to denounce advertising for its manipulation of the emotions is to pay it too great a compliment. But this gigantic mystification, in which both censors and defenders willingly collude, doubtless has a very precise function, which is to deflect attention from the real process, that is to say from the radical analysis of the processes of censorship which 'operate' very effectively underneath all this fantasmagoria. The real conditioning we are subjected to by the machinery of erotic advertising is not some 'deep-level' persuasion or unconscious suggestion, but *rather* the censorship of the deep meaning, the symbolic function, the fantasmic expression in an articulated syntax – in short, the censorship of the living emanation of sexual signifiers. All this is blotted out, censored, abolished in a codified play of sexual signs, in the opaque obviousness of the sexual that is deployed on all sides, in which the subtle destructuring of syntax leaves place only for a closed, tautological manipulation. It is in this systematic terrorism, which operates at the level of signification itself, that all sexuality empties itself of its substance and becomes material for consumption. It is here that the 'process' of consumption takes place, and this is of quite a different order of seriousness from naïve exhibitionism, fairground phallicism and knockabout Freudianism.

The Sexed Doll

The sexed doll is a new toy. But the toys directed at children on the basis of adult fantasies implicate the whole of a civilization. This new doll attests to the general nature of our relation to sex in consumer society which, like our relation to everything else, is governed by *a process of simulation and restoration*. The driving principle of this is an artificial mad desire [*vertige*] for realism: sexuality is confused, in this case, with the 'objective' reality of the sexual organs.

If we look closely, it is the same with colour in television, with nudity in advertising or elsewhere, as it is in participation in the factories or the 'organic and active' participation of spectators in the 'total' spectacle of avant-garde theatre: everywhere we find an effort artificially to restore a 'truth' or a 'totality', *systematically* to restore a totality on the basis of the prior division of labour or functions.

In the case of the sexed doll (the equivalent of sex as *toy*, as infantile manipulation), we must first have split off sexuality as totality, in its symbolic total exchange function, in order to be able to contain it in *sexual signs* (genitals, nudity, secondary sexual characteristics, the generalized erotic signification of all objects) and to *assign these to the individual* as private property or as attributes.

The 'traditional' doll fully performed its symbolic (and thus *also* sexual) function. To deck it out with a specific sexual sign is, in a sense, to strike out that symbolic function and to confine the object to a spectacular function. This is not a special case: this sex *added to* the doll as secondary attribute, as sexual affabulation and, in fact, as *censorship* of the symbolic function is the equivalent, at the level of the child, of the nudist and erotic affabulation, of that glorification of the signs of the body which surrounds us on all sides.

Sexuality is a total, symbolic structure of exchange:

1 *It is deposed from its symbolic function* by substituting for it the realistic, manifest, spectacular significations of sex and 'sexual needs'.
2 *It is deposed from its exchange function* (this is fundamental) by individualizing Eros, by assigning the sex to the individual and the individual to the sex. This is the culmination of the technical and social division of labour. Sex becomes a fragmented function and, in the same process, is allotted to the individual as 'private' property (as also occurs with the Unconscious).

We can see that one thing is going on here and one alone: the denial of sexuality as symbolic exchange or, in other words, as total process beyond *functional* division (that is to say, the denial of sexuality as *subversive*).

Once its total, symbolic exchange function has been deconstructed and lost, sexuality collapses into the dual use-value/exchange-value schema (which two aspects are together characteristic of the notion of *object*). It is objectivized as a separate function, both:

1 use-value for the individual (by way of his/her own sex, 'sexual technique' and 'sexual needs', for in this case, it is a matter of technique and needs, not of desire);

2 exchange-value (though this is no longer symbolic, but either economic and commodity-based – prostitution in all its forms – or, as is much more significant today, conspicuous sign-value – 'sexual status').

It is this whole story which is told by the sexed doll in its guise as 'progressive' toy. Like the naked female rump thrown in as a bonus in an advert for record players or Air India, this dollish sex is a *logical* aberration. It is as grotesque as a brassière on a pre-pubescent girl (a thing you can see on beaches). And, though in appearance opposite to that, it has the same meaning. The one veils, the other 'unveils', but the two are equally affected, and equally puritanical. In each case, there is a *censorship* operating through the artifact, through the conspicuous *simulation* which is always based on a *metaphysics of realism* – the real here being the reified and the opposite of the true.

The more signs/attributes of the real are added and the more the artifact is perfected, the more is truth censored by diverting the symbolic charge towards the cultural metaphysics of reified sex. Everything will now be artificially sexualized in this way (not just dolls), the better to exorcise the libidinal dimension and the symbolic function. But this particular case is an admirable one, for here it is the parents who, in good faith(?) and on the pretext of sexual education, carry out a veritable *castration* on the child by the over-exhibition of sexual signs where they have no place at all.

9

The Drama of Leisure or the Impossibility of Wasting One's Time

In the real or imagined abundance of the 'consumer society', Time occupies something of a privileged place. The demand for that very special kind of good equals the demand for almost all the others taken together. There is, of course, no more an equality of opportunity – or democracy – of free time than there is of other goods and services. Moreover, we know that, though it has some significance between periods or between cultures, the accounting of free time in chronometric units is not at all meaningful for us as an absolute value: the *quality* of that free time, its rhythm and its contents, and whether it is residual to the demands of work or 'autonomous', are all things which make a difference between particular individuals, categories or classes. And even the excess of work and the lack of leisure can become the privilege of the manager or of the high-ranking official. In spite of these disparities, which would only assume their full meaning within a differential theory of signs of status (of which 'consumed' free time is a part), the fact remains that time retains a particular mythic value for its equalizing of human conditions, a value which has been taken up again strongly and thematized in our own day in the concept of leisure time. The old adage that 'all men are equal before time and death', which once encapsulated in its entirety the demand for social justice, today lives on in the carefully tended myth that all are equal in leisure.

> Going harpoon fishing together and sharing the Samos wine created a deep sense of fellow-feeling. On the boat back, they realized that they knew each other only by their Christian names and, wishing to exchange addresses, discovered to their amazement that they worked in the same factory, the one as technical director, the other as nightwatchman.

This delightful little fable, which sums up the entire ideology of the Club Méditerranée, involves several metaphysical postulates:

1   Leisure is the realm of freedom.
2   Every man is, by nature, in substance free and equal to others: he has only to be put back in a state of 'nature' to recover this substantial liberty, equality and fraternity. Thus, the Greek islands and the underwater depths are heirs to the ideals of the French Revolution.
3   Time is an a priori, transcendent dimension, which pre-exists its contents. It is there waiting for you. If it is alienated and subjugated in work, then 'you don't have time.' When you are away from work

or unconstrained, 'you have time.' As an absolute, inalienable dimension, like air or water, in leisure it once again becomes everyone's private property.

This last point is the key one: it hints at the fact that time might well be only the product of a certain culture and, more precisely, of a certain mode of production. In that case, it is *necessarily* subject to the same status as all the goods produced or available within the framework of that system of production: that of property, private or public, that of appropriation, that of the **object**, possessed and alienable, alienated or free, and, like all objects produced by that systematic mode, partaking of the reified abstraction of exchange-value.

Of most objects, one can still say that they have a certain use-value, which is in theory dissociable from their exchange-value. But is this true of time? Where is the use-value that could be defined by some objective function or specific practice? For this is the exigency which lies at the bottom of 'free' time: *that we restore to time its use-value*, that we liberate it as an empty dimension to fill it with its individual freedom. Now, in our system, time can only be 'liberated' as object, as chronometric *capital* of years, hours, days, weeks, to be 'invested' by each person 'as he pleases'. It is already, therefore, no longer in fact 'free', since it is governed in its chronometry by the total abstraction which is that of the system of production.

The demand underlying leisure is, therefore, an insolubly contradictory and truly desperate one. Its fervid hope for freedom attests to the power of the system of constraints which is nowhere so total, precisely, as at the level of time. 'When I speak of time, it is already gone,' said Apollinaire. Of leisure we may say that 'When you "have" time, it is no longer free.' And the contradiction here is not one of terms, but of substance. This is the *tragic* paradox of consumption. Everyone wants to put – believes he has put – his desire into every object possessed, consumed, and into every minute of free time, but from every object appropriated, from every satisfaction achieved, and from every 'available' minute, the desire is already absent, necessarily absent. All that remains is *consommé* of desire.

In primitive societies there is no time. The question of whether one 'has' time or not has no meaning there. Time there is nothing but the rhythm of repeated collective activities (the ritual of work and of feasting). It cannot be dissociated from these activities and projected into the future, or planned and manipulated. It is not individual; it is the very rhythm of exchange which culminates in the act of feasting. There is no name for it; it merges with the verbs of exchanging, with the cycle of men and nature. It is, therefore, 'bound', but not constrained and this 'binding' (*Gebundenheit*) does not stand opposed to some kind of 'freedom'. It is properly symbolic, which is to say that it cannot be abstractly isolated. But to say 'time is symbolic' has no meaning: it simply does not exist there, any more than does money.

The analogy between time and money is, on the other hand, funda-mental to the analysis of 'our' times and what the great significant break between working time and free time might imply. This is a crucial break since the basic options of consumer society are based upon it.

'Time is money': this slogan etched in letters of fire on Remington typewriters is also written above the factory gates, and inscribed in the subjugated time of daily life, in the increasingly important notion of the 'time-budget'. It even governs – and it is this which concerns us here – leisure and free time. And it is this slogan too which defines empty time and is etched on the beach sundials and over the entrances to the holiday villages.

Time is a rare and precious commodity, subject to the laws of exchange-value. This is clearly true of working time, since it is bought and sold. But, increasingly, free time itself has to be directly or indirectly purchased before it can be 'consumed'. Norman Mailer has analysed the production calculation carried out on orange juice, delivered frozen or liquid (in a carton). The latter is dearer because the price includes the two minutes gained over preparing the frozen product: *in this way, the consumer's own free time is being sold to him*. And there is logic in this, since 'free' time is in fact time 'earned'; it is capital on which a return can be had, potential productive power, which has therefore to be bought if one is to have control of it. One could only be amazed or indignant at this if one still held to the naïve hypothesis of a 'natural' time, ideally neutral and available to all. The idea, which is not at all absurd, that one might be able to put a shilling in a juke-box and 'buy back' two minutes' silence illustrates the same truth.

Divisible, abstract, measured time thus becomes homogeneous with the exchange-value system: it forms part of that system on the same basis as any other object. As an object of temporal calculation, it can and must be exchanged against any other commodity (in particular, money). Moreover, the notion of time-as-object [*la notion de temps/objet*] is a reversible one: just as time is an object, so all produced objects can be considered as crystallized time – not just labour time in the calculation of their market value, but also leisure time, in so far as technical objects 'save' time for those who use them and are sold on that basis. The washing machine is free time for the housewife, potential free time transformed into an object so as to be buyable and sellable (free time she may possibly take advantage of to watch TV and the adverts she can see there for washing machines!).

This law of time as exchange-value and as productive force does not stop at leisure's doorstep, as though leisure miraculously escaped all the constraints that rule working time. The laws of the (production) system do not take holidays. On the roads, on the beaches, in the holiday villages – they everywhere continually reproduce *time as productive force*.

The apparent division into working time and leisure time – the latter ushering in the transcendent sphere of liberty – is a myth. This grand opposition, which is increasingly fundamental at the lived level of consumer society, remains nonetheless a formal one. This gigantic orchestration of annual time into a 'solar year' and a 'social year', with the holidays as the solstice of private life and the beginning of spring as the solstice (or equinox) of collective life – this gigantic ebbing and flowing is a seasonal rhythm in appearance only. It is *not a rhythm* at all (a succession of natural moments of a cycle), but a *functional mechanism*. It is a single systematic process which splits two ways into working time and leisure time. We shall see that, as a function of this common objective logic, the norms and constraints which are those of working time are transferred to free time and its contents.

Let us return, for a moment, to the specific ideology of leisure. Rest, relaxation, escape and distraction are, perhaps, 'needs': but they do not in themselves define the specific exigency of leisure, which is the consumption of *time*. Free time is, perhaps, the entire ludic activity one fills it up with, but it is, first of all, *the freedom to waste one's time*, and possibly even to 'kill' it, to expend it as pure loss (this is why it is insufficient to say that leisure is 'alienated' because it is merely the time necessary to reproduce labour power. The alienation of leisure is more profound: it does not relate to the direct subordination to working time, but is linked to the **very impossibility of wasting one's time)**.

The true use-value of time, the use-value which leisure desperately tries to restore, is that of being wasted.[1] The holidays are this quest for a time which one can waste in the full sense of the term, without that waste entering in its turn into a process of calculation, without that time being (at the same time) in some way 'earned'. In our system of production and productive forces, one can only *earn* one's time: this fatality weighs upon leisure as it does upon work. One can only 'exploit [*faire-valoir*] one's time', if only by making a spectacularly empty use of it. The free time of the holidays remains the private property of the holiday-maker: an object, a possession he has earned with the sweat of his brow over the year; it is something owned by him, possessed by him as he possesses his other objects – something he could not relinquish to give it or sacrifice it (as one does with objects in making gifts of them), to yield it back up to total availability, to that absence of time which would be true freedom. He is tethered to 'his' time as Prometheus was tethered to his rock, tethered to the Promethean myth of time as productive force.

Sisyphus, Tantalus, Prometheus: all the existential myths of 'absurd freedom' are reasonably accurate representations of the holiday-maker in his setting, with all his desperate efforts to imitate 'vacation', gratuitousness, a total dispossession, a void, a loss of himself and of his time which **he cannot** achieve, being, as he is, an object caught up in a definitively objectivized dimension of time.

We are in an age when men will never manage to waste enough time to be rid of the inevitability of spending their lives earning it. But you can't throw off time like underwear. You can no longer either kill it or waste it, any more than you can money, since they are both the very expression of the exchange-value system. In the symbolic dimension, gold and money are *excrement*. It is the same with objectivized time. But it is, in fact, very rare – and logically impossible in the current system – for money or time to be restored to their 'archaic', sacrificial function of excrement. That would really be to deliver oneself of them in the symbolic mode. In the order based on calculation and capital, things are, in a sense, precisely the opposite way about: objectivized by it, and manipulated by it as exchange-value, *it is we who have become the excrement of money, it is we who have become the excrement of time.*

Thus, everywhere, in spite of the fiction of freedom in leisure, 'free' time is logically impossible: there can only be constrained time. The time of consumption is that of production. It is so to the extent that it is only ever an 'escapist' parenthesis in the cycle of production. But, once again, this functional complementarity (variously shared out in the different social classes) is not its essential determination. Leisure is constrained in so far as, behind its apparent gratuitousness, it faithfully reproduces all the mental and practical constraints which are those of productive time and subjugated [*asservi*] daily life.

It is not characterized by creative activities: creating, artistically or otherwise, is never a *leisure* activity. Leisure is generally characterized by regressive activities of a type pre-dating modern forms of work (pottering, handicrafts, collecting, fishing). The guiding model for free time is the only one experienced up to that point: the model of childhood. But there is confusion here between the childhood experience of freedom in play and the nostalgia for a stage of social development prior to the division of labour. In each of these cases, because the totality and spontaneity leisure seeks to restore come into being in a social time marked essentially by the modern division of labour, they take the objective form of escape and *irresponsibility*. Now, this irresponsibility in leisure is homologous with, and structurally complementary to, irresponsibility in work. 'Freedom' on the one hand, constraint on the other: the structure is, in fact, the same.

It is the very fact of the functional division between the two great modalities of time which constitutes a system and makes *leisure the very ideology of alienated labour*. The dichotomy establishes the same lacks and the same contradictions on both sides. So, everywhere, we find in leisure and holidays the same eager moral and idealistic pursuit of accomplishment as in the sphere of work, the same **ethics of pressured performance**. No more than consumption, to which it belongs entirely, is leisure a praxis of satisfaction. Or, at least, we may say that it is so only in appearance. In fact, the obsession with getting a tan, that bewildered whirl in which tourists 'do' Italy, Spain and all the art galleries, the gymnastics and nudity which are *de rigueur* under an obligatory sun and, most important of all, the smiles and unfailing *joie de vivre* all attest to the fact that the holiday-maker conforms in every detail to the principles of duty, sacrifice and asceticism. This is the 'fun-morality' Riesman speaks of, that properly ethical dimension of salvation in leisure and pleasure which no one can now escape, except by finding their salvation in other criteria of accomplishment.

The increasingly marked tendency towards the physical concentration of tourists and holiday-makers – which stands in formal contradiction to the declared motive of pursuing freedom and autonomy – obeys the same principle of constraint which is homologous with that experienced in work. Solitude is a value spoken about, but not practised. People flee work, but not physical concentration. Here again, of course, social discrimination plays its part (see *Communications*, 8). Sea, sand, sun and the presence of a crowd are much more necessary to holiday-makers at the bottom of the social scale than to the better-off. This is partly a question of financial resources, but, above all, it is one of cultural aspirations: 'Subjected to passive holidays, they need the sea, the sun and the crowd to feel as though they really are somebody' (Hubert Macé, in *Communications*, 10, 'Vacances et tourisme', 1967).

'Leisure is a collective vocation.' This journalistic headline perfectly sums up the institutional character, the aspect of internalized social norm which free time and its consumption have assumed, in which the privilege of enjoying snow, idleness and cosmopolitan cuisine merely masks deep compliance with:

1   a collective morality of maximization of needs and satisfactions, which reflects point by point in the private and 'free' sphere the principle of maximization of production and productive forces in the 'social' sphere;
2   a code of distinction, a structure of differentiation – the distinctive criterion, which for the well-to-do of earlier ages was 'idleness', having now become the 'consumption' of useless time. It is the constraint that one must do nothing (useful) which governs leisure – and does so very tyrannically – just as it governed the status of the privileged in traditional societies.

Leisure, which is still very unequally distributed, remains, in our democratic societies, a factor of cultural distinction and selection. We may, however, envisage this trend reversing itself (at least we may imagine this): in Aldous Huxley's *Brave New World*, the Alphas are the only ones who work, the mass of the others being condemned to hedonism and leisure. We may admit that, with the progress of leisure, and the generalized 'promotion' of free time, there will be a reversal of this privilege and the great thing will be to set aside less and less time for *obligatory consumption*. If, as is probable, though it is the opposite of what are ideally their goals, leisure activities, as they develop, increasingly sink into competitiveness and the disciplinary ethic, then we may suppose that work (a certain type of work) will become the place and time in which to recover from one's leisure. And work can even now be a mark of distinction and privilege once again, as is the case with the affected 'servitude' of top executives and managing directors who feel they have to work 15 hours a day.

So we come to the paradoxical end-point where it is work itself that is *consumed*. To the extent that work is *preferred* to free time, that it meets a 'neurotic' demand, and that the excess of it is a mark of prestige, we are in the field of the consumption of work. But we know that anything can become a consumer object.

The fact remains that today, and for long into the future, the distinctive value of leisure will remain. Even the reactional valorization of work merely proves *a contrario* the force of leisure as a *noble value* in our deepest conceptions. 'Conspicuous abstention from labour becomes the conventional index of reputability', writes Veblen in his *Theory of the Leisure Class*. Productive work is base: this tradition is still alive. It is perhaps even reinforced with the increased status competition we find in modern 'democratic' societies. This law of leisure-value is assuming the force of an absolute social prescription.

Leisure is not, therefore, so much a function of *enjoyment* of free time, satisfaction and functional repose. Its definition is that of an un- productive consumption of time. And so we come back to the 'wasting' of time we spoke of at the outset, though in this instance to show how *consumed* free time is in fact the time of a *production*. This time, which is economically unproductive, is the time of a production of *value* – distinctive value, status value, prestige value. Doing nothing (or doing nothing productive) is, in this regard, a specific activity. Producing value (signs, etc.) is an *obligatory* social prestation; it is the very opposite of passivity, even if the latter forms the manifest discourse of leisure. In fact, time is not 'free' in leisure; it is *expended*, and not as pure loss, because it is the moment, for the social individual, of a production of status. No one needs leisure, but all are charged to prove their freedom not to perform productive labour.

The *consumption* of empty time is, therefore, a kind of *potlatch*, in which free time serves as a material of signification and sign-exchange (in parallel with all the activities subsidiary and internal to leisure). As in Bataille's *The Accursed Share*, it assumes value in its very destruction, in being sacrificed. And leisure is the site of this 'symbolic' operation.[2]

It is, therefore, within the logic of distinction and the production of value that leisure *is justified* in the last instance. We may verify this almost experimentally: left to his own devices, in a state of 'creative freedom', the leisured individual desperately seeks out a nail to bang in or an engine to strip down. Outside the competitive sphere, there are no autonomous needs, no spontaneous motivation. But still he does not give up doing nothing. Far from it. He imperiously 'needs' to do nothing, for this has a value of social distinction.

Still today, what the average individual seeks in his holidays and free time is not the 'freedom to fulfil himself' (as what? what hidden essence is going to emerge?), but to demonstrate the uselessness of his time, the excess of time he possesses as sumptuary capital, as *wealth*. Leisure time, like consumption time in general, is becoming the highly charged part of social time, the part productive of value – a dimension not of economic *survival*, but of social *salvation*.

We can see now what, ultimately, is the basis of the 'freedom' of free time. This is akin to the 'freedom' to work and the 'freedom' to consume. Just as labour has to be 'freed' as labour power to be able to assume economic exchange-value, and just as the consumer *must* be 'freed' as such, that is to say, left (formally) free to choose and establish preferences for the system of consumption to be established, so time has to be 'freed', that is to say, extricated from its (symbolic, ritual) implications to become: not only (1) *a commodity* (in labour time) in the cycle of economic exchange); but also, (2) *a sign* and sign material assuming, in leisure, a social exchange-value (ludic prestige value).

It is this last modality alone which defines *consumed* time. Labour time, for its part, is not 'consumed' – or, rather, it is consumed only in the sense that an engine consumes petrol, a sense which bears no relation to the *logic* of consumption. As for 'symbolic' time, that time which is neither economically constrained nor 'free' as sign-function, but *bound* – in other words, indissociable from the concrete cycle of nature or reciprocal social exchange – that time is clearly not 'consumed'. In fact it is only by analogy with, and projection of, our chronometric conception that we call it 'time'; it is a rhythm of exchange.

In an integrated and total system like ours, there cannot be any free availability of time. And leisure is not the availability of time, it is its **display**. Its fundamental determination is the *constraint that it be different from working time*. It is not, therefore, autonomous: it is defined by the absence of working time. That difference, since it constitutes the deep value of leisure, is everywhere connoted and marked with redundancy, over-exhibited. In all its signs, all its attitudes, all its practices, and in all the discourses in which it is spoken of, leisure thrives on this exhibition and over-exhibition of itself as such, this continual ostentation, this **marking**, this **display**. Everything may be taken away from it, everything stripped from it but this. It is this which defines it.

10

The Mystique of Solicitude

The consumer society is not simply characterized by the abundance of goods and services but by the more important fact that in this society *everything is a service*. What is available to be consumed never presents itself as pure and simple product, but as a *personal service*, as gratification. From 'Guinness is good for you', via the receptionist's smile and the automatic cigarette machine's 'thank-you', to the politicians' deep concern for their fellow citizens, each of us is beset by a formidable obligingness, surrounded by a conspiracy of devotion and goodwill. The tiniest bar of soap is presented as the fruit of the thinking of a whole council of experts who have been poring for months over the softness of *your* skin. Airborne puts its entire management team at the service of your 'bottom':

> For this is the crux. That is our prime area of study . . . Our business is seating you. Anatomically, socially and, almost, philosophically. All our chairs are the product of detailed observation of your person . . . If a chair has a polyester seat, that is all the better to hug the delicate curve of your posterior, etc.

This chair is no longer a chair, it is a total social service for your benefit.

Nothing is purely and simply consumed today – that is to say, bought, possessed and used for particular ends. Objects no longer serve *a purpose*; first and foremost they serve *you*. Without this direct object, the personalized 'you', without this total ideology of personal service, consumption would not be what it is. It is the warmth of *gratification*, of personal allegiance which gives it its whole meaning – not *satisfaction* pure and simple. It is in the sun of this solicitude that modern consumers bask.

Social Transfers and Maternal Transference

In all modern societies, this system of gratification and solicitude has its official support structure in the form of all the institutions of social redistribution (social security, pension funds, subsidies, insurances, grants and the various benefits) by which, as F. Perroux argues,

> the public authorities have been induced to correct the excesses of the powers of the monopolies by providing social allocations aimed at satisfying needs and not at remunerating productive services. These latter transfers, for which nothing is apparently rendered in return, in the long term reduce the aggressiveness of the so-called dangerous classes.

We shall not discuss the real efficacy of this redistribution here, or the economic mechanisms by which it is effected. What concerns us is the collective psychological mechanism it brings into play. Thanks to their tax levies and their economic transfers, the social authorities (in other words, the established order) arrogate to themselves the psychological benefit of appearing generous, present themselves in a charitable light. A whole maternal, protectionist lexicon is deployed to refer to these institutions: social security, insurance, family allowance, old-age cover, unemployment benefit. This bureaucratic 'charity', these mechanisms of 'collective solidarity' – all of them 'hard-won social gains' – thus act, through the *ideological* operation of redistribution, as mechanisms of *social control*. It is as though a certain part of surplus value were sacrificed to preserve the rest[1] – the overall system of power sustaining itself with this ideology of munificence in which the 'benefit' bestowed conceals the profit taken. This kills two birds with one stone: the wage-earner is quite pleased to receive in the guise of gifts or 'free' services a part of what has previously been taken from him.

This is, in short, what J.M. Clarke refers to as the 'pseudo-market society'. In spite of their commercial spirit, Western societies protect their cohesion by social security legislation, the correction of initial inequalities and various priority allocations. The principle underlying all these measures is an extra-mercantile solidarity. The means is a judicious use of a certain dose of constraint for transfers which in themselves obey not the principles of equivalence, but the rules of a gradually rationalizing redistributive economy.

More generally, it is, in Perroux's view, true of every commodity that

> it is the nexus not only of industrial processes, but of relational, institutional, transferential and cultural ones. In an organized society, people cannot purely and simply exchange commodities. What they hand over to each other are symbols, significations, services and information. Every commodity must be regarded as the nexus of non-chargeable services which qualify it socially.

Now this point, which is correct, means, if we turn it around, that no exchange, no prestation in our society of whatever type is 'free', that the venality of exchange, even exchange of the most apparently disinterested kind, is universal. Everything is bought and sold, but market society cannot concede this either theoretically or legally. Hence the crucial ideological significance of the 'social' mode of redistribution: this induces in the collective mentality the myth of a social order entirely devoted to 'service' and the well-being of individuals.[2]

The Pathos of the Smile

However, alongside the economic and political institutions, there is a whole other – more informal, non-institutional – system of social relations which interests us more precisely here. This is that entire network of 'personalized' communication which is invading everyday consumption. For we are indeed talking of consumption here – the consumption of human relations, of solidarity, reciprocity, warmth and social participation standardized in the form of services – a continual consumption of solicitude, sincerity and warmth, but consumption in fact only of the *signs* of that solicitude, which is even more vital for the individual than biological nourishment in a system where social distance and the atrociousness of social relations are the objective rule.

The loss of (spontaneous, reciprocal, symbolic) human relations is the fundamental fact of our societies. It is on this basis that we are seeing the systematic reinjection of human relations – in the form of *signs* – into the social circuit, and are seeing the *consumption* of those relations and of that human warmth *in signified form*. The receptionist, the social worker, the public relations consultant, the advertising pin-up girl, all these apostles of the social machine have as their secular mission the gratification, *the lubrication of social relations with the institutional smile*. Everywhere we see advertising aping intimate, intimist, personal styles of communication. It attempts to speak to the housewife in the language of the housewife next door, to speak to the executive or the secretary as a boss or a colleague, to speak to each of us as our friend or our superego or as an inner voice in the confessional mode. It thus produces intimacy where there is none – either among people or between people and products – by a veritable process of simulation. And it is this, among other things (though perhaps this above all), which is consumed in advertising.

The whole of group dynamics and similar practices arise out of the same (political) objective or the same (vital) necessity: the accredited psycho-sociologist is well paid to reinject solidarity, exchange and communication into opaque intra-company relationships.

So it is with the whole tertiary sector of **services**. With the shopkeeper, the bank clerk, the salesgirl or the representative, in information services, sales promotion, all these jobs in the packaging, marketing and merchandising of human relations, not forgetting the sociologist, the interviewer, the impresario and the salesman, whose professional rule is one of 'contact', 'participation' and 'gaining the psychological involvement' of others – in all these sectors of employment and roles, the connotation of reciprocity and 'warmth' is written into the planning and exercise of the function. It is the key asset in job-finding, promotion and salary level. Having 'human qualities', 'interpersonal skills', 'warmth', etc. We are surrounded by waves of fake spontaneity, 'personalized' language, orchestrated emotions and personal relations. 'Keep smiling'. *Seid nett miteinander!*':

> The smile of Sofitel-Lyon is the smile we hope to see on your face when you step through our door. It is the smile of everyone who has already spent an enjoyable time at one of our hotels . . . It is the demonstration of our hotel philosophy – service with a smile.

Or there is operation *verres de l'amitié* [literally: friendship glasses]:

> *Verres de l'amitié*, with a dedication from the great names of stage, screen, sport and journalism, will serve as 'free gifts' to be given away with the products of firms which choose to make a donation to the French Medical Research Foundation . . . Among the personalities who have signed and decorated the *verres de l'amitié* are the racing driver Jean-Pierre Beltoise, the cyclist Louison Bobet, Yves Saint-Martin, Bourvil, Maurice Chevalier, Bernard Buffet, Jean Marais and the explorer Paul-Émile Victor.

Or TWA:

> We are handing out a million dollars in bonuses to those among our employees who have surpassed themselves serving you! This hand-out depends on you, our contented passengers. We ask you to vote for the TWA employees who have really delighted you with their service!

A tentacular superstructure which goes far beyond the simple functionality of social exchange to form a 'philosophy', a value system for our technocratic society.

'Playtime' or the Parody of Services

This huge system of solicitude is based on a total contradiction. Not only can it not mask the iron law of market society, the objective truth of social relations, which is competition – social distance increasing with urban and industrial concentration and crowding – and, most importantly, the spread of the abstraction of exchange-value into the very heart of daily life and the most personal relationships, but this system, in spite of appearances, is **itself a system of production**. It is the production of communication, of human relations in the service sector style. What it produces is sociability. Now, as a system of production, it cannot but obey the same laws as those of the mode of production of material goods. It cannot but reproduce in its very functioning the social relations it aims to transcend. Though designed to produce solicitude, it is condemned simultaneously to produce – and reproduce – distance, non-communication, opacity and atrocity.

This basic contradiction makes itself felt in all the fields of 'functionalized' human relations. Precisely because this new sociality, this 'radiant' solicitude, this warm 'ambience' no longer has anything spontaneous about it, because it is produced institutionally and industrially, it would be astonishing if the social and economic truth of it did not show through in its very *tone*. And it is indeed this distortion we find everywhere: everywhere this bureaucratic system of solicitude is skewed by, shot through with, aggressiveness, sarcasm and involuntary (black) humour, and everywhere the services rendered, the obligingness are subtly combined with frustration and parody. And everywhere, linked to this contradiction, one feels the *fragility* of this general system of gratification, and that it is always about to malfunction and collapse (which does indeed happen occasionally).

We are touching here on one of the deep contradictions of our so-called 'affluent' society: that between the notion of 'service', which has feudal origins and traditions, and the dominant democratic values. The serf or feudal servant served 'in good faith', without any mental reservations: however, the system is already visibly in crisis in Swift's *Directions to Servants* (1745), in which the servants, united on the margins of their masters' society, form a society apart, a parasitic, cynical, parodic and sarcastic society. This is the collapse, where the manners of the day were concerned, of the fealty-based society of 'service': it leads to a fierce hypocrisy, to a kind of latent, shamefaced class struggle, to reciprocal shameless exploitation between masters and servants under cover of a system of values which, formally, has not changed.

Today we have democratic values: as a result, there is an irresolvable contradiction at the level of 'services', the provision of which is irreconcilable with the formal equality of persons. The only outcome is a generalized social **game** (for it is everyone's lot today – and not just in private life but also in their social and occupational practice – to receive or provide services. Everyone is, to a greater or lesser extent, everyone else's tertiary sector). This social game of human relations in a bureaucratic society differs from the fierce hypocrisy of Swift's domestics. It is a gigantic 'simulation model' of the absent reciprocity. We no longer have dissimulation here, but functional simulation. The vital minimum of social communication is only achieved by this pressurized relational 'performance', in which everyone is engaged. It is a magnificent *trompe-l'oeil*, designed to smooth over the objective hostility and distance inherent in all present relationships.

Our world of 'services' is still largely Swift's world. The spite of the functionary, the aggressiveness of the bureaucrat are archaic forms that are still Swiftian in inspiration. For example, the servility of the ladies' hairdresser, the deliberate, unreserved importunity of the commercial traveller are still violent, forced, caricatural forms of the service relationship. Theirs is a rhetoric of servility in which an alienated form of *personal* relationship nonetheless shows through, as it did between Swift's masters and servants. The way the bank clerk, the bellboy or the postmistress express, by their acrimony or their hyper-devotion, that they are paid to do what they do is the very thing that makes them human, personal and irreducible to the system. Their coarseness, insolence, affected reserve, calculated slowness, open aggressiveness or, conversely, their excessive respect is plainly and simply that which, within them, is battling against the contradiction of having to embody, *as though it were natural*, a systematic devotion for which they are also paid. Hence the unwholesome ambience, constantly verging on veiled aggression, of this exchange of 'services' *in which the real persons resist the functional 'personalization' of the exchanges*.

But this is merely an archaic residue: the true functional relationship today has resolved all tension. The 'functional' service relationship is no longer violent, hypocritical or sado-masochistic; it is openly warm, spontaneously personalized and definitively pacified. We find it in the extraordinary, vibrant atonality of the announcers at major airports or on TV; in the atonal smile, so 'sincere' and calculated (though, ultimately, it is neither of these things for it is no longer a question of sincerity or cynicism here, but of 'functionalized' human relations, cleansed of all temperamental or psychological aspects, cleansed of all real, affective harmonics, and reconstituted on the basis of the calculated vibrations of the ideal relationship – in a word, freed from any violent moral dialectic of being and appearance, and restored to the simple functionality of the *system* of relations).

We are still, in our service consuming society, at the crossroads of these two orders. This was very well illustrated by Jacques Tati's film *Playtime*, which moved from traditional, cynical sabotage, the wicked parodying of services (the whole episode in the fancy restaurant, with the cold fish passing from one table to another, the malfunctioning systems, all the perversion of 'reception structures', and the breakdown of a world that is simply too new) to the useless instrumental functionality of reception rooms, armchairs and pot-plants, glass façades and 'impeccable' communication, all in the icy solicitude of the countless gadgets and a perfect ambience.

Advertising and the Ideology of the Gift

The social function of advertising is to be understood in the same extra-economic perspective as the ideology of the gift, of free offers and service. For advertising is not merely sales promotion or the use of suggestion for economic ends. It is perhaps not even these things *first and foremost* (its economic effectiveness is increasingly being questioned): the specific message of 'the language of advertising' is the denial of the economic rationality of commodity exchange under the auspices of a general exemption from payment.[3]

That exemption assumes minor economic dimensions in the form of reductions, discounts and free gifts, all the little 'gizmos' and 'freebies' offered when one makes a purchase. The profusion of free offers, games, competitions and bargains is the outer trappings of promotional activity, its external aspect, as it appears to the ordinary housewife. An identikit picture:

> In the morning, the housewife/consumer throws back the shutters of her house – that happy house she has won in the Floraline competition. She takes her tea from the splendid Persian-style breakfast cups she got with Triscottes (only 9 francs 90 plus five tokens). She puts on a little dress – a bargain from 3J (20 per cent off) and sets off to the Prisunic, not forgetting her Prisu Card which allows her to make cashless purchases . . . No problem finding a main course! At the supermarket she played the Buitoni magic lantern game and won 40 centimes off a tin of *poulet impérial* (5 francs 90). And, for her son,

something cultural: the Peter Van Hought painting free with Persil soap powder. Thanks to Kellogg's Corn Flakes, he has built himself an airport. In the afternoon, to relax, she puts on a record, a Brandenburg Concerto. The LP cost her 8 francs with the San Pellegrino three-pack. In the evening, a great new experience: a colour TV loaned free of charge by Philips for three days (simply on approval, no obligation to buy), etc.

'I sell less and less washing powder and more and more gifts,' sighs the marketing director of a detergent manufacturer.

These are just the little touches, the window dressing of public relations. The point is, however, that the whole of advertising is merely a gigantic extrapolation of this 'something extra'. In advertising, the little daily gratuities assume the dimensions of a total social fact. Advertising is something 'bestowed'. It is a continual free offer to and for everyone. It is the prestigious image of affluence, but above all it is the repeated gage of the virtual miracle of 'something for nothing'. Its social function is, therefore, that of a public relations sector. We know how public relations proceeds: the works visit (Saint-Gobain), executive refresher courses in Louis XIII chateaux, the photogenic smile of the MD, artworks in the factories, group dynamics: 'the task of a PR man is to maintain a harmony of mutual interests between public and managers.' In the same way, it is the function of advertising in all its forms to set in place a *social fabric* ideologically unified under the auspices of a collective super-patronage, a kindly super-feudality, which provides all these 'extras' the way aristocrats laid on feasts for their people. Through advertising, which is already a social service in itself, all products are presented as services, all real economic processes are staged and reinterpreted socially as effects of giving, of personal allegiance and affective relations. No matter that this munificence, like that of potentates, is only ever a functional redistribution of a part of the profits. The trick of advertising is precisely to *substitute everywhere the magic of the cargo cult* (the total, miraculous abundance the natives dream of) *for the logic of the market.*

All the artful moves of advertising tend in this direction. See how discreet it is everywhere, how benevolent, self-effacing and disinterested. An hour's radio programme against a one-minute 'ad' for its product. Four pages of poetic prose and the company trademark placed shame-facedly(?!) at the foot of a page. And all its games with itself, piling on the self-effacement and the 'anti-advertising' parodies. The blank page for the millionth Volkswagen: 'We can't show it to you. We've just sold it.' All these things, which could be included in a history of the rhetoric of advertising, are logically deducible from advertising's need to dis-tance itself completely from the level of economic constraints and to fuel the fiction of a game, a party, a charitable institution, a disinterested social service. The conspicuous display of disinterestedness plays its part as a social function of wealth (Veblen) and an integrating factor. And even a play of aggressiveness towards the consumer – antiphrasis – is admissible. All is possible and everything works, though not so much to sell as to restore consensus, complicity, *collusion* – in short, here again, to produce relationship, cohesion, communication. The fact that the consensus produced by advertising can *then* result in attachment to objects, acts of purchase and implicit conformity to the economic imperatives of consumption is certain, but it is not the essential point. And, at any event, that economic function of advertising is *consequent* upon its overall social function. This is indeed why it is never safely assured.[4]

The Shop-Window

The shop-window – all shop-windows – which are, with advertising, the foci of our urban consumer practices, are also the site *par excellence* of that 'consensus operation', that communication and exchange of values through which an entire society is homogenized by incessant daily acculturation to the silent and spectacular logic of fashion. That specific space which is the shop-window – neither inside nor outside, neither private nor wholly public, and which is already the street while maintaining, behind the transparency of its glass, the distance, the opaque status of the commodity – is also the site of a specific social relation. Tracking along the shop-windows, with their *calculated riot of colour*, which is always at the same time a frustration, this hesitation-waltz of shopping is the Kanak dance in which goods are exalted before being exchanged. Objects and products are offered there in a glorious *mise-en-scène*, a sacralizing ostentation (this is not a pure and simple displaying, any more than is the case in advertising, but, as G. Lagneau says, a 'setting-off', a 'showcasing'). This symbolic giving, aped by the objects themselves on their stage-set, this symbolic, silent exchange between the proffered object and the gaze, is clearly an invitation to real, economic exchange inside the shop. But not necessarily, and at any event the communication which is established at the level of the shop-window is not so much between individuals and objects as a generalized communication between all individuals, not via the contemplation of the same objects but via the reading and recognition in the same objects of the same system of signs and the same hierarchical code of values. It is this acculturation, this training, which takes place at every moment everywhere in the streets, on the walls and in the underground stations, on advertising hoardings and neon signs. Shop-windows thus beat out the rhythm of the social process of value: they are a continual adaptability test for everyone, a test of managed projection and integration. The big stores are a kind of pinnacle of this urban process, a positive laboratory and social testing ground, where, as Durkheim writes in *The Elementary Forms of Religious Life*, the collectivity reinforces its cohesion, as in feasts and spectacles.

Therapeutic Society

The ideology of a society which is continually taking care of you culminates in the ideology of a society which is actually treating you medically, as a potential patient. The social body surely must be thought rather ill then, and its citizen consumers rather fragile – always on the verge of collapse, of becoming unhinged – for this 'therapeutic' discourse to be so widespread among professionals, in the public prints and among analytical moralists.

Bleustein-Blanchet: 'In my view, Gallup polls are an indispensable gauge of opinion, which the advertiser must use, like a *doctor* calling for tests and X-rays.'

An ad man: 'What the client is looking for is security. He needs to be reassured, taken care of. At times you are a father to him, at times a mother or a son.' 'Our profession is akin to the art of medicine.' 'We're like medics, we give advice. We don't force anything on anyone.' 'My job is a vocation, like a doctor's.'

Architects, advertising executives, town planners, designers all see themselves as demiurges or, rather, as *thaumaturges* of social relations and the environment. 'People live in ugliness': this we have to cure. Psycho-sociologists, too, see themselves as *therapists* of human and social communication. This is even true of industrialists, who present themselves as missionaries of well-being and general prosperity. 'Society is sick': this is the refrain of all the well-meaning souls in power. The consumer society is a canker; 'we have to give it back some soul,' says M. Chaban-Delmas. It must be said that this great myth of the Sick Society, a myth which evacuates all analysis of the real contradictions, is one those contemporary medicine-men the intellectuals very largely connive in. They, however, tend to locate society's ills at a fundamental level. Hence their prophetic pessimism. Professionals, in general, tend rather to maintain the myth of the Sick Society, as a society that is sick not so much organically (in which case it would be incurable) but functionally, at the level of its interchanges and metabolism. Hence their dynamic optimism: it only has to be cured to re-establish the *functionality* of interchanges, to speed up the metabolism (that is to say, once again, to inject communication, relationship, contact, human balance, warmth, efficiency and the controlled smile). These are all tasks they undertake cheerfully and profitably.

The Ambiguity and Terrorism of Solicitude

What has to be stressed about this whole liturgy of solicitude is its profound ambiguity. An ambiguity which coincides very exactly with the double meaning of the verb 'to solicit':

1   The dimension of 'solicitude', in the 'caring', 'favouring', 'mothering' sense. The **gift**.
2   The opposite meaning it assumes in the sense of **'requesting'** (soliciting a reply), 'demanding', or even 'commandeering'. This is a sense which is even more clearly seen in the modern usage of the term ('soliciting information', etc.). What is involved here is a diverting, a seizing of something; turning it to one's own ends. This is precisely the opposite of what is meant by solicitude.

Now, the function of all the apparatuses of solicitude, institutional or otherwise (public relations, advertising, etc.), which surround us – and are, indeed, proliferating – is both to care for and to satisfy, on the one hand, and surreptitiously to gain by enticement and abduction on the other. The average consumer is always *subjected* to this two-pronged undertaking. He is solicited in every sense of the word – the ideology of the **gift** which is conveyed by 'solicitude' serving always as an alibi for the real conditioning which is that of his 'solicitation' or entreaty.[5]

This rhetoric of thaumaturgy and solicitude which stamps the consumer society, the affluent society, with a particular emotional tone has precise social functions:

1   The emotional re-education of individuals isolated within bureaucratic society by the technical and social division of labour and by the parallel technical and social division – *itself equally total and bureaucratic –* of consumption practices.
2   A political strategy of formal integration which covers – and covers up for – the failings of the political institutions: just as universal suffrage, referendums and parliamentary institutions are designed to establish a social consensus through *formal* participation, so advertising, fashion, human and public relations can be interpreted as a kind of *perpetual referendum* – in which citizen consumers are entreated [*sollicités*] at every moment to pronounce in favour of a certain code of values and implicitly to sanction it. This *informal* system of mobilization of assent is safer: it leaves practically no way of saying 'no' (admittedly, the political referendum is also a democratic staging of the affirmative response). In every country today we see 'participationist' modes of integration taking over from the *violent* processes of social control (repressive, state, political constraints). This they do, first, in the parliamentary, electoral form, and, subsequently, through the informal processes of *solicitation* we are discussing. It would be interesting to analyse in this light the 'public relations' operation mounted by Publicis/Saint-Gobain in the great sociological event that was Boussois's hostile takeover bid for Saint-Gobain: public opinion was mobilized, and called upon as a witness and a 'psychological stakeholder' in the operation. In the objective restructuring of the capitalist enterprise, the public found itself, under the guise of 'democratic' information, integrated as jury, and, through the symbolic

group of the shareholders in Saint-Gobain, manipulated as an actor in the drama. One can see how advertising activity, understood in the broadest sense, can shape and totalize social processes, how it can substitute itself daily – and no doubt even more effectively – for the electoral system in psychological mobilization and control. A whole new political strategy is coming into being at this level, contemporaneous with the objective development of the 'technostructure' and monopoly productivism.

3 'Political' control by solicitation and solicitude is accompanied by a more intimate control over motivations themselves. This is where the term 'solicit' assumes its double meaning, and it is in this sense that all solicitude is basically *terroristic*. Let us examine the admirable example of advertising which runs: 'When a girl tells you she adores Freud, what she means is that she loves comic strips: 'a girl is a "little wild thing", full of contradictions. Now, beyond these contradictions, it is up to us, advertisers, to understand that girl. More generally, to understand the people whom we wish to address.' People, then, are incapable of understanding themselves, of knowing what they are and what they want, but *we* are there to do that. We know better than you do about yourselves. A repressive position of paternalistic analysis. And the ultimate ends of this 'higher understanding' are clear: 'Understanding people in order to be understood by them. Knowing how to speak to them in order to be heard by them. Knowing how to please them in order to interest them. In short, knowing how to sell them a product – your product. This is what we call "communication".' A marketing trick? Not just that. This girl *has no right to like Freud*. She is wrong and, for her own good, we are going to foist upon her what it is that she secretly likes. The whole of the social inquisition is here, the whole of psychological repression. Advertising in general does not admit these things so clearly. Yet, at every moment, it operates the same mechanisms of charitable and repressive control.

It is the same with the advert for TWA: 'the airline which understands you'. And just look how it understands you:

> We cannot bear to think of you all alone in your hotel room, frantically twiddling the controls of your TV . . . We'll do everything we can to enable you to take your better half with you on your next business trip, with our special family tariff etc. With your better half alongside you, at least you'll have someone to change channels . . . That's what love is.

There is no question of being alone then. You don't have the right to be alone: 'We cannot bear the idea.' If you don't know what it is to be happy, we'll teach you. We know better than you. And even how to make love: your better half is your erotic 'second channel'. You didn't realize that? We'll teach you that too. We are there to understand you. That is our role.

Sociometric Compatibility

Sociability or the ability to 'relate to people', to sustain relationships, to stimulate exchanges, to intensify the social metabolism, becomes in this society a mark of 'personality'. Consuming, spending and following fashion and, through these things, communicating with others is behaviour which forms a keystone of the contemporary sociometric 'personality' outlined by David Riesman in *The Lonely Crowd*. The whole system of gratification and solicitude is, in fact, merely the affective modulation (itself functionalized) of a system of relations in which the status of the individual is changing totally. To enter the cycle of consumption and fashion is not simply to surround oneself with objects and services as one pleases; it is to change one's being and directedness. It is to move from an individual principle based on autonomy, character, the inherent value of the self to a principle of perpetual recycling by indexation to a code in which the value of the individual becomes rational, diffracted, changeable: it is the code of 'personalization', which no individual himself possesses, but which traverses each individual in his signified relation to the others. The person as a determining instance disappears and is replaced by personalization. From this point on, the individual is no longer a centre of autonomous values, but merely the expression of multiple relations in a process of shifting interrelationships. 'The other-directed person is, in a sense, at home everywhere and nowhere, capable of a rapid if sometimes superficial intimacy with and response to everyone.'[6] He is, in fact, caught in the toils of a kind of sociometric graph and is perpetually redefined by his position in these bizarre spiders' webs (these threads which connect A, B, C, D, E, in a web of positive, negative, unilateral and bilateral relations). He is, in short, a sociometric being, whose definition is that he is *at the point of intersection with others.*

This is not simply an 'ideal' model. This *immanence of others, and this immanence in others,* governs all status behaviour (and hence the whole field of consumption) according to a process of unlimited interrelationship, where there is not, strictly speaking, any individualized Subject with its 'freedom', or 'Others' in the Sartrean sense of the term, but a generalized 'ambience', in which the relative terms only assume meaning by their differential mobility. The same tendency can be read at the level of the objects/elements and their combinatorial manipulation in modern interiors. In this new type of integration, then, it is a matter not of 'conformism' or 'non-conformism' (although these terms are still constantly found in journalistic language, they relate to traditional bourgeois society), but of optimum sociality, *of maximum compatibility with others* and with the various situations and professions (retraining, versatility), of mobility at all levels. To be universally 'mobile', dependable and versatile: that is what 'culture' is in the era of human engineering. So, molecules form on the basis of the multiple valencies of particular atoms;

they can be unformed and reorganized differently or turned into large, complex molecules. This adaptive capacity coincides with a social mobility which is different from the rise of the 'traditional' parvenu or self-made man. There is no severing of ties in the course of making one's individual career, no breaking out of one's class to make one's way, no meteoric rise. It is, rather, a question of *being mobile with everyone else*, and rising up the coded rungs of a strictly demarcated hierarchical ladder.

There is, indeed, no question of not being mobile: mobility is a warrant of morality. We also have here, then, in every case, an enforced *mobilization*. And the unceasing compatibility is also an *accounting* [*comptabilité*]: in other words, the individual, who is defined as the sum of his relations, of his 'valencies', is also always accountable as such: he becomes a unit of calculation and enters voluntarily into a sociometric (or political) plan/calculation.

Proving Oneself and Approval (*Werbung und Bewährung*)

In this network of anxious relations, in which there is no longer any absolute value, but only functional compatibility, it is no longer a question of 'asserting oneself', of 'proving oneself' (*Bewährung*), but of relating to and gaining the approval of others, soliciting their judgement and their positive affinity. This mystique of gaining approval is everywhere gradually supplanting the mystique of proving oneself. The traditional individual's objective of transcendent accomplishment is giving way to processes of reciprocal solicitation (in the sense in which we defined it above: *Werbung*). Everyone 'solicits' and manipulates, everyone is solicited and manipulated.

This is the foundation of the new *morality*, in which individualistic or ideological values give way to a kind of *generalized relativity*, of receptivity and agreement, of anxious communication – others must 'speak to' you (and *speak you*: they must address you, but must also express you and say what you are), love you, rally round you. We have seen the orchestration of this in advertising, which does not so much seek to inform you (or even, in the end, to mystify you) as to 'speak to' you. 'It is not important,' writes Riesman, 'whether Johnny plays with a truck or in the sandbox, but it matters very much whether he involves himself with Bill – via any object at all.'[7] We are reaching a point where the group is less interested in what it produces than in the human relations within it. Its essential work may be, more or less, to *produce relationship*, and to consume this as it goes along. This process may even suffice to define a group quite apart from any external objective. The concept of 'ambience' sums all this up quite well: 'ambience' is the diffuse sum of relations, produced and consumed by the group – the presence of the group to itself. If it does not exist, it can be programmed and produced industrially. This is, indeed, the most common case.

In its broadest sense, which goes well beyond common usage, this concept of ambience is characteristic of the consumer society which may be defined as follows:

1   Values related to 'objectives' and transcendence (final, ideological values) give way to ambience-related (relational, immanent, objective-less) values, which exhaust themselves in the moment of relating ('consumed' values).

2   The consumer society is simultaneously a society of the production of goods and of the *accelerated production of relations*. Indeed, this latter is the defining aspect. This production of relations, which is still craft-based at the intersubjective level or the level of primary groups, is, however, tending gradually to become aligned to the mode of production of material goods or, in other words, to the generalized industrial mode. It then becomes, by this same logic, the province (if not, indeed, the monopoly) of specialized (private or national) enterprises, and indeed constitutes their social and commercial *raison d'être*. The consequences of this development are as yet difficult to foretell. It is difficult to accept that (human, social, political) relationships are produced in the same way as objects, and that, once they come to be produced in that same way, they become, similarly, objects of consumption. Yet this is, in fact, the case. But we are merely at the beginning of a long process here.[8]

Cult of Sincerity – Functional Tolerance

For it to be produced and consumed, relating must – like material goods, like labour power, and according to the same logic – be 'liberated', 'emancipated'. In other words, it must free itself from all the traditional social conventions and rituals. This marks the end of courtesy and etiquette, which are incompatible with generalized functional relations. But the disappearance of etiquette does not mean that we come to relate spontaneously to one another. Our relating simply falls under the sway of industrial production and fashion. But because it is the opposite of spontaneity, it will imperiously take over all the marks of that spontaneity. Riesman has noted this in his description of the 'cult of sincerity'.[9] This is a mystique parallel to those of 'warmth' and 'solicitude' we have discussed above, as of all the *obligatory* signs and rites of *absent* communication: '[This] yearning for sincerity is a grim reminder of how little they can trust themselves or others in daily life.'[10]

It is, in fact, the ghost of lost sincerity which haunts all this contact-based friendliness, these perpetual 'live link-ups', this aping and forcing of dialogue at all costs. The authentic relationship is lost, long live sincerity! Behind this obsession with 'honest pricing', with sporting, sentimental and political fair play, with the 'simple ways of the "great and the good"', the straight-talking confessions of cinema or other idols, or telephoto-lens shots of the daily life of royal families – and in this frantic demand for sincerity (like that for seeing the materials in modern building) – there is perhaps also (from a more 'sociological' point of view) the acculturated classes' immense mistrust of – and immense reaction against – traditional culture and rites, of whatever kind, which have always served to mark social distance. A massive obsession, which runs through the whole of mass culture – a class expression of the *déclassés* of culture: the fear of being had, of being duped and manipulated by signs as they have been historically over centuries – or, alternatively, the fear or rejection of high, ceremonial culture, a fear repressed beneath the myth of a culture of the 'natural' and of instant communication.

At all events, in this industrial culture of sincerity, it is still the *signs* of sincerity which are consumed. And that sincerity is no longer opposed to cynicism or hypocrisy as it was within the register of being and appearance. In the field of functional relations, cynicism and sincerity *alternate* without contradicting each other, in the same manipulation of signs. Naturally, the moral schema (sincerity = good; artificiality = evil) still operates, but it no longer connotes real qualities. It now connotes only the difference between the *signs* of sincerity and the *signs* of artificiality.

The problem of 'tolerance' (liberalism, laxism, the 'permissive society', etc.) takes the same form. The fact that those who were once mortal enemies are now on speaking terms, that the most fiercely opposed ideologies 'enter into dialogue', that a kind of peaceful coexistence has set in at all levels, that morality is less strict than it was, in no sense signifies some 'humanist' progress in human relations, a greater understanding of problems or any such airy nonsense. It indicates simply that, since ideologies, opinions, virtues and vices are ultimately merely material for exchange and communication, all contradictory elements are equivalent in the play of signs. Tolerance in this context is no longer either a psychological trait or a virtue: *it is a modality of the system itself*. It is like the total compatibility and elasticity of the elements of fashion: long skirts and mini-skirts 'tolerate' each other very well (indeed they signify nothing other than the relationship which holds between them).

Tolerance connotes morally the generalized relativity of functions/signs, objects/signs, beings/signs, relations/signs, ideas/signs. In fact, we are beyond the opposition between fanaticism and tolerance, as we are beyond that between sincerity and fakery. 'Moral' tolerance is no greater than it was before. We have simply changed systems; we have moved on to functional compatibility.

11

Anomie in the Affluent Society

Violence

The consumer society is at one and the same time a society of solicitude and a society of repression, a pacified society and a society of violence. We have seen that 'pacified' daily life thrives on a daily diet of consumed violence, 'allusive' violence: news reports of accidents, murders, revolutions, the atomic or bacteriological threat – the whole apocalyptic stock-in-trade of the mass media. We have seen that the affinity between violence and the obsession with security and well-being is not accidental: 'spectacular' violence and the pacification of daily life are homogeneous, because they are each equally abstract and each is a thing of myths and signs. We might also add that violence is nowadays inoculated into daily life in homoeopathic doses – a vaccine against fatality – to ward off the spectre of the *real* fragility of that pacified life. For it is no longer the spectre of scarcity which haunts the civilization of affluence, but the spectre of **fragility**. And that spectre, which is much more menacing because it concerns the very equilibrium of individual and collective structures, and which has to be warded off at all costs, is in fact kept at bay by this roundabout solution of consumed, packaged, homogenized violence. This violence is not dangerous violence: blood on the front page no more compromises the social and moral order than does sex (despite the emotional blackmail on the part of the censors who wish to persuade themselves of this, and to persuade us of it). It simply attests to the fact that the balance is a precarious one, that the social and moral order is made up of contradictions.

The real problem of violence arises elsewhere. It is the problem of the *real*, uncontrollable violence secreted by plenty and security once a certain threshold has been reached. This is no longer integrated violence, consumed with the rest, but the uncontrollable violence which well-being secretes in its very achievement. That violence is characterized (precisely like consumption as we have defined it, though not as superficially understood) by the fact that it is *aimless and objectless*.[1] It is because we base our lives on the traditional idea of the pursuit of well-being as a *rational* activity that the eruptive, unaccountable violence of the Stockholm youth gangs, of the Montreal riots, of the Los Angeles murderers, seems an incredible, incomprehensible manifestation and one which stands in apparent contradiction to social progress and affluence. It is because we base our lives on the *moral* illusion of the conscious finality of all things, of the basic rationality of individual and collective choices (the whole system of values rests on this: there is in the consumer an absolute instinct which inclines him by essence towards his preferential ends – the *moral* myth of consumption which is the direct heir to the idealist myth of man as naturally inclined towards the Beautiful and the Good), that this violence seems unspeakable to us, absurd, diabolical. Now, perhaps it quite simply means that something far exceeds the conscious objectives of satisfaction and well-being by which this society justifies itself (in its own eyes) or, rather, by which it reinstates itself within the norms of conscious rationality. In this sense, this unexplained violence must cause us to reassess all our thinking on affluence: affluence and violence go together; they have to be analysed together.

The more general problem of which this 'objectless' violence is a part, a violence which is as yet sporadic in certain countries, but virtually endemic in all developed or overdeveloped countries, is that of the *fundamental contradictions of affluence* (and not just its sociological disparities). It is the problem of the multiple forms of **anomie** (to use Durkheim's term) or of **anomaly**, depending on whether we look at them in terms of the rationality of institutions or the lived evidence of normality – forms which run from *destructiveness* (violence, delinquency), through collective escapist behaviour (drugs, hippies, non-violence), to contagious *depressiveness* (fatigue, suicide, neuroses). Each of these characteristic aspects of the 'affluent' or 'permissive' society raises in its way the problem of a fundamental imbalance.

It is not easy to adapt to affluence, say Galbraith and the 'strategists of desire': 'our economic attitudes are rooted in the poverty, inequality, and economic peril of the past' (or in centuries of puritan morality in which humanity lost the habit of happiness).[2] This difficulty of living in affluence should itself show us, if such a demonstration were needed, that the alleged 'naturalness' of the desire for well-being is not so natural as all that. Otherwise, individuals would not have so much trouble getting used to it; they would embrace plenty with open arms. This should indicate to us that there is in consumption something quite different, and perhaps even something opposite: something for which people have to be educated, trained, even tamed. It should tell us that there is here, in fact, a new system of moral and psychological constraints which has nothing to do with the realm of freedom. The vocabulary of the neo-philosophers of desire is significant in this connection. According to them, it is a question simply of *teaching* people to be happy, of teaching them to *devote* themselves to happiness, of *creating* within them the *reflexes* of happiness. Affluence is not, then, a paradise. It is not a leap beyond morality into the ideal immorality of plenty. It is a new objective situation governed by a new morality. Objectively speaking, it is not therefore an advance, but quite simply *something different*.

There is, then, this ambiguity about affluence: it is always simultaneously experienced as euphoric myth (of resolution of tensions and conflicts, of happiness beyond history and morality) and *endured* as a process of more or less enforced adaptation to new types of behaviour, collective constraints and norms. The 'Revolution of Affluence' does not usher in the ideal society; it simply leads into a different type of society.

Our moralists would like to reduce this social problem to one of 'mentalities'. So far as they are concerned, the key shift has already occurred: real affluence is here and we simply have to move from a mentality of scarcity to a mentality geared to affluence. And they deplore how difficult this is and are horrified to see forms of *resistance to plenty* emerging. However, one has only to accept for a moment that affluence itself is merely (or is *also*) a system of constraints of a new type to understand immediately that the new (more or less unconscious) social constraint must be accompanied by a new type of demand for freedom. In the event, this takes the form of a rejection of the 'consumer society' in violent and Erostratic[3] form (the blind destruction of material and cultural goods) or non-violent, abdicationist form (refusal to engage in it through either production or consumption). If affluence were freedom, then this violence would indeed be unthinkable. If affluence (growth) is constraint, then that violence is easy to understand; it follows *logically*. If it is wild, objectless, formless, this is because the constraints it is contesting are themselves also unformulated, unconscious, illegible: they are the very constraints of 'freedom', of controlled accession to happiness, of the totalitarian ethic of affluence.

This sociological interpretation leaves space for (I even believe it connects at a deep level with) a psychoanalytic interpretation of these apparently aberrant phenomena of the 'rich' societies. The moralists we have referred to, who also regard themselves as psychologists, all speak of *guilt*. By this they always mean a residual guilt, a hangover from puritan times, which, in terms of their logic, must now be on the decline. 'We are not yet ready for happiness.' 'The prejudices which do us so much harm.' Now it is clear that this guilt (let us accept the term) is, on the contrary, increasing as our affluence progresses. A gigantic process of primitive accumulation of anxiety, guilt and rejection runs parallel to the process of expansion and satisfaction and it is this source of discontent which fuels the violent, impulsive subversion of – and murderous 'acting-out' against – the very order of happiness. It is not therefore the past and tradition or any other of the stigmata of original sin which cause human beings, rendered fragile by happiness, to become uneasy in a state of affluence and, on occasion, to rise up against it. Even though that old burden is still there, it is no longer the key factor. Guilt, 'malaise' and profound incompatibilities are at the heart of the *current* system itself, and are produced by it in the course of its *logical* development.

Forced to adapt to the **principle of need**, to the **principle of utility** (the principle of economic reality) or, in other words, to the ever full and *positive* correlation between a product of some kind (object, good or service) and a satisfaction through the one being indexed to the other; forced into this concerted, unilateral and ever positive finality, *the whole of the negativity of desire*, the other side of **ambivalence**, and hence all the things which do not fit into this positive vision, *are rejected, censored by satisfaction itself* (which is not enjoyment [*jouissance*]: enjoyment, for its part, is ambivalent), and, no longer finding any possible outlet, crystallize into a gigantic fund of anxiety.[4]

This explains the basic problem of violence in the affluent society (and, indirectly, all the symptoms of anomaly, depression or abdication). That violence, which is radically different from the violence engendered by poverty, scarcity and exploitation, is the emergence, in action, of the negativity of desire which is omitted, occulted, censored by the total positivity of need. It is the opposite mode of the ambivalence which resurfaces at the very heart of the smug equivalence of man and his environment in satisfaction. It is – against the imperative of productivity/consummativity – the emergence of *destructiveness* (the death drive) for which there can be no bureaucratic reception structures, since these would then become a part of a process of planned satisfaction and, hence, a system of positive institutions.[5] We shall see, however, that, just as there are models of consumption, so society suggests or sets up 'models of violence' through which it seeks to tap, control and mass-mediafy these irruptive forces.

Indeed, in order to prevent this fund of anxiety, accumulated as a result of the *breakdown of the ambivalent logic of desire* and hence of the *loss of the symbolic function*, from resulting in that uncontrollable, anomic violence, society acts at two levels:

1   On the one hand, it attempts to diminish this anxiety by the proliferation of caring agencies: innumerable collective services, roles and functions are created; soothing, guilt-dispelling balm and smiles are injected into the system – psychological lubricants, not unlike the cleansing agents in washing powder. Enzymes gobbling up anxiety. And tranquillizers, relaxants, hallucinogens and therapies of all kinds are also on sale. An endless task, in which *the affluent society, the provider of satisfaction without end, exhausts its resources producing the antidote to the anxiety generated by that satisfaction*. An increasingly large budget goes into consoling the beneficiaries of the miracle of affluence for their anxious satisfaction. We may liken this to the economic deficit (which is not in fact calculable) created by the disbenefits of growth (pollution, built-in obsolescence, crowding, scarcity of natural resources), but it undoubtedly exceeds that by a very long way.

2   Society may try – and does try systematically – to claw back that anxiety as a means of stimulating consumption, or to claw back the guilt and the violence in their turn as consumable goods or distinctive cultural signs. There is, then, an intellectual luxury of guilt characteristic of certain groups, a 'guilt exchange-value'. Or, alternatively, the cultural malaise[6] is offered for consumption like everything else; it is resocialized

as a cultural commodity and an object of collective delectation, which merely leads more deeply into anxiety, since this cultural metaconsumption is tantamount to a new censorship and starts the process off again. At any event, violence and guilt are mediated here by cultural *models* and turn back into the consumed violence we discussed at the beginning of this chapter.

These two control mechanisms have powerful effects, but they are not, however, capable of forestalling the critical process of the turning – the subversive conversion – of affluence into violence. And it is useless to hold forth and gripe on, as *all* the critics do, about this 'inevitability' of violence, the 'unstoppable spiral', the possible social and moral solutions or, on the other hand, about paternalistic permissiveness ('young people have to have an outlet for their energies'). Some will look back longingly to the days 'when violence had a meaning', the good old violence of war, patriotism, passion and, ultimately, rationality – violence sanctioned by an objective or a cause, ideological violence or the individual violence of the rebel, which was still of the order of individual aestheticism and could be regarded as one of the fine arts. People will go on trying to fit this new violence into old models and apply known treatments to it. But we have to see that this violence, which is no longer strictly historical, no longer sacred, ritualistic or ideological – nor yet again, for all that, pure act or expression of individual singularity – is structurally linked to affluence. This is why it is irreversible, always imminent and so fascinating to everyone, whatever their explicit attitudes to it: this is because it is rooted in the very process of growth and increased satisfaction in which everyone is now involved. From time to time, within our closed universe of consumed quietude and violence, this new violence very briefly takes over *for everyone* a part of the lost symbolic function, before resolving back into a consumer object.

Serge Lentz (on *The Chase*): 'The last scenes of the film are so savage that, for the first time in my life, my hands were shaking as I left the cinema. In the New York theatres where the film is currently showing, these same scenes spark incredible reactions. When Marlon Brando throws himself on a man, wild, hysterical members of the audience jump up screaming "Kill him! kill him!"'

July 1966: Richard Speck breaks into a nurses' home in Chicago's south side. He binds and gags eight young women all aged about 20. Then he executes them one by one by stabbing or strangulation.

August 1966: C.J. Whitman, an architecture student at the University of Austin, Texas, sets himself up with a dozen guns on a 300-foot block overlooking the university campus and starts shooting: 13 dead, 31 injured.

Amsterdam, June 1966: For the first time since the war, there was fighting of extraordinary violence for several days in the very heart of the city. The Telegraaf building was stormed. Lorries were burned, windows smashed, hoardings torn down. Thousands of demonstrators running rampant. Millions of florins' worth of damage. One dead, some 10 injured. The revolt of the 'Provos'.

Montreal, October 1969: Grave disorder broke out on Tuesday following a strike of policemen and fire fighters. Two hundred taxi drivers ransacked the premises of a transport company. Shots were fired and two people were killed. After that attack, 1,000 young people descended on the city centre, smashing shop-windows and looting. There were 10 bank raids, 19 armed attacks, three terrorist explosions and a host of burglaries. Given the scale of these events, the government put the army on standby and passed an emergency law conscripting police officers.

The murder at the Polanski villa: five persons of varying degrees of celebrity killed at a villa in the Los Angeles hills, including the wife of Polanski, a director of sado-fantastic films. A murder of idols exemplary because, by a kind of fanatical irony, it lent material form, in the very details of the murder and its staging, to some of the characteristics of the films which had won fame and success for the victims. And interesting because it illustrated the paradox of that violence: both savage (irrational, with no obvious objective) and ritualistic (indexed to spectacular models imposed by the mass media – in this case, Polanski's very own films). Like the Austin murder, this was not a crime of passion, not committed by the criminal underworld or done for gain; it lay outside the traditional criteria of the legal system or of individual responsibility. Mindless, unreflected murders and yet *'reflected' in advance* (here, astonishingly, to the point of precise imitation) *by mass-media models*, and being reflected along this same route in similar murders or forms of 'acting-out' (cf. also suicides by fire). This alone defines them: their spectacular connotation as news items, such that they are conceived from the outset as film scenarios or as reportage, and their desperate attempt in pushing back the limits of violence to be 'irrecuperable', to transgress and smash that mass-media order, to which they are in fact party even in their asocial vehemence.

Subculture of Non-Violence

Indissociable from these new-style phenomena of violence, though formally opposed to them, are the modern manifestations of non-violence. From LSD to flower-power, psychedelia to hippies, zen to pop music, all have in common the rejection of socialization through status and the principle of productivity, the rejection of this whole contemporary liturgy of affluence, social success and gadgetry. Whether this rejection paints itself as violent or non-violent, it is always the rejection of the activism of the society of growth, of enforced well-being as the new repressive order. In this sense, violence and non-violence, like all anomic phenomena, have a litmus function. This society which gives itself out to be, and sees itself as, hyperactive and pacified is revealed by the beats and the rockers on the one hand, and the hippies on the other, to be characterized at a deep level by *passivity* and *violence*. The one group lays hold of the latent violence of this society and turns that violence against it, taking it to extremes. The other group extends the secret, orchestrated passivity of this society (behind its façade of hyperactivity) into a practice of abdication and total asociality, thus causing that society to deny itself, in accordance with its own logic.

Let us leave aside here all the Christic, Buddhist, lamaistic themes of Love, Awakening and Heaven on earth, the Hindu litanies and total tolerance. The question would seem rather to be the following: do the hippies and their community represent a real alternative to the processes of growth and consumption? Are they not merely the inverted and complementary image of those processes? Are they an 'anti-society', ultimately capable of overturning the whole social order, or are they merely a decadent outgrowth of that order – or even simply one of the many versions of the visionary sects which have always cast themselves out of the world in order imperatively to bring about the earthly paradise? Here again, we must not mistake the mere metamorphosis of an order for its subversion.

> We want to have time for living and loving. The flowers, the beards, the long hair and the drugs are secondary. . . Being 'hip' first and foremost means being a friend to humanity. Someone who tries to take a fresh, non-hierarchical look at the world: a non-violent person, who respects and loves life. Someone who has true values and a true sense of proportion, who puts freedom before authority and creation before production, who values cooperation and non-competition . . . Just someone kind and open who avoids doing others harm. That's the main thing.

Or again:

> As a general rule, doing what you think is right whenever and wherever it may be, without worrying about approval or disapproval, on the sole express condition that it causes no harm or offence to anyone.

The hippies immediately made headlines in the West. With its fondness for primitive societies, the consumer society immediately seized on them as part of its folklore, like a strange, inoffensive flora. Are they not ultimately, from a sociological point of view, merely a luxury product of rich societies? Are not they, with their orientalist spirituality, their gaudy psychedelia, also marginals who merely exacerbate certain traits of their society?

They are, or remain, conditioned by the basic mechanisms of that society. Their asociality is communal, tribal. We may speak, in their regard, of McLuhan's 'tribalism', that resurrection on a planetary scale, under the aegis of the mass media, of the oral, tactile, musical mode of communication which was that of archaic cultures before the visual, typographical era of the Book. They advocate the abolition of competition, of the defensive system and functions of the ego. But this is merely to translate into more or less mystical terms what has already been described by Riesman as 'other-directedness', an objective evolution of personal character structure (organized around the ego and the superego) towards a group 'ambience' in which everything comes from, and is directed towards, others. The hippies' mode of guileless emotional transparency is reminiscent of the imperative of sincerity, openness and 'warmth' of the 'peer group'. As for the regression and infantilism which constitute the seraphic, triumphant charm of the hippie communities, these needless to say merely reflect, in glorificatory mode, the irresponsibility and infantilism to which modern society confines each of its individuals. In short, the 'Human', almost hounded out of existence by productivist society and the obsession with social standing, celebrates its *sentimental resurrection* in the hippie community, where, beneath the apparent total anomie, all the dominant structural features of the mainstream society persist.

Writing of American youth, Riesman, referring to the cultural models defined by Margaret Mead, speaks of a 'Kwakiutl' style and a 'Pueblo' style. The Kwakiutl are violent, agonistic, competitive and rich, and engage in unrestrained consumption in the potlatch. The Pueblos are gentle, kind and inoffensive; they live frugally and are content to do so. Our current society can thus be defined by the formal opposition between a dominant culture which is one of unrestrained, ritualistic, conformist consumption, a culture which is violent and competitive (the potlatch of the Kwakiutl) and a permissive, euphoric, 'drop-out' sub-culture of the hippie/Pueblo type. But everything indicates that, just as violence is immediately reabsorbed into 'models of violence', the contradiction here resolves itself into functional coexistence. The extreme of acceptance and the extreme of rejection here meet up, as on a Moebius strip by means of a simple twist. And the two models ultimately develop in concentric zones around the same axis of the social order. John Stuart Mill put it brutally: 'In this age, the mere example of non-conformity, the mere refusal to bend the knee to custom, is itself a *service*.'[7]

Fatigue

Just as there is a world hunger problem, so there is now also a worldwide problem of fatigue. Paradoxically, the two are mutually exclusive: endemic, irrepressible fatigue – like the irrepressible violence we have discussed above – is the prerogative of rich societies and is a product of, among other things, the overcoming of hunger and endemic scarcity which remains the major problem for pre-industrial societies. Fatigue, as a collective syndrome of the post-industrial societies, thus represents one of the profound anomalies, one of the 'dysfunctions' of prosperity. As a new *mal du siècle*, it should be analysed in conjunction with the other phenomena of anomie, whose recrudescence marks our age, at a time when such problems ought in fact to be disappearing.

Just as the new violence is 'objectless', so this fatigue is 'groundless'. It has nothing to do with muscular fatigue or lack of energy. It does not arise from physical exertion. There is, of course, much spontaneous talk of 'nervous strain', of 'depression' and psychosomatic illness. This kind of explanation is now part of mass culture: it is in all the newspapers (and all the conferences). Everyone can fall back on this, as though it were something that could now be taken for granted, and can hence derive gloomy pleasure from being a martyr to their nerves. Admittedly, this fatigue signifies one thing at least (in this respect it has the same revelatory function as violence and non-violence): this society which claims to be – which regards itself as being – in constant progress towards the abolition of effort, the resolution of tension, greater ease of living and automation, is in fact a society of stress, tension and drug use, in which the overall balance sheet of satisfaction is increasingly in deficit, in which individual and collective equilibrium is being progressively compromised even as the technical conditions for its realization are being increasingly fulfilled.

The heroes of consumption are tired. Various interpretations for this may be advanced on the psycho-sociological level. Instead of equalizing opportunities and reducing social competition (economic and status competition), the consumption process makes competition more violent and more acute in all its forms. Only in the consumer age are we at last in a society of generalized, *totalitarian* competition, which operates at all levels – the economy, knowledge, desire, the body, signs and drives. These are all things which are now *produced* as exchange-value in an endless process of differentiation and super-differentiation.

We may also take it, with Chombart de Lauwe, that, rather than matching up 'aspirations, needs and satisfactions' as it claims to do, this society creates ever greater disparities both among individuals and among social groups who are wrestling, on the one hand, with the imperative of competition and upward social mobility and, on the other, with the – now highly internalized – imperative to maximize their pleasures. Under so many opposing constraints, the individual comes apart. The social discrepancy of inequalities is added to the internal discrepancy between needs and aspirations to make this society one that is increasingly at odds with itself, disunited, suffering from a 'malaise'. Fatigue (or 'asthenia') will then be interpreted as a response on the part of modern man – a response in the form of a passive refusal – to his conditions of existence. But it has to be seen that this 'passive refusal' is in fact a *latent violence*, and that it is, by this token, only one possible response, the others being responses of *overt violence*. Here again, we have to restore the principle of ambivalence. Fatigue, depression, neurosis are always convertible into overt violence, and vice versa. The fatigue of the citizen of post-industrial society is not far removed from the 'go-slow' or 'slowdown' of factory workers, or the schoolchild's 'boredom'. These are all forms of passive resistance; they are 'ingrowing' in the way one speaks of an 'ingrowing toenail', turning back in towards the flesh, towards the inside.

In fact, we must reverse all the terms of the spontaneous view: fatigue is not passivity set against the social hyperactivity outside. It is, rather, *the only form of activity* which can, in certain conditions, be set against the constraint of general passivity which applies in current social relations. The tired pupil is the one who passively goes along with what the teacher says. The tired worker or bureaucrat is the one who has had all responsibility taken from him in his work. Political 'indifference', that catatonia of the modern citizen, is the indifference of the individual deprived of any decision-making powers and left only with the sop of universal suffrage. And the physical and mental monotony of work on the production line or in the office plays its part, too: the muscular, vascular, physiological catalepsy of positions imposed (both standing and seated), of stereotyped gestures, of all the inertia of the chronic underemployment of the body in our society. But this is not the essential point, and this is why 'pathological' fatigue will not be cured by sport and muscular exercise as naïve specialists contend (any more than it will by stimulants or tranquillizers). For fatigue is a concealed form of protest, which turns round against oneself and 'grows into' one's own body because, in certain conditions, that is the only thing on which the dispossessed individual can take out his frustration, just as the blacks rebelling in the cities of America begin by burning down their own neighbourhoods. *True passivity is to be found in the joyful conformity to the system* of the 'dynamic' young manager, bright-eyed and broad-shouldered, ideally fitted to continual activity. Fatigue is an activity, a latent, endemic revolt, unconscious of itself. This explains its function: the 'slowdown', in all its forms, is (like neurosis) the only way to avoid total, genuine breakdown. And it is because it is a (latent) activity that it can suddenly go over into open revolt, as the month of May [1968] everywhere showed. The spontaneous, total contagion, the 'powderkeg' of the May movement can only be explained by this hypothesis: what was taken for lifelessness, disaffection and generalized passivity was in fact a potential of forces *active* in their very resignation, in their ebbing – and hence immediately available. There was no miracle. And the ebbing since May is not an inexplicable 'reversal' of the process either. It is the *conversion* of a form of open revolt into a modality of latent *protest* (the term *'protest'* should indeed be applied only to this latter form: it refers to the many forms of refusal cut off momentarily from a practice of radical change).

Having said this, the fact remains that, in order to grasp the meaning of fatigue, we have to resituate it, beyond psycho-sociological inter-pretations, in the general structure of depressive states. Insomnia, head-aches, migraines, pathological obesity or anorexia, atony or compulsive hyperactivity: though formally different or opposed, these symptoms can in reality be *interchanged*, can substitute one for another, somatic 'conversion' being always accompanied, and even defined by, the virtual 'convertibility' of all symptoms. Now – this is the crucial point – this logic of depressiveness (namely that, being no longer linked to organic lesions or real dysfunctions, symptoms 'wander around') echoes the very logic of consumption (namely that, being no longer linked to the objective function of objects, needs and satisfactions succeed one another, link up one to another, substitute one for another on the basis of a fundamental dissatisfaction). It is the same elusive, unlimited character, the same systematic convertibility which regulates the flow of needs and the 'fluidity' of depressive symptoms. We shall turn once again here to the principle of ambivalence, which we have already mentioned in connection with violence, to sum up the total, structural interrelatedness of the system of consumption and the system of abreaction/somatization (of which fatigue is merely one aspect). All the processes of our societies tend towards a deconstruction, a dissociation of the ambivalence of desire. That ambivalence, totalized in *jouissance* and the symbolic function, is split apart, but, in going off in two different directions, it obeys a single logic: all the positivity of desire passes into the series of needs and satisfactions, where it resolves itself in terms of managed aims; all the negativity of desire, however, passes into uncontrollable somatization or into the acting-out of violence. This explains the profound unity of the whole process: no other hypothesis can account for the multiplicity of disparate phenomena (affluence, violence, euphoria, depression) which, taken together, characterize the 'consumer society' and which we sense are all necessarily inter-linked, though their logic remains inexplicable within the perspective of a classical anthropology.

Though this is not the place to do it, we ought to go further into:

1   the analysis of consumption as a general process of 'conversion', or, in other words, of 'symbolic' transfer of a lack to a whole chain of signifiers/objects successively invested as part-objects;
2   generalizing the theory of the part-object to the processes of somatization – here again a symbolic transfer and an investment – on the basis of a theory of the body and its status as object within the system of modernity. We have seen that this theory of the body is essential to the theory of consumption, the body being an epitome of all these ambivalent processes: both invested narcissistically as an object of eroticized solicitude and invested 'somatically' as an object of concern and aggressivity.

'It's absolutely classic,' comments a specialist in psychosomatic illness. 'You take refuge in your headaches. It could be anything else at all, such as colitis, insomnia, various kinds of pruritus or eczema, sexual difficulties, obesity, respiratory, digestive or cardiovascular problems . . . or quite simply, and indeed most often, insurmountable *fatigue*.'

Significantly, depression comes to the surface at the point where one is released from the constraints of work and where the time for satisfaction begins (or should begin) – the managing director with migraines from Friday night to Monday morning; suicide or death following hard upon retirement, etc. It is very well known too that, beneath the now institutional, ritual demand for free time, the 'age of leisure' has seen the development of a growing demand for work, for activity, a compulsive need to 'be doing' or 'acting' in which our pious moralists immediately saw a proof that work was man's 'natural vocation'. It seems more likely that this non-economic demand for work is an expression of all the aggressivity that has not been satisfied in leisure and satisfaction. But it can find no resolution by that route since, arising from the depths of the ambivalence of desire, it here reformulates itself as a demand or a 'need' for work and thus re-enters the cycle of needs, from which we know there is no way out for desire.

Just as violence can be turned to domestic use, to heighten the enjoyment of security, so fatigue, like neurosis, can become a cultural trait of distinction. Then the whole ritual of fatigue and satisfaction comes into play, most often among the cultivated and the privileged (though this cultural 'alibi' is filtering down very quickly). At this stage, fatigue is no longer anomic at all, and nothing of what we have just said of it applies to this 'obligatory' fatigue: this is 'consumed' fatigue and forms part of the social ritual of exchange and status.

CONCLUSION

On Contemporary Alienation or the End of the Pact with the Devil

The Student of Prague

The *Student of Prague* is an old silent film from the 1930s, an expressionist film of the German school.[1] It tells the story of a poor but ambitious student impatient for a more prosperous life. As he is taking part in a drinking bout in a café near Prague, a hunt is in progress all around in which that city's high society is finding what amusement it can. Someone rules over that society and is pulling the strings. He can be seen manoeuvring the animals at will and regulating the movements of the hunters. And this man of relatively advanced years, with his top hat, gloves, knobbed stick, slight paunch and little turn-of-the-century goatee beard, looks like one of the hunters. He is the Devil. He contrives to have one of the women from the hunt lose her way. She meets the student – love at first sight! But the woman, being rich, is beyond his grasp. Returning home, the student broods on his ambition and dissatisfaction, which have now assumed a sexual dimension.

The Devil then appears in the student's seedy room, which contains only books and a life-size mirror. In exchange for his image in the mirror, he offers him a pile of gold. The deal is struck. The Devil peels the specular image from the mirror as though it were an etching or a sheet of carbon paper, rolls it up, puts it in his pocket, and leaves, in suitably obsequious and sardonic fashion. Here the film's real argument begins. Thanks to his money, the student enjoys success after success, avoiding, with cat-like tread, the mirrors with which the fashionable society in which he moves unfortunately surrounds itself. At the beginning, however, he retains his peace of mind; he is not greatly vexed at no longer seeing his own image. But then, one day, he sees his own flesh-and-blood image. This double, which now frequents the same circles and clearly takes an interest in him, follows him around and never lets him rest. It is, we surmise, his own image – the image he sold – which the Devil has revived and put back into circulation. As the good image it is, it remains attached to its model; but, as the bad image it has become, it now accompanies him not only when he chances to pass by mirrors, but in life itself, wherever he goes. He runs the risk of being compromised by it at any moment, if the two are seen together (a number of small incidents of this kind have already occurred). And if he flees society to avoid it, it takes his place and completes what he had begun, distorting his actions to the point of rendering them criminal. One day when he has provoked a duel, but has resolved to make his excuses on the duelling ground, he arrives at the appointed place at dawn. But he is too late: his double has passed that way before him and the opponent is already dead. The student hides. His image continues to hound him, as though to be avenged for having been sold. He sees the image everywhere. It appears to him behind tombs, or at the edge of the cemetery. He is no longer able to have any social life; his existence is impossible. In this despairing state, he rejects even a sincere offer of love and, to put an end to all his troubles, settles on the plan of killing his own image.

One day, the image pursues him into his room. In the course of a violent scene between the two, it happens to pass in front of the mirror from which it came. At the memory of this initial scene, nostalgia for his image, mingled with fury at what he is enduring on its account, pushes the student to the brink. He fires at it. Naturally, the mirror is smashed and the double, become again the phantasm it once was, vanishes into thin air. But at the same moment, the student slumps to the ground; it is *he* who is dying. For, by killing his image, he is killing himself, since, without his noticing it, the image has become living and real in his stead. In his death throes, however, he grasps at one of the fragments of the mirror scattered about the floor and realizes that *he can see himself again*. He loses his body, but, by paying that price, his *normal* likeness is restored to him just before he dies.

The mirror image here symbolically represents the meaning of our acts. These build up around us a world that is *in our image*. The transparency of our relation to the world is expressed rather well by the individual's unimpaired relation to his image in a mirror: the faithfulness of that reflection bears witness, to some degree, to a real reciprocity between the world and ourselves. Symbolically, then, if that image should be missing, it is the sign that the world is becoming opaque, that our acts are getting out of our control and, at that point, we have no perspective on ourselves. Without that guarantee, no identity is possible any longer: I become another to myself; I am *alienated*.

This is the first element, then, which the film presents. But it is not content merely to tell a general tale. It immediately supplies the concrete meaning of the situation. The image is not lost or abolished by chance: it is *sold*. It falls into the commodity sphere, we might say, and this is indeed the sense of *concrete, social* alienation. At the same time, the fact that the Devil can pocket this image as an object is also the fantastic illustration of the real process of commodity fetishism: from the moment they are produced, our works and our acts fall out of our grasp and are objectivized; they fall, literally, into the Devil's hands. Thus, in Chamisso's *Peter Schlemihl* the shadow too is separated from the person maleficently and becomes a pure thing, an article of apparel one might leave at home if one were not careful and which could get stuck to the ground if there were too sharp a frost. Schlemihl, who has lost his shadow, fancies he might have one drawn for him by a painter – one which will follow him about. And Egyptian legends say that one should not walk too close to water, since crocodiles have a taste for passing shadows. The plots of the two tales are equivalent: whether we are speaking of image or shadow, it is in each case the transparency of our relation to ourselves and to the world that is shattered, and life then loses its meaning. But there is one thing in the fables of *Schlemihl* and *The Student of Prague* that is superior to many other pacts with the Devil: the fact that they put Gold, and Gold alone – that is to say, commodity logic and exchange-value – at the centre of alienation.

The two fables do, however, proceed in quite different ways after that, with the logic of the Schlemihl story – in which Chamisso does not carry through the consequences of the shadow being transformed into an object – lacking rigour. Chamisso fills out his tale with fantastical, comic episodes, like the chase over the 'sunlit sandy plain' after a wandering, masterless shadow, which might be his, or when the Devil gives him back his shadow to try out again for a few hours. But Schlemihl does not suffer directly from his alienated shadow; he suffers only the social reprobation which attaches to the absence of a shadow. Once it has escaped, it does not turn against him to become the instrument which destroys his very being. Schlemihl is condemned to solitude, but *he remains the same*. Neither his consciousness nor his life is taken from him, only life in society. Hence the final compromise, in which he stoically rejects the second bargain proposed by the Devil, which would give him back his shadow in exchange for his soul. Thus, *he loses his shadow, but he saves his soul*.

The Student of Prague follows a much tighter logic. As soon as he has sold his image or, in other words, has sold a part of himself, the student is hounded *to his death* by it in real life. This translates the unvarnished truth of the process of alienation: nothing of what is alienated runs off into some neutral circuit, into an 'external world' over against which we might be said to remain free – suffering, with each dispossession, only a loss in our *having*, but always retaining possession of ourselves in our 'private' sphere and ultimately remaining intact in our *being*. This is the reassuring fiction of the 'inner self' or 'heart of hearts' [*for intérieur*], where the soul is free of the world. Alienation goes much deeper than that. There is a part of us which gets away from us in this process, but we do not get away from it. The object (the soul, the shadow, the product of our labour become object) *takes its revenge*. All we are dispossessed of remains attached to us, but negatively. In other words, it *haunts* us. That part of us sold and forgotten is still us, or rather it is a caricature of us, the ghost, the *spectre* which follows us; it is our continuation and takes its revenge.

We encounter the troubling atmosphere of this inversion of subject and object, this sorcery of the otherness of the same, in the most everyday expressions: 'He followed him about like a shadow.' And also in our cult of the dead – a propitiating of a part of us which is alienated once and for all, and from which, as a consequence, we can expect only ill. Now, there is a part of ourselves by which, *when living*, we are collectively haunted: social labour power, which, once sold, returns, through the whole social cycle of the commodity, to dispossess us of the meaning of labour itself; labour power which has become – by a social, not a diabolical, operation, of course – the materialized obstacle to the fruits of our labours. It is all this which is symbolized in *The Student of Prague* by the sudden emergence, live and hostile, of the image, and by the long suicide (for such we must call it) which that image imposes on the one who sold it.

What is crucial here, and is dramatically demonstrated to us, is that the alienated human being is not merely a being diminished and impoverished but left intact in its essence: it is a being turned inside out, changed into something evil, into its own enemy, set against itself. This is, on another level, the process Freud describes in repression: the repressed returning through the agency of repression itself. It is the body of Christ on the cross changing into a woman to obsess the monk who has taken a vow of chastity. In alienation, it is the human being's objectivized life-forces which at any moment change *into him to his cost*, and thus drive him to his death.

In the end, Schlemihl gives relative meaning to his life and dies a natural death, like a solitary American industrialist, in a charitable institution he himself founded in the days when he was wealthy. He saved his soul by rejecting the second bargain. This division of the action flows necessarily from the ambiguity of the initial idea and, as a result, the fable entirely loses its rigour.

In *The Student of Prague*, there is no second bargain. The student dies inexorably from the *logical* consequences of the first. This means that, for Chamisso, it is possible to sell one's shadow – that is to say, to be alienated in all respects of one's behaviour – and *still to save one's soul*. Alienation leads only to a conflict in social *appearances*, and, that being the case, Schlemihl can very easily overcome it *abstractly* in solitude, whereas *The Student of Prague* develops the *objective* logic of alienation in all its rigour and shows that *there is no way out but death*. Every ideal solution for overcoming alienation is cut off. Alienation cannot be overcome: it is *the very structure of the bargain with the Devil*. It is the very structure of market society.

The End of Transcendence

The Student of Prague is a remarkable illustration of the processes of alienation, that is to say, of the generalized pattern of individual and social life governed by commodity logic. Moreover, since the early Middle Ages, the Pact with the Devil has been the central myth of a society engaged in the historical and technical process of the domination of Nature, that process being always simultaneously a process of the taming of sexuality. Among the forces of evil, indexed to the Devil, the Western 'Sorcerer's Apprentice' has served constantly to thematize the immense guilt attaching to the puritanical, Promethean enterprise of Progress, of sublimation and labour, of rationality and efficiency. That is why this medieval theme of the re-emergence of the repressed – of being haunted by the repressed and selling one's soul (the 'pact' reflecting the irruption of market processes into early bourgeois society) – was revived by the romantics in the very earliest years of the 'industrial age'. Since then, the theme has continued to run (parallel to the myth of the 'miracle of technology') beneath the myth of the *inevitability of technology*. All our current science fiction is steeped in it, as is the whole of everyday mythology, from the peril of the atomic catastrophe (the technological suicide of civilization) to the theme, played out in a thousand variations, of the fatal gap between technical Progress and human social morality.

We may, therefore, suggest that the age of consumption, being the historical culmination of the whole process of accelerated productivity under the sign of capital, is also the age of radical alienation. Commodity logic has become generalized and today governs not only labour processes and material products, but the whole of culture, sexuality, and human relations, including even fantasies and individual drives. Everything is taken over by that logic, not only in the sense that all functions and needs are objectivized and manipulated in terms of profit, but in the deeper sense in which everything is *spectacularized* or, in other words, evoked, provoked and orchestrated into images, signs, consumable models.

But the question then is: in so far as it revolves around *the alterity of the selfsame* (that is to say, around an alienated, abducted, essence of man), can this schema (or this concept) of alienation still be operative in a context in which the individual is no longer ever confronted with his own split image? The myth of the Pact and the Sorcerer's Apprentice is still a *demiurgic myth*, the myth of the Market, Gold and Production, the transcendent objective of which turns around against human beings themselves. By contrast, consumption is not Promethean; it is hedonistic and regressive. Its process is no longer one of labour and self-surpassing, but *a process of absorption of signs and absorption by signs*. It is, therefore, characterized, as Marcuse says, by the *end of transcendence*. In the generalized process of consumption, there is no longer any soul, no shadow, no double, and no image in the specular sense. There is no longer any contradiction within being, or any problematic of being and appearance. There is no longer anything but the transmission and reception of signs, and the individual being vanishes in this combinatory and calculus of signs. Consumer man never comes face to face with his own needs, any more than with the specific product of his labour; nor is he ever confronted with his own image: *he is immanent in the signs he arranges*. There is no transcendence any more, no finality, no objective: what characterizes this society is the absence of 'reflection', of a perspective on itself. There is, therefore, no *maleficent agency* either, like that of the Devil, with whom one could enter into a Faustian pact to gain wealth and glory, since one is given these things by a *beneficent*, maternal *ambience* – the affluent society itself. Or, alternatively, we must suppose that it is society as a whole, as a *société anonyme*, as a thing of 'limited liability', which has struck a contract with the Devil, has bartered all transcendence and finality for affluence, and is now haunted by an absence of ends.

In the specific mode of consumption, there is no transcendence any more, *not even the fetishistic transcendence of the commodity*. There is now only immanence in the order of signs. Just as there is no agonizing ontological struggle, but a logical relation between the signifier and the signified, so there is no longer an ontological struggle between the being and its double (its shadow, its soul, its ideal), whether divine or diabolic; there is logical calculation of signs and absorption into the system of signs. There is no longer any mirror or looking-glass in the modern order in which the human being would be confronted with his image for better or for worse; there is only the *shop-window* – the site of consumption, in which the individual no longer produces his own reflection, but is absorbed in the contemplation of multiple signs/objects, is absorbed into the order of signifiers of social status, etc. He is not reflected in that order, but absorbed and abolished. *The subject of consumption is the order of signs*. Whether we define this latter structurally, as the instance of a code, or empirically as the generalized ambience of objects, the involvement of the subject is no longer, at any event, that of an 'alienated' essence in the philosophical, Marxist sense of the term. It is not that of an essence which is dispossessed, taken over by some alienating agency and become foreign to itself. For there is no longer, properly speaking, any 'selfsame', any 'subject itself', or, therefore, any 'alterity of the selfsame', and therefore no alienation in the strict sense. The situation is rather like that of the child kissing his image in the mirror before going to bed: he doesn't entirely mistake the image for himself, since he has already 'recognized' it. Nor is it an alien double in which he is reflected: he *plays* with it, *somewhere between sameness and otherness*. So it is with the consumer: he 'plays out' his personalization between one term and another, one sign and another. Between signs there is no contradiction, just as there is no exclusive opposition between the child and his image: there is collusion and ordered involvement. The consumer defines himself by his choice within a 'game' played between different models or, in other words, by his combinatorial involvement in that game. It is in this sense that consumption is ludic and that *the ludic dimension of consumption has gradually supplanted the tragic dimension of identity*.

From Spectre to Spectrum

We have today no myth equal to that of the Pact with the Devil or the Sorcerer's Apprentice (which thematized the fatal contradiction between the individual being and his Double) to thematize the peaceful coexistence – in the guise of a paradigmatic declension – of the successive terms which define the 'personal' model. Tragic duality (which the situationists are again restoring in the concept of the 'spectacle', the 'society of the spectacle', and radical alienation) had its great myths, all of them linked to the notion of a human essence and the inevitability of losing it – linked to Being and its **spectre**. But the ludic ramification of the person into a spectrum of signs and objects, nuances and differences, which constitutes the basis of the consumption process and totally redefines the individual not as alienated substance but as shifting difference – this novel process, which is not analysable in terms of the person (what an admirable amphibology we have in the French word *personne* which, on its own, means 'no one'!) and the alterity of the person, has not found an equivalent myth to embody the Metaphysics of Consumption – a metaphysical myth to represent what the Double and Alienation represented for the order of production. *This is no accident*. Myths, like the faculties of speech, reflection and transcription, are indissociable from transcendence, and disappear with it.

Consumption of Consumption

If the consumer society no longer produces myth, this is because *it is itself its own myth*. The Devil, who brought Gold and Wealth (the price of which was our soul), has been supplanted by Affluence pure and simple. And the pact with the Devil has been supplanted by the contract of Affluence. Moreover, just as the most diabolical aspect of the Devil has never been his existing, but his making us believe that he exists, so Affluence *does not exist*, but it only has to make us believe it exists to be an effective myth.

Consumption is a myth. That is to say, it is *a statement of contemporary society about itself*, the way our society speaks itself. And, in a sense, the only objective reality of consumption is the *idea* of consumption; it is this reflexive, discursive configuration, endlessly repeated in everyday speech and intellectual discourse, which has acquired the force of *common sense*.

Our society thinks itself and speaks itself as a consumer society. As much as it consumes anything, it consumes *itself* as consumer society, as *idea*. Advertising is the triumphal paean to that idea.

This is not a supplementary dimension; it is a fundamental one, for it is the dimension of myth. If we did nothing but consume (getting, devouring, digesting), consumption would not be a myth, which is to say that it would not be a full, self-fulfilling discourse of society about itself, a general system of interpretation, a mirror in which it takes supreme delight in itself, a utopia in which it is reflected in advance. In this sense, affluence and consumption – again, we mean not the consumption of material goods, products and services, but the consumed image of consumption – do, indeed, constitute our new tribal mythology – the morality of modernity.

Without that anticipation and reflexive potentialization of enjoyment in the 'collective consciousness', consumption would merely be what it is and would not be such a force for social integration. It would merely be a richer, more lavish, more differentiated mode of subsistence than before, but it would no more have a *name* than ever it did before, when nothing designated as collective value, as reference myth what was merely a mode of survival (eating, drinking, housing and clothing oneself) or the sumptuary expenditure (finery, great houses, jewels) of the privileged classes. Neither eating roots nor throwing feasts was given the name 'consuming'. Our age is the first in which current expenditure on food and 'prestige' expenditure have both been termed **consumption** by everyone concerned, there being a total consensus on the matter. The historic emergence of the *myth* of consumption in the twentieth century is radically different from the emergence of the technical concept in economic thinking or science, where it was employed much earlier. That terminological systematization for everyday use changes history itself: it is the sign of a new social reality. Strictly speaking, there has been consumption only since the term has 'passed into general usage'. Though it is mystifying and analytically useless – a veritable 'anti-concept' indeed – it signifies, nonetheless, that an ideological restructuring of values has occurred. The fact that this society experiences itself as a consumer society must be the starting point for an objective analysis.

When we say that this 'affluent' society is its own myth, we mean that it takes over, at a general level, that admirable advertising slogan which might happily serve as its motto: **the body you dream of is your own**. A kind of immense collective narcissism is inducing society to merge itself into – and absolve itself in – the image it presents of itself, to be convinced of itself in the way that advertising ends up convincing people of their bodies and the prestige values of those bodies. In short, it is becoming its own 'self-fulfilling prophecy'.[2] Boorstin has shown how this immense process of self-demonstrative tautology works in the USA, where a whole society speaks itself in the mode of prophecy, but a prophecy which does not have future ideals or transcendent heroes for its substance, but solely the reflection of itself and of its immanence. Advertising is dedicated entirely to this function: the consumer can at any moment read, as in Till Eulenspiegel's mirror, what he is and what he desires – and fulfil that desire in the process. There is no longer any ontological distance or fissure. The suture is immediate. It is the same with opinion polls, market research surveys and all those actions in

which the great Delphic Oracle of Public Opinion is made to speak and
to rave: they foretell social and political events and substitute themselves, like identikit pictures, for the real events, which end up reflecting
them. Hence, as Boorstin writes, 'public opinion – once the public's
expression – becomes more and more an image into which the public fits
its expression. Public opinion becomes filled with what is already there.
It is the people looking in the mirror.'[3] So it is too with celebrities, stars
and 'heroes of consumption':

> The hero stood for outside standards. The celebrity is a tautology . . .
> Celebrities are known primarily for their well-knownness. Yet the celebrity is
> usually nothing greater than a more publicized version of us. In imitating him,
> in trying to dress like him, talk like him, look like him, think like him, we are
> simply imitating ourselves . . . By imitating a tautology, we ourselves become
> a tautology standing for what we stand for . . . We look for models, and we see
> our own image.[4]

And of television, Boorstin remarks: 'At home we begin to try to live
according to the script of television programmes of happy families,
which are themselves nothing but amusing quintessences of us.'[5]

Like every great myth worth its salt, the myth of 'Consumption' has its
discourse and its anti-discourse. In other words, the elated discourse on
affluence is everywhere shadowed by a morose, moralizing, 'critical'
counter-discourse on the ravages of consumer society and the tragic end
to which it inevitably dooms society as a whole. That counter-discourse
is to be heard everywhere. Not only is it found in intellectualist discourse, which is always ready to distance itself by its scorn for 'simple-
minded values' and 'material satisfactions', but it is now present within
'mass culture' itself: advertising increasingly parodies itself, integrating
counter-advertising into its promotional technique. *France-Soir, Paris-
Match*, the radio, the TV, and ministerial speeches all contain as an
obligatory refrain the lament on this 'consumer society', where values,
ideals and ideologies are giving way to the pleasures of everyday life. We
shall not soon forget Chaban-Delmas's famous flight of oratory: 'We
have to control consumer society by giving it back some soul!'

This endlessly repeated indictment is part of the game: it is the
critical mirage, the anti-fable which rounds off the fable – the discourse
of consumption and its critical undermining. *Only the two sides taken
together constitute the myth.* We have, therefore, to allot to the 'critical'
discourse and the moralizing protest their true responsibility for the
elaboration of the myth. It is that discourse which locks us definitively
into the mythic and prophetic teleology of the 'Civilization of the Object'.
It is that discourse which, being itself much more fascinated by the
Object than either common sense or the grassroots consumer, transfig-
ures it into a mythic and fascinated anti-object critique. The rebels of
May 1968 did not escape this trap of reifying objects and consumption
excessively by according them diabolical value, of denouncing them as
such and building them up into a determining instance. And the real

work of myth-making lies here. If all the denunciations, all the disquisitions on 'alienation', and all the derisive force of pop and anti-art play so easily into establishment hands, that is because they are themselves part of the myth, which they round out by providing the counter-melody within the formal liturgy of the Object we spoke of at the beginning – and do so in a manner that is without doubt more perverse than the spontaneous adherence to consumer values.

In conclusion, we shall say that this counter-discourse, which establishes no *real* distance, is as immanent in consumer society as any of its other aspects. This negative discourse is the intellectual's second home. Just as medieval society was balanced on God **and** the Devil, so ours is balanced on consumption **and** its denunciation. Though at least around the Devil heresies and black magic sects could organize. Our magic is white. No heresy is possible any longer in a state of affluence. It is the prophylactic whiteness of a saturated society, a society with no history and no dizzying heights, a society with no other myth than itself.

But here we are once again speaking in morose, prophetic terms, caught in the trap of the Object and its apparent plenitude. Now, we know that the Object is nothing and that behind it stands the tangled void of human relations, the negative imprint of the immense mobilization of productive and social forces which have become reified in it. We shall await the violent irruptions and sudden disintegrations which will come, just as unforeseeably and as certainly as May 1968, to wreck this white Mass.

Notes

Chapter 1

1 K. Marx, *A Contribution to the Critique of Political Economy*, Lawrence and Wishart, London, 1971, p. 87.

2 Contrary to a rather odd assertion in Mark Poster's book *Jean Baudrillard: Selected Writings* (Polity, 1988, p. 55, note 4), Flaine is not 'Baudrillard's parody of suburban communities around Paris' but a genuine ski resort in Haute-Savoie (Tr.).

Chapter 2

1 This situation is almost ideally realized by a city like Berlin. Moreover, almost all science-fiction novels have as their theme the situation of a rational and 'affluent' Great City *threatened* with destruction from without or within by some great hostile force.

Chapter 3

1 Tables appearing in the original French have been removed at the author's request (Tr.).

2 J.K. Galbraith, *The Affluent Society*, Penguin in association with Hamish Hamilton, Harmondsworth, 1962, p. 210.

3 There is in this sense an absolute difference between waste in our 'affluent societies', a waste that is a *nuisance integrated into the economic system*, which is a functional wastage not productive of collective value, and the destructive prodigality engaged in by all the so-called 'societies of scarcity' in their festivals and sacrifices, this latter being waste 'by excess', in which the destruction of goods was a source of collective symbolic values. Breaking up old cars that have gone out of fashion or burning coffee in locomotives is in no sense festive. It is a deliberate, systematic destruction for strategic ends. So too is military expenditure (perhaps only advertising . . .). The economic system cannot transcend itself in an act of festive waste, caught up as it is in its own alleged 'rationality'. It can only devour its excess of wealth as it were shamefully, practising a calculated destructiveness that is complementary to its productivity calculations.

Chapter 4

1 The term 'inequality' is inappropriate. The equality/inequality opposition, ideologically linked to the system of modern democratic values, only fully covers economic disparities and cannot figure in a structural analysis.

2 Or the 'Great Society', recently imported into France.

3 On this point, see Chapter 7 in relation to 'lowest common culture' and 'lowest common multiples'.

4 It is, of course, in its functioning as a system of social differentiation (2 above) that consumption takes on this unlimited dimension. As a system of communication and

exchange (1 above), where it may be compared to language, a *finite* range of goods and services (like the finite material of linguistic signs) can very well suffice, as we see in primitive societies. Language [*la langue*] does not proliferate because there is no *ambivalence* of the sign at that level, that ambivalence being grounded in social hierarchy and simultaneous double determination. By contrast, a certain level of *parole* and style does give rise again to distinctive proliferation.

5   On this point, see Chapter 5, section 'Consumption as the Emergence and Control of New Productive Forces'.

6   This is the 'reserve army' of needs.

7   This growing differentiation does not necessarily signify *a growing distance from the top to the bottom* of the scale, a 'greater overall imbalance', but *increasing discrimination*, an increase in the quantity of distinctive signs *within* a hierarchy whose extremes have moved closer together. Relative 'democratization' and homogenization are accompanied by a related intensification in status competition.

8   In this sense, the distinction between 'real' and 'artificial' needs is also a false problem. 'Artificial needs' do, of course, mask the non-satisfaction of 'essential' needs (television instead of education). But this is secondary to generalized determination by growth (the expanded reproduction of capital), in respect of which the terms 'natural' and 'artificial' have no meaning. We might even say that this natural–artificial opposition, which implies a theory of human finalities, is *itself an ideological product of growth*. It is reproduced by growth and is functionally linked to it.

9   *Les Temps modernes*, October 1968.

Chapter 5

1   Quoted by Galbraith, *The New Industrial State*, Signet, New York, 1967, epigraph to Chapter 10.

2   In the survey carried out by *Sélection du Reader's Digest* (A. Piatier, 'Structures et perspectives de la consommation européenne'), the pattern which emerges is not one of an immense middle class, as in the case of the USA, but that of a minority, a consumer elite (the As) serving as a model for a majority which does not yet possess that range of luxury goods (sports car, stereo, second home) which every European worthy of the name must have.

3   Galbraith, *The New Industrial State*, p. 215.

4   Ibid., p. 222.

5   This is the 'anti-coagulant' effect of advertising (Elgozy).

6   Galbraith, *The New Industrial State*, p. 281.

6   Ibid., p. 279.

8   Ibid., p. 280.

9   On this, see this chapter, section 'Consumption as the Emergence and Control of New Productive Forces'.

10   J. Baudrillard, 'The ideological genesis of needs', in *For a Critique of the Political Economy of the Sign*, Telos, St Louis, 1981, pp. 63–87.

11   This paragraph has been slightly modified by the author (Tr.).

12   *La Nef*, no. 37.

13   Galbraith, *The New Industrial State*, p. 49.

14   On this point, see Chapter 10, 'The Mystique of Solicitude'.

Chapter 6

1   It is the same with relationships. The system is built upon a total liquidation of personal ties, of concrete social relations. It is to this extent that it becomes necessarily and

systematically productive of relationship (public relations, human relations, etc.). The production of relationships has become one of the key sectors of production. And because they no longer have anything spontaneous about them, because they are *produced*, those relationships are necessarily fated, like all that is produced, to be consumed (unlike *social relations*, which are the unconscious product of social labour and not the result of deliberate, controlled industrial production: these are not 'consumed' but are, in fact, the site of *social contradictions*).

On the production and consumption of human relations and social relationships, see Chapter 10, 'The Mystique of Solicitude'.

2 D. Riesman, *Abundance for What? And Other Essays*, Chatto and Windus, London, 1964, p. 129.

3 D. Riesman (with N. Glazer and R. Denney), *The Lonely Crowd: A Study of the Changing American Character*, Doubleday Anchor, New York, n.d., pp. 98–9.

4 See Chapter 11, section 'Violence'.

Chapter 7

1 The reference is to the Le Président health clubs. See note 4 to Chapter 8 (Tr.).

2 If beauty is to be found in the 'figure', the career is defined by its 'profile'. Such connivances of vocabulary are significant.

3 See this chapter, section 'Pseudo-Event and Neo-Reality'. The term 'gadget' covers a rather different semantic field in French, referring in particular to objects which are not necessarily technical implements, but merely useless objects of a 'gimmicky' kind. However, since the French usage will be reasonably clear from the author's argument here, I have generally retained the term 'gadget', which has at least equally pejorative connotations in English (Galbraith writes, 'The word gadget is itself a pejorative term for durable goods', *The Affluent Society*, p. 162) (Tr.).

4 *Tirlipot* is the name of a 1960s radio quiz game.

5 *Le Monde*, 28 September 1969.

6 There is, in this sense, a relationship of sorts between kitsch and snobbery. However, snobbery is linked, rather, to the aristocracy/bourgeoisie acculturation process and kitsch essentially to the rise of the 'middle' classes in a bourgeois industrial society.

7 But it is not a toy, as the toy has a symbolic function for the child. However, a 'new look' toy, a fashionable toy becomes a gadget once again simply by dint of such modishness.

8 The *pure* gadget, defined as something totally useless to anyone at all, would be an absurdity.

9 An annual French competition for artisans and inventors (Tr.).

10 See Daniel J. Boorstin, *The Image, or What Happened to the American Dream*, Penguin, Harmondsworth, 1963.

11 The cubists were still searching for the 'essence' of space, seeking to unveil a 'secret geometry', etc. In Dada, Duchamp or the surrealists, objects were wrenched from their (bourgeois) functions to be set up in their subversive banality, in a reminder of their lost essence and of an order of authenticity evoked by way of the absurd. In Francis Ponge, the apprehension of the naked, concrete object is still the act of a – poetic – consciousness or source of perception. In short, whether poetic or critical, the whole of art, 'without which things would merely be what they are', is fuelled (before pop) by transcendence.

12 Cf. the Conclusion, section 'The Consumption of Consumption'.

13 Mario Amaya, *Pop as Art: A Survey of the New Super Realism*, Studio Vista, London, 1965.

14 In this sense, the truth of pop might be said to be wage labour and the advertising hoarding, not the contract and the art gallery.

15 'Popular' art is concerned not with objects, but always primarily with human beings and their actions. It would not paint cooked meats or the American flag, but a-man-eating or a-man-saluting-the-American-flag.

16 In fact we often read this 'terroristic' humour in it, but we do so out of critical nostalgia on our part.

17 Marshall McLuhan, *Understanding Media: The Extensions of Man*, Sphere, London, 1967, p. 27.

18 It is easy to see how one can, in this sense, 'consume' language [*du langage*]. As soon as it becomes loaded with in-group connotations, and, instead of being a vehicle for meaning, turns into a group lexicon, a class or caste heritage (the style of the 'smart set', intellectual jargon; the political jargon of a party or grouping); as soon as it ceases to be a *means of exchange* and becomes a *material of exchange* for the internal usage of a group or class – its real function, under cover of conveying a message, being one of collusion and recognition; and as soon as, rather than putting meaning into circulation, it begins itself to circulate as password, as shibboleth, in a process of group tautology (the group speaking itself), then language is an object of consumption, a fetish.

It is no longer being used as a language [*langue*], as a system of distinctive denotative signs, but consumed as a system of connotation, as a distinctive code.

We find the same process in 'medical consumption'. There has been an extraordinary inflation of the demand for health care, closely linked to the rise in the standard of living. The line between 'justifiable' demand (though on what definition of a vital minimum and bio-psychosomatic equilibrium might it be considered justified?) and the consumer compulsion for medical, surgical and dental treatment is becoming blurred. Medical practice is turning into *the use of the doctor him/herself* and this sumptuary, conspicuous use of the doctor/object, the medicine/object, joins the second home and the car as part of the panoply of social standing. Here again, the medication – and, particularly where the wealthier classes are concerned, the doctor (Balint: 'The medication most frequently dispensed in general practice is the doctor himself') – cease to be the means of achieving health, considered as a final goal, and become themselves the focus of the ultimate demand. They are then consumed, on the selfsame pattern of a diverting of the objective practical function into a mental manipulation and a sign-based calculus of a fetishistic type.

We have, properly speaking, to distinguish between two levels of this 'consumption': the 'neurotic' demand for the giving of medication, for anxiety-reducing medical care. This demand is just as objective as the demand which arises from an organic ailment, but it leads into 'consumption' in so far as the doctor no longer has any specific value at this level: he is substitutable, as anxiety-reducer or care-provider, for any other process of partial regression: alcohol, shopping or collecting (the consumer 'collects' the doctor and medicines). The doctor is consumed as one-sign-among-others (just as a washing machine may be consumed as a mark of status and ease – see Chapter 7).

At a deep level, then, what institutes 'medical consumption' is – beyond the neurotic logic of individuals – a social logic of status, which incorporates the doctor as sign (quite apart from any objective performance and on the same basis as any other value *attribute*) into a generalized system. We can see that it is on the abstraction (the reduction) of the medical function that medical consumption is established. We find this pattern of systematic abduction or rerouting [*détournement*] everywhere as the very principle of consumption.

19 Boorstin, *The Image*, p. 209.

20 This is why all forms of resistance to the introduction of advertising on TV or elsewhere are merely moralizing or archaic reactions. The problem lies at the level of the system of signification as a whole.

21 Boorstin, *The Image*, p. 213.

22 Ibid., p. 217.

23 Ibid., p. 219.

Chapter 8

1   The reference in the hymn is, however, not to the body, but to the soul (Tr.).

2   The original *cartes du tendre* were, of course, actual 'maps' or charts depicting the course of love (Tr.).

3   See also this exemplary text from *Vogue*:

A new wind is blowing through the world of beauty, a fresher, freer, healthier, less hypocritical wind of *pride in one's body*. Not pretentiousness, which is vulgar. But the honest awareness that our bodies are worth accepting, caring for, loving, *if they are to be well used*. We are happy that our knees are more supple, we are delighted with the length of our legs, with our lighter feet . . . (for these we use a mask as we do for the face . . . we massage our toes with an extraordinary 'supersonic' cream, we find ourselves a good chiropodist . . . see how on page 72). We are all for the new body-spray perfumes, which give a satiny finish right down to our toes. Left, mules in South African ostrich-feathers with embroidery by Lamel (Christian Dior).

Etc.

4   In French. *le phrynéisme*. The reference here is to the Greek courtesan Phryne, who 'when she saw that in spite of the eloquence of her defender Hyperides she was going to be condemned, . . . unveiled her bosom, and by this sudden display of her charms so influenced her judges, that she was immediately acquitted' (*Lemprière's Classical Dictionary*, Bracken, London, 1984, p. 526) (Tr.).

5   The male equivalent of the *Elle* text is the advert for Le Président entitled 'No pity for executives?' This is an admirable text, which encapsulates all the themes we have analysed here (narcissism, the revenge of the neglected body, functional 'recycling'), except that here the masculine model centres on 'physical fitness' and social success, whereas the feminine model focused on 'beauty' and 'seduction'.

Forty years old. Modern civilization commands him to be young. The paunch which was once a symbol of social success is now synonymous with decline and the scrapheap. His superiors, his subordinates, his wife, his secretary, his mistress, his children and the girl in the microskirt he's chatting to at his table outside the café (with who knows what in mind) all judge him on the quality and style of his clothes, his choice of tie and after-shave, the suppleness and slenderness of his body.

He has to keep a watchful eye on everything: the crease in his trousers, his collar, his puns, his feet when he dances, his diet when he eats, his stamina when he is climbing stairs, his back when he makes a violent effort. If, only yesterday, efficiency in his work was enough, today *he is required to possess both physical fitness and elegance.*

The myth of the healthy American businessman, part James Bond, part Henry Ford, confident and sure of himself, physically and psychologically well balanced, has taken its place in our civilization. Finding and keeping *dynamic* co-workers with pep and drive is the major concern of every business manager.

The forty-year-old falls in with this image. *This neo-Narcissus of modern times* likes to take care of himself and tries to enjoy himself. He savours his diet, his medication, his physical training, the difficulty he has stopping smoking.

Aware that his social success depends entirely on the image others have of him, *that physical fitness is his trump card*, the man of forty is looking for his second wind and his second youth.

There follows the advert for Le Président. There, it is chiefly fitness that is being: fitness, the magic word, that 'fairy godmother's gift' (after Narcissus, the fairies!), which managing directors, senior executives, journalists and doctors pursue 'in an air-conditioned, cocooned atmosphere' and 'using 37 sets of apparatus with pedals, wheels, weights, vibrations, levers and steel cables' (as one can see, both athleticism and phryneism, both 'fitness' and 'beauty', are partial to gadgetry).

6   In the technical sense of simulations where the conditions of weightlessness are simulated experimentally – or of mathematical models.

7   The truth of the body is desire. And this, being lack, cannot be shown. The most exhaustive exhibition of that desire merely highlights it as absence, and ultimately, merely

censors it. Will we one day see photos in which erections are shown? This would still be done under the heading of fashion. The censors thus ultimately have nothing to fear, except from their own desire.

8   Norman O. Brown, *Life against Death: The Psychoanalytical Meaning of History*, Wesleyan University Press, Middletown, CT, p. 252.

9   On this point, see Chapter 6, section 'The Structural Models'.

10   Sexuality is no longer a celebration [*une fête*]. It is an erotic *festival*, with all that implies in terms of organization. Within the framework of that festival, everything is done also to revive 'polymorphous, perverse' sexuality. Cf. the first world fair of pornography in Copenhagen [this chapter, section 'The Sex-Exchange Standard'].

11   We find the same process in the 'consumption' of Technology. Without wishing to contest the enormous impact of technological progress on social progress, one can see how technology itself falls into the domain of consumption, dividing into a daily practice 'liberated' by innumerable 'functional' gadgets and a transcendent myth of (capital T) Technology, the combination of the two making it possible to head off all the revolutionary potentialities of a *total social* practice of technology. See *Utopie*, no. 2–3, May 1969, 'La Pratique sociale et la technique'.

12   The French verb *solliciter* contains an ambiguity, referring at times to a demand or even manipulation [the expression *solliciter des textes* implies forcing texts or documents to yield significations which they do not clearly contain (Tr.)], at times to solicitude and gratification. See Chapter 10, 'The Mystique of Solicitude'.

13   The Danish parliament (Tr.).

14   This line does not actually seem to appear in either of Rimbaud's 'Villes' poems (commonly known as 'Villes I' and 'Villes II') (Tr.).

15   This phrase occurs with slight variations of emphasis in two letters which Rimbaud wrote in May 1871. The first of these is to Georges Izambard, the second to Paul Demeny. Originals and translations of both letters are to be found in Wallace Fowlie's *Rimbaud: Complete Works, Selected Letters*, University of Chicago Press, Chicago and London, 1966, pp. 302–11 (Tr.).

Chapter 9

1   It might be thought that time is, in this respect, opposed to all other objects, whose 'use-value' traditionally lies in being possessed, utilized, employed to advantage. But this is without doubt a profound error. The true use-value of objects is doubtless also to be consumed, to be expended 'as pure loss' – a 'symbolic' use-value which is everywhere scored out [*barrée*] and replaced by 'utilitarian' use-value.

2   But the goal of the operation here remains strictly individual. In the archaic festival, time is never expended 'for oneself': it is the time of collective prodigality.

Chapter 10

1   Twenty per cent of national income for France.

2   Advertising itself, as an economic process, may be regarded as a 'free celebration', financed by social labour but delivered to everyone 'with nothing apparently given in return' and presenting itself as collective gratification (see later in this chapter).

3   Cf. Lagneau in *Le Faire-Valoir*, 'Advertising is the wrapping up of an unbearable economic logic in the thousand seductive artifices of "exemption from payment", which negate it the better to allow it to operate.' G. Lagneau, *Le Faire-Valoir*, E.M.E., Paris, 1969.

4   On this problem, see the articles by J. Marcus-Steiff and P. Kende in the *Revue française de sociologie*, 1969, X, 3.

5   In German, the word *werben*, which means to ask for someone's hand in marriage and

hence implies loving concern [*sollicitude amoureuse*], also means competition, rivalry and advertising (commercial solicitation).

6   Riesman et al., *The Lonely Crowd*, p. 41.

7   Ibid., p. 83.

8   To take an example, 'In fact,' writes a specialist in sales promotion, 'if, before it was presented to the public, Giscard d'Estaing's programme had been got into shape by an agency like Publicis, using the methods that were so successful in the Saint-Gobain affair, then French voters would probably have backed him.' And he adds: 'When you think of all the trouble you take to win the public's favour when you launch a new bar of soap, bringing all the modern resources of radio, TV and cinema into play, you are amazed by the antiquated methods the government employ when they want to "sell" an economic and financial programme running into billions of francs to the mass of the French people.'

9   Riesman et al., *The Lonely Crowd*, p. 224ff.

10   Ibid., p. 225.

Chapter 11

1   'Objectless craving' has its counterpart in 'objectless raving'.

2   Galbraith, *The Affluent Society*, p. 14.

3   Erostratus or Eratostratus was an Ephesian who burnt down the temple of Diana solely with the object of achieving eternal fame. The Ephesians subsequently passed a law making it illegal to mention his name (Tr.).

4   Economists and psychologists base their thinking wholly on equivalence and rationality: they postulate that, in all processes, the subject is always positively orientated, in a state of need, towards the object. If the need is satisfied, that is all there is to it. They forget that there is no 'satisfied need'; a completed process, where there is only positivity, is something which is never found: there is only desire and desire is ambivalent.

5   Hence the very logical (American) idea of a motel for the suicidal where, for a reasonable price, a 'suicide service', provided like any other social service (though not covered by social security!), ensures that you enjoy optimum conditions for death and undertakes to effect your suicide effortlessly, with a smile.

6   The original French text here is 'le malaise de la civilisation', the title of the standard French translation of Freud's *Das Unbehagen in der Kultur* (English: *Civilization and its Discontents*) (Tr.).

7   J.S. Mill, *On Liberty*, ed. H.B. Acton, Dent/Dutton, London/New York, 1972, p. 124 (my italics, JB).

Conclusion

1   There have been at least three versions of this film. From what he says, Baudrillard is clearly not referring to the first of these (Stellan Rye, 1913) and it seems most likely that he is familiar with the 1926 film by the Dutch-born writer-director Henrik Galeen (who was also involved in the earlier production). A further German version was made in 1936 by the Chicago-born director Arthur Robison (Tr.).

2   Like all myths, this one also seeks to ground itself in an original event. In this case, it is the so-called 'Revolution of Affluence', a historical revolution of Well-Being, the last revolution of Western man after the Renaissance, the Industrial Revolution and the Political Revolutions. Consumption thereby presents itself as the opening of a new era – the final era of achieved Utopia and the end of history.

3   Boorstin, *The Image*, p. 240.

4   Ibid., p. 83.

5   Ibid., p. 259.

Index